# Increasing Executive Productivity

*A Unique Program for Developing the Inner Skills of Vision, Leadership, and Performance*

## Phil Nuernberger

**PRENTICE HALL**
Englewood Cliffs, New Jersey 07632

Prentice-Hall International (UK) Limited, *London*
Prentice-Hall Of Australia Pty. Limited, *Sydney*
Prentice-Hall Canada, Inc., *Toronto*
Prentice-Hall Hispanoamericana, S.A., *Mexico*
Prentice-Hall of India Private Limited, *New Delhi*
Prentice-Hall of Japan, Inc., *Tokyo*
Simon & Schuster Asia Pte. Ltd., *Singapore*
Editora Prentice-Hall do Brasil, Ltda., *Rio de Janeiro*

© 1992 *by*

Prentice Hall, Inc.

Englewood Cliffs, New Jersey

10  9  8  7  6  5  4  3  2  1

**Library of Congress Cataloging-in-Publication Data**

Nuernberger, Phil, 1942—

    Increasing executive productivity: a unique program
for developing the inner skills of vision, leadership, and
performance/ by Phil Nuernberger.

    p.     cm.
    Includes index.
    ISBN 0-13-463811-5
    1. Executive ability.    2. Leadership.    I. Title.
HD38.2.N84    1992
658.4'90—dc20                          91-30176
                                          CIP

ISBN 0-13-463811-5

**PRENTICE HALL**
Business Information & Publishing Division
Englewood Cliffs, NJ 07632
Simon & Schuster. A Paramount Communications Company

Printed in the United States of America

# Dedication

This book is dedicated to my Spiritual Master who through love and example has shown me the power of humanity; to my Karate Sensei who has shown me the value of focused movement and respect; to my teachers, one and all, who have traveled the journey of personal fulfillment and have willingly shared their knowledge, skill, and love with me.

# Acknowledgments

My special thanks to:

Anne Mazer Futterman for her patience and expertise in editing my work, and teaching me how to improve my writing skills;

Ron Oehl for providing both encouragement and financial help in the early stages of this book;

Kim Breese for graciously reviewing the manuscript and writing the foreword;

Richard Ruch, Farrel Reynolds, Bob Bostrom, and Oded Lurie for contributing to my appreciation of executive life and for their feedback and help with the manuscript.

Don Miller, Bob Fuller, Horst Rechelbacher, Clarence Cleer, and others who have given me many examples of personal effectiveness;

The executives and students who have attended my seminars and have challenged and stimulated me to develop my ideas clearly;

My wife, Deborah, my two daughters, Santosha and Raka, and my son Sam, for their loving patience and support.

# Foreword

by Kim Breese
Chief Executive Officer
Dow Jones & Co.

In 1987 I became chairman of the advisory board of the business school at Rider College in Lawrenceville, New Jersey. Richard Ruch, the young dean, had recruited me for the board several years earlier as a representative of my company, Dow Jones. At the end of my three-year term he asked me to stay on for another term as chairman.

In 1980, Richard came to Rider as one of the youngest business school deans in the country. He brought a strong belief that business schools in general were missing the boat. They were so busy teaching traditional disciplines by traditional methods that they had failed to see some fundamental changes in business. To Richard, it was clear the next generation of corporate executives, members of his generation, would face challenges much different from those of their predecessors. And they would have much different expectations from their employers. These baby-boom managers would run companies with employees from diverse ethnic and racial groups, with women moving into the executive suite, with employees who put their families and personal lives ahead of the company. They would run companies competing in a global business environment requiring understanding and appreciation of other cultures. They would have to understand what made others tick and, more important, what made themselves tick.

So, Richard set out to break new ground. His goal: to put Rider in the forefront of institutions preparing businessmen and businesswomen to thrive in the new business environment.

One of his most innovative initiatives was to bring in Phil Nuernberger as adjunct professor. Phil was a nontraditional business professor in several ways. His doctorate is in psychology. He had worked with businesses but never for one. For twenty years he had studied eastern philosophy and yoga as a science of the mind. He also had practiced as a psychotherapist and was a pioneer in the use of biofeedback.

Richard, also a student of eastern philosophy, had met Phil several years earlier. He soon realized that Phil not only was a gifted teacher but also had expertise and experience that could add a new dimension to the Riders program.

He invited Phil to teach, on an experimental basis, an MBA course that would help students understand themselves and understand others. Particularly, the course would teach students how to use inner resources to develop skills such as vision, intuition, concentration, self-confidence, creativity—skills executives need but don't often know how to develop. This was ground breaking stuff. Some thought it weird.

But it was a huge success. More that half the students taking the course in the summer of 1987 wrote unsolicited letters to the dean heaping praise on the course and on Phil. Some said it was their most valuable academic experience. As a result, the course was offered again in the spring of 1988. By this time, news of the course had spread and it was filled immediately.

I had just taken the advisory board chairmanship. I reasoned that if I wanted to make a real contribution I should learn first hand what was going on in the school. So I asked Richard and Phil for permission to audit Phil's course that spring. They both readily agreed. So, every Monday night during the spring, after working all day, I spent three hours at Rider in class with 35 MBA students, most of whom had also worked all day.

Phil is a natural teacher. I was in awe for the whole semester. He was enthusiastic—and his energy generated enthusiasm in the students. He was captivating. He was fascinating. I found myself eagerly awaiting the next class.

Soon I found myself breathing diaphragmatically, meditating and, in stressful situations, "going to the breath." I began to consciously think about how to concentrate, how to be intuitive, how to be creative. I began to pay attention to my thoughts and to determine where they came from. Were some really the thoughts of others "fluttering through my mind" as Phil had said? I looked at myself differently each morning as I shaved. I looked at others around me differently.

In essence, the world as I perceived it was no longer the same. This new level of awareness was powerful.

Most of what Phil taught me and the MBA students is contained in this book. And Phil has written it in the same entertaining, conversational style he uses in his lectures.

Phil looks at business people first as human beings. He tries to teach them how to develop the power of their minds. This makes them better businessmen and businesswomen. But mostly, it helps make them better human beings.

# Introduction

*...a time of turbulence is also one of great opportunity for those who can understand, accept, and exploit the new realities.*
—*Peter Drucker*

Several months ago, I was speaking with a colleague, a consultant in organizational development, about the pressures we face as we try to cope with the the faster and faster pace of modern life.

"I have a client," he told me with concern, " who has so much to do to run her business that she doesn't even have time to take care of the critical decisions anymore. It's not a matter of prioritizing. We have already done that. She has eliminated all non-essential decisions, and has delegated every possible responsibility. But there are so many opportunities and challenges that she *still* doesn't have time to take care of the crucial problems. How does she sort it all out?"

My consultant friend knew he could not manufacture time for his client, nor make the world more simple. Nor can we do those things for ourselves. We all have the same twenty-four hours day to balance work, career, family life, social responsibilities, hobbies, dining, relaxation, and sleep in a world that has become increasingly chaotic and turbulent.

Much of the chaos and turbulence stems from our dramatically increased ability to gather and transmit information quickly. This improved information technology has helped bring about political, economic, and environmental changes and significantly altered the world in which we live. Our society, our work, every aspect of our lives, has been transformed—and continues to be changed very quickly. At the same time, we have sped up the pace of our lives so much that we are in serious danger of losing ourselves.

We know that the amount of information now reaching us, and the increasing speed of its delivery, can overwhelm us. Today's time pressures, intensified by the improved information technology, create a constant crisis mentality and desperate pressures for a quick fix in Corporate America. This, in turn, has given rise to crisis management, short-term thinking...and long-term disaster.

## CLEAR AND PRESENT DANGERS

Among business executives, the levels of fear and stress are spiraling upward. Those pressures, in turn, are leading to more opportunistic thinking, unethical behavior, and stress-related diseases. The result is that we have become dissatisfied and cynical about ourselves and our ability to make a real difference. We feel powerless and ineffectual, and our levels of productivity are plunging. At the same time, *we are becoming even more dependent on our technology to solve problems.*

We are also modeling our ourselves after our technology. We have become so enamored of its power and speed that we increasingly ignore the nearly infinite power of our own mind. We foster "fast-food thinking" that provides the same superficial nutrition for the mind that junk food provides for the body. Instead of really thinking, we now want to be entertained. Instead of building for the future, we want to take what we can get now. Instead of developing our character, we strive to create an image.

The more we treat ourselves and others as machines, the more we lose touch with our own inner human resources and power, and these are the foundation of our community, our ethics, and our personal fulfillment. We pay an enormous price for this superficiality at all levels of our society. At one extreme we find the selfish greed of the Marcoses, the Boeskys, and those who engineered savings & loan rip-offs. At the other, we see how chronic poverty, homelessness, and drugs keep draining away enormous amounts of human talent and resources. Meanwhile, between those extremes, we suffer from psychosomatic diseases, failed marriages, and the frantic emptiness of middle-class life.

These well-known social problems distract us from a much greater danger—the abdication of our powerful human capacities for understanding and problem-solving in favor of technological decision-making.

Preoccupied with technology, we ignore two important, fundamental questions:

- What are the *personal* resources, qualities and characteristics necessary for success in the age of information technology?
- And how do we develop them?

## NEEDED—A NEW WAY OF THINKING

Keeping up your productivity and succeeding in the age of information technology demand new ways of solving problems and structuring organizations. We also must make dramatic transformations in the way we think about time, space, and matter. Most importantly, we must make a profound change in how we see and understand ourselves, and how we educate ourselves to deal with these new realities.

For in the end analysis, it is not the technology, the computer, the space satellite, or the sophisticated competitive information systems that we develop that really make the difference. What counts is people—the human resource, the mind behind the system.

## UPGRADING THE HUMAN ELEMENT: THE EMPOWERED MIND

The inescapable demand for fast, accurate response makes the old ways of using our mind obsolete. We can't, nor should we try, to put an end to technological advance. But, we need to make at least the same effort to develop our crucial human capacities as well. We must become as sophisticated in the use of our inner resources as we are our technological resources. The human mind, our most powerful resource, includes a sophisticated arsenal of innate skills. When we consciously command these innate skills, and use them to execute our decisions and enhance our effectiveness and personal power, we are exercising what I call an Empowered Mind.

I have seen executives think more clearly, be more creative, communicate more effectively, and take command by learning how to access and rely on their own innate mental abilities. I recall vividly the time that a senior vice-president of Malaysian Airlines came to me after one seminar, and told me with great excitement:

"Today, for the first time in my life, I was able to pay attention without my mind wandering here and there. I never realized that I had the power to direct my mind and focus attention where I wanted it to be instead of where it wanted to be. I can't tell you how much of a thrill this is for me."

## DEVELOPING YOUR INNER SKILLS

*Increasing Executive Productivity: A Unique Program for Developing the Inner Skills of Vision, Leadership, and Performance* is a personal training manual that can show you how to develop your inner resources and expand your abilities to produce, make leadership decisions, and achieve greater career and personal satisfaction. In the following chapters, information and techniques are included to help you build an effective self-training program. By taking charge of your own inner training, you can develop the following qualities that characterize a more productive executive.

### Self-Knowledge

Through self-knowledge, the executive with an Empowered Mind identifies, develops, and involves all the subtle resources of the mind. When we do not know how we function on different levels, we unwittingly create problems for ourselves. Through self-knowledge, we tap our hidden resources, become skillful in their use, and guarantee our success.

### Fearlessness

Probably the most important quality of an executive with an Empowered Mind is fearlessness. *Fear is the single greatest enemy of personal effectiveness.* It inhibits concentration and creativity, prevents intuitive insight, and distorts our instincts. When we become aware of our inner strengths, however, we gain the power to live without fear. Where others see danger and threats, an executive with an Empowered Mind sees opportunities and challenges. He is unafraid to make mistakes. An executive with an Empowered Mind evaluates actions in terms of their consequences, obtains data and valuable feedback, and creates opportunities for effective action.

## Balance

To succeed in this turbulent world, we need an internal gyroscope, an inner balance and stability, so that we don't lose our bearings and get tossed about by the strong winds of change. An executive with an Empowered Mind creates and maintains inner balance both physically and mentally. This inner stability, characterized by mental alertness and flexibility, allows him to respond with control and choice. By remaining calm and tranquil in the face of adversity and danger, he can seize opportunity and take effective actions.

## Curiosity

An executive with an Empowered Mind is never satisfied with her level of knowledge. Driven by a desire to know about all of life, she constantly seeks to expand knowledge and opens her creative force to new input and diverse ideas. By allowing curiosity to grow throughout life, an Empowered Mind remains forever youthful.

## Integration

An executive with an Empowered Mind successfully integrates the various demands and roles that life offers. No magic boundary line exists between our personal life and our work life, just as no magic boundary exists between our emotional life and our thinking life. The various "departments" of our human resource must work in harmony if we are to be successful.

## Flexibility

An executive with an Empowered Mind adapts easily and accurately to changing conditions. One of the greatest challenges of information technology is the speed and intensity of change. But thought can move quickly, too. By taking control of our mind, we can take control of technology and its insatiable demands for action as well. Our ability to adapt, use, and benefit from the speed and intensity of change of modern life will determine whether we succeed or fail.

## Visionary Sensitivity

An executive with an Empowered Mind has the capacity to anticipate and create the unexpected. This is long-range, strategic thinking. He can operate within the bounds of conventional wisdom with ease, but just as easily allow his mind to discard conventional wisdom and travel in unconventional ways. While others see what is, the executive with an Empowered Mind sees what will be.

## Perceptual Sensitivity

Attuned to the shifting currents, an executive with an Empowered Mind develops great strategic sense. This executive sees distant things as if they were close. In this way, she discriminates and understands the direction and course of events. And she takes a distant view of close things to avoid pressure and maintain objectivity.

## Leadership

Through self-knowledge, an executive with an Empowered Mind gains sensitivity to others and provides better leadership and more effective management. Sensitive to natural rhythms, this executive develops an acute sense of timing. He understands when to approach and when to fall back, and when to maintain the status quo. This gives him the patience necessary to build the future and enhance the present. His objectivity, fearlessness, and flexibility allow him to learn from mistakes, bring order out of chaos, and inspire others.

## Skill

Through awareness, self-discipline and practice, an executive with an Empowered Mind acts consciously and expertly. With perceptual skill, she understands the hidden or subtle meaning of another's words and behavior. With skillful use of will, this executive marshalls her resources to achieve her goals, and avoids dissipating energies through conflict and opposition. Spiritually whole, and unafraid of loss, an executive with an Empowered Mind acquires the power of absolute negotiation. With skillful use of visionary powers, this executive gains the insight to guide her future with confidence.

## HOW TO USE THIS BOOK

There is no "quick fix" that will empower your mind, develop your inner skills and increase your productivity. Building an Empowered Mind takes time and effort. Just as it takes time to develop and use the world's most powerful computer, it takes time to develop and use your even more powerful mind. The more time and effort you invest, the more skilled and empowered you become.

The job of this book is to help you put it all together, to create a discipline of skills. If you look in a dictionary, you will find the following definitions associated with the word *discipline*:

- a set of methods or rules of conduct
- a specific branch of knowledge or of teaching
- training intended to elicit a specified pattern of behavior or character
- behavior that results from that training.

All of these definitions apply to the process of building an Empowered Mind. An executive with an Empowered Mind is disciplined, commited to be the finest and most productive executive he or she can be. What you achieve depends entirely on the effort you make.

The journey to self-empowerment and increased executive productivity is not difficult, however. You will find that the techniques are quite simple, yet effective. Some of the exercises in this book will bring immediate benefit and satisfaction. However, genuine skill and lasting benefit will take time and practice.

For example, you will quickly learn how to calm your mind and focus attention, but to maintain a calm and focused mind is a much higher order of skill that will take some time and effort to achieve.

To help your journey have the best chance for success, this book draws upon very ancient traditions of wisdom and knowledge as well as the most modern scientific findings. This book is structured to:

- help you develop a practical and comprehensive map of the different levels of your personality and the innate resources of your mind
- detail the specific capacities for leadership, vision and performance found within each of these personality levels
- provide the techniques that will allow us to access these innate capacities and develop them into conscious skills
- provide a unique understanding of the power of our human spirit to bring about fearlessness
- detail the methods by which you can experience the unbounded strength of your own humanity.

If you just read the book and do not take the time to become skilled, you will accomplish very little. If you do the exercises without understanding their purpose, you'll get stuck on the technique, and won't learn how to generalize the experience into everyday life.

The magic is not in any technique, but in your own mind. The techniques in this book can make you more sensitive to what your mind already knows, and give you greater access and control in using this power and knowledge. The goals are enhanced awareness, increased productivity in your work, and greater personal fulfillment.

Any skill, whether playing tennis, predicting economic trends, or using your intuitive knowledge, requires practice, patience and persistence.

Many of the exercises in this book will be difficult to read and do at the same time. One of the best ways to solve this problem is to first record the exercise in your own voice on a cassette tape, and then listen to the cassette tape. Do not be in a hurry to finish the book. Take the time to work with, and enjoy, the exercises in each of the chapters.

You already have all the resources you need to negotiate the age of information technology, an age in which change and pressure are constants. You are already more capable than any computer, than any technology, to create and direct your future. You just have to learn how to tap into, focus, and use your inner power. So, welcome to the world where the name of the game is flexibility, vision, command, and risk. Welcome to the world of the Empowered Mind, and prepare yourself for the rich, productive, rewarding future that is now.

# Contents

**FOREWORD** iv

**INTRODUCTION** vii

Clear and Present Dangers   ix
Needed: A New Way of Thinking   x
Upgrading the Human Element: The Empowered Mind   x
Developing Your Inner Skills   xi
How to Use This Book   xii

**CHAPTER 1 / THE EMPOWERED MIND:**
**Tapping the Executive Potential   1**

Drawing Personal Power from Inner Resources   3
How the Unconscious Mind Affects the Conscious Mind   4
Focused Attention: The Secret Power of the Conscious Mind   6
Awareness as a Conscious Choice   7

   *An Exercise in Awareness   7*

The Consciousness of Choice   8
Mastering the Skill of Concentration   9
How to Tap into Your Potential   10
Health/Wellness Skills: Laying the Foundation   11

   *Executive "Response Ability"   12*

*An Exercise in Taking Responsibility   13*

Performance Skills: Perceptual Sensitivity and Creative Options   14

Visionary Skills: Commanding the Future   16

Directing Your Leadership Skills   17

Spiritual Skills: Values, Ethics, and the Human Spirit   18

The Empowered Mind: Personal Power in Action   20

Summary of Principles   21


## CHAPTER 2 / A MAP OF PERSONAL POWER: The Journey Within   23

Journeying Through the Five Levels of Self-Power   24

*A Traveling Exercise   26*

*An Analogy: The Computer and You   27*

Personality Level 1: The Body—Your Mobile Home   28

*Health, Performance, and Skill   28*

*Corporate Stress Management   30*

*The Body as an Information Resource   31*

*Body Check Exercise   32*

*Tuning In to Knowledge   32*

*Sensitivity Exercise   33*

*Accessing the Unconscious Mind Through Sensitivity   33*

Personality Level II: Energy—Mind/Body Connection   35

*Body-Energy -Mind Exercise   37*

*Mind and Energy Level   37*

*The Mind—Our Ultimate Resource   37*

Personality Level III: The Sensory Mind—Making Sense of the World   38

*Facts and Instincts: Two Kinds of Knowledge   40*

*Perception: Creating Personal Reality   41*

*Language: The Power to Define Reality 42*

*Emotional Power 43*

*The Power of Habit 44*

*An Exercise in Habit Sensitivity 44*

*Habits and Energy 45*

Personality Level IV: Discriminating Mind—Decision
And Intuition 46

*Analysis and Thinking 46*

*Intuition—Direct Awareness of Cause/Effect
Relationships 48*

Personality Level V: Balanced Mind—Source of
Inner Strength 50

The Center of Control 51

Being Human: More Than a Machine 51

Integration, Balance and Power 53

Summary of Principles 55


**CHAPTER 3 / THE BALANCE FACTOR:
Productivity and Stress Management 57**

Stress: Mismanaged Resources 58

Stress: The Myth and the Reality 58

*Myth Number 1: There Is Good Stress and Bad Stress 58*

*Myth Number 2: Stress Is Something That Happens to You 59*

*Myth Number 3: To Excel, to Really Produce, We
Need Stress 59*

Stress: A Question of Balance 60

Fight-or-Flight: Only Halfway There 61

The Possum Response: The Other Half of Stress 63

The Worst of Both Worlds 64

Stress: The Answer Is Balance 64

Taking Charge of Our Controls 67

When Normal Means Stressed   68
Learning Diaphragmatic Breathing   72

     *Step 1: The Relaxation Posture   72*

     *Step 2: Diaphragmatic Breathing   72*

     *Step 3: Balanced Diaphragmatic 2:1 Breathing   73*

     *Step 4: The Two-Minute Breath Break   73*

Deep Relaxation—A Crucial Skill   74
The Three Levels of Relaxation   75

     *Structural Relaxation   75*

     *Autonomic Relaxation   78*

     *Concentration: Achieving The Deepest State Of Relaxation   82*

The Opportunities of Imbalance   83
Summary of Principles   84


## CHAPTER 4 / MANAGING THE REALITY GENERATOR: Mastery of the Sensory Mind   86

The Chattering Mind: Invitation to Disaster   87
Breath Awareness and Task Absorption:
  Managing the Mind   91

     *Breath Awareness   92*

     *Breath Awareness and Emotional Control   92*

     *Breath Awareness and Content Control   93*

     *The Green Frog Exercise   95*

Playing With Words   97

     *Clarity Exercise   98*

     *The Equalizer   98*

     *Word Play   99*

     *Mind—the Sly Fox   99*

Your Choice: Stress or Personal Power   100
The Three Mistakes of the Sensory Mind   101

*Fear: Negative Use of Creative Imagination 101*

*Four Steps to Controlling Fear 103*

*Self-Rejection: Creating Impotency 104*

*An Exercise for Solving the "Should" Problem 105*

*The "Should" Stopper Exercise 106*

*Laziness: Path to Nowhere 106*

Balance and Choice: The Door to Self-Mastery 107

*An Exercise in Letting Go 108*

Summary of Principles 109

## CHAPTER 5 / CONCENTRATION:
### The Executives Ultimate Skill 111

Focusing the Mind 112

Concentration: The Mind as Laser 112

*From Homo Haphazardous to Homo Sapiens 113*

*Taking Control: Increasing the Power 115*

*61 Points 116*

*A Calm Mind Brings Awareness 118*

*Refining Concentration: Making the Mind a Laser 118*

*Unitary Consciousness: The Crown Jewel of Concentration 120*

Making a Conscious Choice 120

*Building the Force: Expansion or Contraction 121*

*Fear and Awareness: Diminishing Returns 122*

*Steps to Positive Motivation 124*

The Ins and Outs of Concentration 124

*External Concentration: Peak Performance at Work 125*

*Inner Concentration: The Realization of Power 126*

*Gazes: From Vision to Skill 126*

*Gaze Exercise 127*

Energy: Balance and Conservation  128

    *Energy Requirements: The Lows and the Highs    128*

    *Energizing Exercises    129*

    *Calming Breath    129*

    *Concentration and Conservation    131*

    *Pseudo-Concentration: Blowing Our Energy Fuse    133*

Skill: The Fifth Dimension    133

    *Success Insurance: Knowing How to Practice    134*

    *Commitment: Dedicating Time to Personal Power    134*

    *Stress Control    134*

    *Posture    134*

    *Make Transitions Gently    135*

Unlearning the Habit of Distraction    135

More Concentration Techniques    136

    *Breath Awareness as a Concentration Exercise    136*

    *A Meditation Practice    137*

    *Centering Exercise    138*

    *Meditation Exercise    139*

    *Points to Remember    139*

The Empowered Mind: Step by Step    140

    *Fifteen Minutes to Personal Power    140*

    *Building Day-to-Day Skills    141*

Summary of Principles    141


**CHAPTER 6 / CLEAR PERCEPTION—OPTIMUM
               PERFORMANCE:
               Enhancing Day-to-Day Skills    143**

Instinct: In Touch with the World    145

Breath Awareness: Listening With the Whole Mind    147

Trusting Your Senses    148

*The Walking Exercise   148*

*Standing in Another's Shoes   149*

Creativity: Playing with Perception   151

*The Creative Matrix   152*

*A Brief Exercise in Creative Thought   154*

*Taking Control of Creativity   155*

*The Creative Impulse—Stage One: Inner Balance   156*

*Steps to Managing the Creative Matrix   157*

*The Creative Impulse—Stage Two: Germination   158*

*The Creative Impulse—Stage Three: Discovery   161*

*Techniques of Discovery: Spontaneous Association   162*

*Free Association Exercise   162*

*Techniques of Discovery: Directed Association   163*

*Reframing Exercise: Changing the Rules of the Game   164*

Mind Traps and Power Blockers   164

Imagination: Shaping Mind Power   165

Emotional Energy: The Mind's Power Source   166

*Engaging the Power   166*

The Wide World of Imagery Work   167

*Imagery Exercise for Neutralizing Negative Feelings   168*

*A Positive Start to the Day   169*

*Creating Success   170*

Summary of Principles   170


**CHAPTER 7 / THE VISIONARY MIND:**
**Tapping the Inner Wisdom For**
**Executive Decision Making   172**

Why Linear Models Do Not Work   173

*The Sensory Mind as Linear   174*

Discrimination: The Non-Linear Mind   174

Intuition—The Power of Pure Knowledge    175

    *What Is Intuition?    176*
    *Building the Knowledge Base for Intuition    177*
    *Focused Attention: Loading the Computer    178*
    *Increase Attention to Enhance Discrimination    179*
    *The Balance Factor    179*

Needed: An Open, Flexible Mind    181

    *Maintaining a Flexible and Open Mind    181*

Quiet Time: The Need for Incubation    182
The Path to Wisdom: Tapping Your Intuition    183

    *The Art and Science of Paying Attention    183*

The Body Knows    184
The Quiet Thoughts    185
A Picture of the Future    186

    *A Journey into Wisdom    187*
    *The Room    190*

Direct Access    191
Things to Watch For    192
Discrimination—The Power Behind Reasoning    193

    *Intuition and Critical Thinking: Dynamic Duo for
      Problem-Solving    194*

    *Four Critical Steps to Critical Thinking    194*

    *Problem-Solving Through Sleep    195*

Decisiveness: Knowing When and How to Take Action    196

    *Taking Fear Out of the Decision-Making Process    197*

    *Bypassing Self-Doubt: Becoming an Experimenter    198*

Three Steps to Effective Decision-Making    198
A Summary of Principles    199

# CHAPTER 8 / EXECUTIVE LEADERSHIP:
## The Mastery of Inner Strength  201

Will—Directing Your Mind Power   202

*Three Steps to a Powerful Will   203*

Building the Foundation   203

Will Power—The Battle Already Lost   204

Conflict Management: Changing 'Will Power' to a
Powerful Will   206

*Step 1: Relax   207*
*Step 2: Accept   208*
*Step 3: Restrain   209*
*Step 4: Explore   209*

Readiness: Building an Inner Consensus   210

The Levels of Self-Confidence   210

*Steps to Increased Self-Confidence   212*
*Unlimited Self-Confidence: The Gift We Already Have   213*
*A Confidence Exercise   214*

Integrity: The Value of Knowing Your Values   214

*Discovering Priorities: An Exercise in What Is
Important to You   217*

Execution: The Staying Power for Success   218

A Program for Training Self-Discipline   219

*A Personal Self-Training Program in Concentration   220*

Doubting Doubts   221

Affirmation: Using Mind Power   223

*Using Affirmations Successfully   224*

Will—The Undeniable Force   224

Summary of Principles   225

## CHAPTER 9 / LOVE, PERFORMANCE AND PRODUCTIVITY: Bringing Spiritual Skills to Work   227

Cooperation: The Experience of Wholeness and Community   230
Building Cooperation   232

*Personal Empowerment   233*
*Empowering Others: Building Community   233*
*An Exercise in Empowerment   234*
*Four Critical Elements to Creating Positive Relationships   235*
*Reinforcing Strengths   235*

Humility: The Power of a Healthy Ego   236

*Humility and Curiosity: The Desire to Know   237*
*I Am, Therefore I Think: The Ego Faculty   237*
*Ego: The Biggest Problem in Life   239*
*The Qualities of a Strong Ego   240*
*Five Steps to a Strong Ego   240*

Love—The Final Power   242

*Pain Release Exercises   242*
*Shrinking Headache Exercise   243*
*Imagery Release Exercise   242*
*Love: Letting Go of Self-imposed Limitations   243*

Selfless Love—The End of Fear   245
Love and the Business World   245
Love as Service   246
Quality Leadership Based on the Principles of Service   246
Love and Strength   247
Non-Attachment: Foundation for Selfless Love   248
The Power of a Reflective Mind   250
Coming Home to the Center   251
Summary of Principles   252

## APPENDIXES   254

Appendix A: Summary Of Exercises   254
Appendix B: Details of 61 Points Exercise   261

## INDEX   264

INDEX   264

# 1 The Empowered Mind: Tapping the Executive Potential

*...What a piece of work is man!*
*—Shakespeare*

Have you ever had the sense that you were working at far less than your real capacity? Most of us feel that somewhere locked within our mind is a creative genius, a powerful and influential will, and a great capacity for wisdom and joy. We suspect that we have an untapped potential for balance and harmony to create a strong, healthy mind and body, free from stress and disease. At times, we catch glimpses of such a creative and dynamic will within us, as well as the wisdom to know how to use it. Yet, as we struggle along with our thoughts and habits, most of the time we cannot seem to reach—and use—that hidden power when we need it.

So we buy books on unlocking our hidden potential, take seminars on creative thinking, learn a few meditation techniques, and join a health club. But, after the first burst of inspiration, ordinary life and its demands reassert themselves, and the techniques we have learned never quite live up to their promises. The books soon are put on the shelf, the seminar material is filed away, and we get to the club maybe once a month, or less. We still know in our hearts that there is greatness to be unlocked, but....well... maybe next time.

It is time to get out of that rut and onto the path toward higher productivity. You can start right now by taking a quick inventory on how you feel about yourself—size up the situation, so to speak. Study the qualities listed in Figure 1:1, then check the percentage of real capacities you think *you* use for each one. And get ready for a surprise.

When you have finished, look over your figures. Most people mark somewhere in the 20-30 percent range. They feel that they have quite a bit of unused capacities. But here is the surprise: even those low estimates

1

are too high. For nearly all of us, the actual answers lie in the 5–10 percent range. Even the brilliant physicist Albert Einstein once surmised that he used only about 10 percent of his potential.

In other words, most of the time, we do not even use 90–95 percent of our true capacities.

| Capacity Inventory | | | | | | | | | | | |
|---|---|---|---|---|---|---|---|---|---|---|---|
| Personal Quality | Percentage Used | | | | | | | | | | |
| | 0-5 | 10 | 20 | 30 | 40 | 50 | 60 | 70 | 80 | 90 | 100 |
| Health | | | | | | | | | | | |
| Optimism | | | | | | | | | | | |
| Contentment | | | | | | | | | | | |
| Instinct | | | | | | | | | | | |
| Creativity | | | | | | | | | | | |
| Imagination | | | | | | | | | | | |
| Intuition | | | | | | | | | | | |
| Reasoning | | | | | | | | | | | |
| Decisiveness | | | | | | | | | | | |
| Will | | | | | | | | | | | |
| Self-Confidence | | | | | | | | | | | |
| Self-Discipline | | | | | | | | | | | |
| Cooperation | | | | | | | | | | | |
| Humility | | | | | | | | | | | |
| Love | | | | | | | | | | | |

Figure 1:1

That means we have enormous capacity for improvement. But improvement where, how, and with what? Our formal education has not truly helped us understand this dimly grasped potential. In fact, most of us barely understand how our bodies function, let alone the subtle intricacies of the mind. At the same time, we constantly create conditions (beliefs, emotions, habits) that interfere with the use of our inner resources.

We go to school to learn skills and gain knowledge, to acquire something that will help us get along in life. But who teaches us to understand and become skillful with our mind tools, such as the power of concentration, mental clarity, self-confidence, and creativity? These factors determine our competency and success far more than the book learning and professional skills we gain through education and training. Our own mind is our most important tool, but we seldom, if ever, learn how to develop this tool or use it to its full potential.

Now go back to the inventory. Take your pencil and mark the percentages you feel you achieve when you have a peak experience such as a particularly creative insight or intuition, or when you really feel confident. Now imagine what your career and life would be like if you could operate at this higher level of efficiency and power all of the time. Yet even when we have peak experiences, we suspect that there is more we could achieve. A peak experience shows us the limits of our *current* capacity, and that can be expanded greatly if we take better command of our inner resources. How far can that capacity be expanded? We simply do not know the limits of the human mind.

By taking command of our inner resources, we can build the tools and habits we need to express our inner strength and capacity. **To do so, we must find a way to access our inner resources and turn them into conscious skills.** This journey of self-discovery and transformation marks the beginning of the journey toward developing an Empowered Mind, and it could be the most important journey you will ever make.

## DRAWING PERSONAL POWER FROM INNER RESOURCES

Personal empowerment does not depend on external conditions. It can't be earned through university degrees or granted by government decree. Many of us think that if we become rich and famous, we'll be happy and content, and fulfill our potential. Personal power doesn't work that way either. Personal power is simply that—personal. It arises out of the innate resources found in every human mind. As the following examples show, we become empowered by learning how to use these inner resources:

- An oil company executive learned how to control his anger. By doing so, he created a better atmosphere for honest communications with his subordinates. This led to an improvement in staff productivity, better morale and fewer sick days. When he took command of himself, his entire department benefited.

- A patient in my biofeedback program freed herself of headaches after twenty years of pain and suffering. She stopped relying on pain killers, which had only relieved, but not cured her headaches. Instead, she learned how to create an inner balance and harmony that prevented the headaches from occurring.

- A couple learned how to listen to each other without feeling threatened. As a result, they created greater intimacy and closeness in their relationship. Each benefited from their own as well as from the other's personal empowerment.

- Even though Steven Hawking's body is disabled by Lou Gehrig's disease and he can only function and speak through the aid of computers, this brilliant English physicist creates personal empowerment through the command of his intellect.

## HOW THE UNCONSCIOUS MIND AFFECTS THE CONSCIOUS MIND

The human mind has many resources. But how well we use them depends on our ability to access them, not how much education we have. Our greatest handicap is our own ignorance. We often simply ignore, or are unaware of, most of the vast resources that our minds hold. Rather than capitalize on this knowledge and power, we leave it buried in the deep recesses of the unconscious mind.

Psychologists often liken the mind to an iceberg, which only shows its tip above the water. When you are awake, you operate in the world from your conscious mind. Yet this is only the surface, the tip of your own mental iceberg.

The greatest part of your mind operates on the unconscious level. The unconscious is a vast storehouse of knowledge, habits, emotions, memories, and complexes, all of which form your personality, regulate your body, and even determine how you think and what you see. This is where the real power and potency of the mind lies.

The process where the conscious and unconscious merge is called the *subconscious*. The subconscious corresponds to the part of the iceberg that we can see beneath the waves. Our subconscious is that part of our experience that we are unaware of, because we aren't paying attention to it. Yet, as soon as we direct our attention to some experience in the subconscious, we become aware of it. Or when we remember something, that memory comes from the subconscious level of the mind.

Meanwhile, the experiences embedded in the unconscious mind are like the vast part of the iceberg which is too deep to see. They lie beyond our awareness. We don't have the capacity to pay attention to them. This is what makes them "unconscious."

For instance, you are aware of the words and pages in this book as you read them. They are part of your conscious experience, your conscious mind. Now, what does the bottom of your left foot feel like? Before you paid attention, the feelings of the bottom of your left foot were in the subconscious, and you weren't aware of them. But the moment you directed your attention, these feelings and sensations become part of your conscious experience. If, on the other hand, I ask you what your spleen feels like, you may start placing your hands on different areas of your abdomen. You may even wonder if you have one or not. Your experience of your spleen lies totally in the unconscious, and isn't accessible to your conscious awareness.

My friend Michael Wright has a more poetic example. He remembers sailing on a ship across the sea, and watching porpoises swimming alongside of the boat. The water was very calm and clear, and he could watch the porpoises dive until they were so deep he could no longer see them. As he continued to watch, he saw them emerge from the depths, rising up through the water until they jumped into the air. To Michael, the porpoises jumping and swimming on the surface were like our conscious mind—busy with all sorts of activity. The porpoises emerging from the depths, swimming towards the surface, represented the knowledge, thoughts and feelings that lie in our subconscious mind. Of course, the porpoises which were so deep that he could no longer see them represented the activity of our unconscious mind.

Since the days of Freud, we have become accustomed to the fact that our unconscious mind is a reservoir of great power. Our conscious mind mostly serves as an excuse maker for what is determined in the unconscious. Think about the last time you became table-thumping angry about something—really angry! A few moments before you exploded, I'll bet you did *not* consciously and rationally think *"Golly gee whiz, this situation calls for a drastic expression of anger in order to correct this person's attitude. I guess I better demonstrate some real anger here."*

Instead, you just felt an explosion of anger that came right out of your unconscious reactions to the situation.

Many advertising agencies make a fortune because they understand that our unconscious emotional habits influence what we buy. Not only do these emotional habits influence what we may buy, but how we think, and even what we perceive. On a conscious level, we talk to ourselves and decide on a course of action, unaware that the real decisions are being made by our unconscious emotional habits.

## FOCUSED ATTENTION: THE SECRET POWER OF THE CONSCIOUS MIND

Many scientists, psychiatrists and psychologists speak knowingly of the hidden power of our unconscious mind. But there is an even greater power that lies undeveloped in our conscious mind which few recognize. Our conscious mind has one unique power: *the power to direct attention, to focus the energy of the mind.* Through attention, our conscious mind can direct the entire mind and all of its resources—knowledge, creativity, will, emotional energy, even habits. By paying attention, we become more aware of our inner reality. Whatever we become aware of, we gain the power to command.

For example, habits—when we do things out of habit, we don't have to think about them. Basically, our habits are unconscious. For a habit to control behavior, it must remain on the unconscious level. The moment you become conscious of a habit, you have the ability to choose to do something different.

In a recent seminar, one of the participants was a jogger. While jogging with a colleague, he developed a habit of discussing work problems. Over a period of time, he noticed that he did not enjoy the jogging as much. He was running slower and could not maintain his speed. During the seminar, he realized that his habit of thinking about work problems while jogging had unconsciously created stress and reduced his efficiency. The very next day, he re-focused his attention on the running, and did not allow his mind to follow the habit of going over work problems. As a consequence, he ran almost as fast as his best time. His joy of running returned, and he felt better than he had for months.

The moment he became sensitive to the habit of thinking about work, he took charge of his thoughts. By choosing different thoughts, he altered the pattern. By doing so, he improved his efficiency in running. He tapped the secret power of his conscious mind.

# AWARENESS AS A CONSCIOUS CHOICE

Through awareness, we alert the conscious mind to what we are doing and allow ourselves the opportunity of choosing another course. However, we must remember that awareness does not mean "thinking about." Awareness means *direct experience*.

For example, you can "think about" ice cream, or you can taste it. Which do you think will give you greater understanding of ice cream and whether or not you like it? What we "think" has little power to change a habit. It is our awareness of the incidents that lead up to the behavior and all the consequences of the behavior—not just the immediate ones—that gives us the power to change a habit.

I remember trying to quit smoking. I knew that smoking was bad for me, but I was not very conscious of the pain my body felt when I smoked. Like others, I quit a number of times, but my desire for nicotine was too strong, and I started smoking again. One day, after a particularly intense practice of meditation, I lit a cigarette. I was so aware of my inner feelings that I felt the impact of the smoke in my lungs and the depressing effect that the carbon monoxide and other gases had on my body. My enhanced sensitivity to the subtle pain killed my desire for smoking, and I was able to quit without any difficulty.

Through biofeedback and the scientific study of yoga, we learn that we can consciously control physical events, such as blood flow, heart rate, and the firing of neurons, events that thirty years ago, science told us were totally beyond conscious control. Many think that biofeedback teaches us how to control our body. This is not true. We already know how to control the body. Everything that happens in the body is regulated by the mind, but it happens on the unconscious level. We use a biofeedback instrument to help us become more aware of both the physical event and the thoughts and feelings associated with it. By bringing the physical event out of the unconscious mind into our conscious mind, we have more choices. By being conscious, we can control the physical event by choosing our thoughts and feelings.

## An Exercise in Awareness

Try it for yourself. If you pay attention, you don't need a biofeedback machine to tell you when your muscles are tense and when they are relaxed. Sit quietly for a moment, and pay attention to the muscles in your face—the jaws, around the eyes, and the forehead. What do you feel? Now be aware of the muscles in the back of your neck and your shoulders. Most people carry excess tension in these areas, and if it becomes chronic, it can lead to tension headaches.

Picture these muscles as being very relaxed and loose. Imagine yourself sitting in your favorite vacation place, relaxing in the sun. Pay attention to what happens to the muscles in your face, neck and shoulders. Notice how your thoughts about being in your favorite spot seem to relax these muscles.

Now let your mind think about the last conflict you got involved with at work. Go over the situation clearly in your mind as if you were reliving it. What is happening to your muscles now? Which thoughts and feelings would you rather have? Which condition would you choose for your muscles? Your awareness gives you the choice.

## THE CONSCIOUSNESS OF CHOICE

When you function on the unconscious level, you do not choose. You take whatever the habit gives you. We all have powerful minds, but the habits we have built deny and distort our power. In business, entrepreneurs all too often provide examples of how untrained personal power cuts both ways.

One of my clients, Harry, the owner and CEO of a growing company, has a powerful and creative mind. Unfortunately, his emotional habits distort his abilities and tend to propel him toward chronic problems in his business.

When Harry stays balanced and in control of himself, he becomes a creative force that leads the company forward. He is a visionary, full of confidence, very loving and generous to his staff. But when he's emotionally out of control, Harry is egotistic, unwilling to listen to alternatives. He becomes vindictive, moody and suspicious, with an overpowering need to be in control of every little thing. He breaks promises, berates individuals in front of their peers, and doesn't allow any independent decision-making. All this creates an atmosphere of fear and intimidation. As a consequence, his managers tell him only what he wants to hear. He has trouble retaining talented people, and he feels alone and isolated.

The most interesting part of this is that Harry always talks about commitment, power-sharing, independent thought, and treating people with respect. He has read all the right books on motivating others, and can talk about the latest theories on effective management. But this isn't what Harry *does*. He only intellectualizes. His behavior, ways of thinking, and attitudes are controlled by his unconscious emotional habits, which are: to not listen to alternatives, to be in contol of everything, and to be egotistic.

There is a bit of Harry in all of us. At times we have flashes of real brilliance and understanding, but then our habits take over, and we become anxious and fearful, or egotistic and overbearing. But most often, we simply function in a routine, habitual manner, using only a small percentage of our real power. Being unaware of our power means that we either do not use it or, like Harry, we use it in abusive and unproductive ways.

That does *not* mean we are doomed to be a slave to our habits. We have all met people who seem intentionally insensitive to other people's feelings. They have a way of expressing themselves that communicates intolerance, impatience, or even callousness. Yet, after we get to know them, we discover that they didn't feel that way at all, nor did they really wish to communicate those attitudes. But when we confronted them with their behavior, they were genuinely surprised. They were not aware of how they affected others. When they recognized their habits, they immediately took steps to change them, and became more effective communicators. Awareness gave them a choice.

## MASTERING THE SKILL OF CONCENTRATION

Think about the three most important skills that you bring to your work, the reasons why you were hired instead of someone else. Take a sheet of paper and write them down. I have asked that question to thousands of executives, and their answers have been very consistent: communication skills, organizing abilities, experience, knowledge, ability to work with others, creativity and problem-solving skills, and so forth.

Look at the skills you have written down. No doubt, they are important skills. But how well could you use them if you were distracted? No matter how skillfully you communicate, solve problems, or organize your work, the moment you do not pay attention, you cannot do anything well. Yet, less than three percent of all the people asked this question list the ability to pay attention as one of their three most important skills.

Above all else, the Empowered Mind commands an enormous ability to concentrate. Without concentration, you cannot be creative, you cannot learn, and you will not do anything well, whether it's having sex or developing a successful marketing plan. Your mind has great power, but if that power is scattered by a thousand and one distractions, you are not using your mind to its full potential.

You must master the ability to focus attention, to concentrate. By training your power of concentration, you can expand your awareness. By being more aware, you can access your inner resources and enhance your performance and productivity. Concentration is the mind's executive skill. Through concentration, you can take command of your mind's energy and direct it towards the goals you want to achieve.

Mikhail Gorbachev, who has influenced world events directly or indirectly in the 1980s and 1990s while leading the Soviet Union, exemplifies this ability to pay attention. As one diplomat has stated, "When you are with Gorbachev, you feel as if you are the only person in the world. He pays complete attention to you, and you feel as if every word you say is being given complete and careful consideration."

## HOW TO TAP INTO YOUR POTENTIAL

We rarely think it strange if someone studies and practices to be a better scientist or accountant, or to play a better game of tennis or golf. So why do some of us think it is strange to practice being a better human being? Think of the personality as a tapestry constantly being created as we go through life. Whatever we do either reinforces or changes the pattern of the tapestry. The older we get, the more difficult it is to change the pattern, but it's not impossible. We constantly create ourselves. So, *why not create what we want, instead of allowing our mind to re-create the same patterns out of habit?* With persistent effort, we can tap the strength, knowledge and wisdom that lie within our vast unconscious mind, and create a powerful, more productive, and successful personality.

Take a moment and think about the kind of person you would really like to be. Include the personal qualities that seem almost too ideal to be real. Before you read any further, write these qualities down. You might be surprised to know that what you write down corresponds fairly closely to your actual innate capacities.

Why be satisfied with using only a small part of your potential? By developing these innate human qualities into usable skills, you can become more of who you really are. This is personal empowerment—learning the skills to actualize your human qualities to their fullest. You may not think of yourself as insightful as Einstein, or as creative as Picasso, but who knows what you might do once you learn how and where to focus your attention.

## HEALTH/WELLNESS SKILLS: LAYING THE FOUNDATION

The first step you must take toward an Empowered Mind is to create a healthy mind and body, free of stress and disease. Let's face it. It is difficult to be creative, intuitive and full of confidence when you suffer from painful ulcers or worry about your blood pressure. A balanced mind and body provide the foundation for personal empowerment.

When we feel good mentally and physically, we do our best work and our relationships run more smoothly. But we seldom think of staying healthy as a skill, nor do we fully appreciate the power we have to stay healthy.

Of course wellness is more than just being fit and doing exercises. It includes optimism and joy, the fundamental faith in our capacity to face the challenges of life, and the thrill we experience when we engage these challenges. When we are pessimistic or down in the dumps, nothing is much fun, nor can we really put our heart into what we're doing. It's a medical fact that happy people are healthier people. It's also a fact that those who love to work do better work.

We cannot fake joy, nor can we program it. We can get uplifted by an inspiring speaker. But if the uplifting does not come from within, the next day it's back to the same grind. *Optimism and joy are inner qualities that arise naturally from a balanced mind.*

The ability to remain calm when everything around you is falling apart is a crucial skill. Two researchers, Morgan McCall and Michael Lombardo, discovered that the most frequent reason executives failed as leaders was that they couldn't handle adversity under stress (Psychology Today, Feb., 1983). We've all "blown up" at some time or the other. Work pressures, money problems, and family difficulties upset our balance, and we become disturbed.

While we cannot control the world, we *can* learn to control our own reactions. We can face the world with equanimity, which comes from inner balance and the freedom from compulsive needs and wants.

Ted, a successful labor negotiator, is famous for his astute and tough negotiating abilities. His secret is simple. He walks into every negotiation completely convinced that he personally has nothing to gain or lose. He describes the feeling as one of "complete freedom. I walk into every negotiating session completely content with what I have, and with no need to have anything more." Because he maintains his equanimity and sense of contentment, Ted seldom walks away without achieving his objectives. When he does walk away, he does so without any regrets, leaving his mind clear to work on the next project.

## Executive "Response Ability"

As a labor negotiator, Ted takes control of the situation by being in control of his mind. The successful executive similarly must take full responsibility for himself or herself. The term responsibility is actually two words: response ability, the ability to respond based on knowledge and skill. Naturally, the greater your knowledge and skill, the greater is your ability to respond to the situations and challenges you face.

Too often, we use the word "responsibility" to blame or accuse others. We misuse it to find fault with someone else when we don't want to be responsible for our own thoughts and feelings.

The problem is that *blaming never solves any problems*. It only creates distorted states of mind, such as guilt, fear, resentment and depression. We become depressed and feel inferior, which makes us even weaker and more prone to making mistakes. Or we become defensive and create a siege mentality, erecting barriers to outside interference. Unfortunately, these barriers also block our inner resources.

By blaming, we deny our own inner power, our ability to take charge of our life and circumstances. This denial of personal response ability turns us into victims, and we lose any possibility of becoming strong and free. We see ourselves as weak, helpless, and dependent on others for our happiness, our livelihood, even our very existence. Then, the more dependent we become, the lower our self-respect sinks, and we enter a negative spiraling pattern of blame, dependency, and disrespect.

Just examine your own experience. How much work do you accomplish when you feel bad about yourself? And what is the quality of your work? It is not hard to see how the negativity engendered by blaming affects your performance and productivity.

Individuals and circumstances *can* create all sorts of problems for us. But life is full of problems for everyone. The stark truth is that we have enormous response ability, because we have enormous power. Successful people refuse to be victims, or to shoulder blame. By taking responsibility for yourself and what happens in your life, you begin to find ways to maximize your potential. Try the following experiment:

## An Exercise in Taking Responsibility

The next time you become angry with someone, blame them by saying "You really make me angry." Pay attention to how that feels when you give someone else the power to make you feel a certain way. Do you notice any feelings of helplessness? What are the reactions of the person you are talking to?

The next time you get angry, change the sentence. Say to that person: "I get really angry when you do that." Is there any difference in how you feel about yourself by staying responsible for your own feelings? How does the other person act? Which way of talking about your anger leaves you with more self-respect and feelings of self-worth and power?

Our health is an excellent example of the power of personal responsibility. It is only recently that we have begun to take responsibility for our own health. Not too many years ago, medical science was telling us that we had little control over what happened in our body, and even less over disease. When we became sick, we went to the doctor, the "expert" who assumed total responsibility for our illness. We took our pills, underwent our operations, and hoped for the best.

But in the early 1960s, we found that by using biofeedback we could begin to control and change physical events in our body that, according to the experts, were uncontrollable. Suddenly, we were learning how to consciously regulate blood flow, control the firing of muscle neurons, even change brain-wave patterns. Almost overnight, everything science had told us about the so-called "involuntary" nervous system was overturned. Since then, we have begun to make changes in what we eat and how we exercise. Some of us have even learned a few stress management techniques. As a result, we are beginning to see a decline in the incidence of heart disease in this country.

We are beginning to realize that our mind has a great deal to do with whether or not we stay healthy. A whole new area of research, called psychoneuro-immunology, has sprung up. It is the study of the influence of the mind and emotions on the immune system. Studies are done to see how depression inhibits our immune system and opens the way to cancer, and how anger and cynicism play a key role in the development of heart disease. The evidence is increasingly clear: our mind, through attitudes, emotions and mental imagery, plays a significant role in whether we suffer from disease such as cancer, heart attacks, and ulcers, or whether we enjoy increasing levels of wellness and health.

The importance of personal responsibility has led to a new philosophy and practice of medicine called "wholistic health," which involves the whole person—mind, body and spirit—in creating health and wellness. Prevention, patient participation, and responsibility are key principles. Instead of just prescribing medication to reduce hypertension, the cardiologist oriented towards wholisitic health involves the patient in a complete program of education and training in deep relaxation exercises, aerobic exercise, proper diet and techniques of emotional management. The physician's strategy not only includes immediate control through medication, but long-term resolution of the disease through education and training in self-management as well. The patient must take responsibility for his or her own state of health, and learn the skills necessary to change the internal conditions that cause the hypertension.

We can develop the same response ability for the inner resources of our mind. The more aware we are of our inner resources, and the more skilled we become at using these resources, the greater our personal response ability, and the more effective and productive we become.

This is personal empowerment: taking charge of our inner resources and refining the power of our mind. Once we manage our stress effectively, we can begin to explore the more subtle resources of our mind that directly impact on our level of performance, productivity, and success.

## PERFORMANCE SKILLS: PERCEPTUAL SENSITIVITY AND CREATIVE OPTIONS

Peter Drucker, one of the most influential teachers of management theory, makes the point that young executives stall in their career because they don't develop the skill to walk into a situation and grasp the whole picture at once—the gestalt. They are too busy analyzing to pay attention to what is already there in front of them.

To understand the world around us, we have to pay attention to what's out there. It's amazing how little we do this, and how much information we fail to hear, sense, or even see. We get distracted by our own thoughts, and only hear the words, not the real message communicated through changes in voice tone, tightening of jaw muscles, tension in the shoulders, or through subtle changes in the eyes.

Some very powerful resources depend on our perceptual sensitivity—our instinct, creativity and imagination. Our instincts are a powerful source of information. If you have ever sensed that a car was going to swerve into your lane, and you slowed in time to prevent a problem, you used your instincts. Or the time you "just knew" that someone in your family needed help, and you called them just at the right time. This is the power of instinct.

Our instincts tell us about anything and everything in our environment that directly affects our well-being. This knowledge comes from direct experience. We don't have to stop and figure things out, or analyze a situation. We know because we see, or smell, or sense the danger, or the opportunity. It's right there in front of our senses.

As we weave the pattern of our life, our creativity not only solves problems and makes us more effective; it adds color and beauty to our life as well. We would all like to be creative, but few of us feel that we really are. The big secret is that *your mind* is the creative force. Creativity is a natural and constant process of our mind. To unlock it, all you have to do is set your mind free from the rules and restrictions that you impose on it. Creativity requires flexibility, willingness to experiment and change the rules, and awareness of how your mind structures your perceptions. You can be as creative as you want, *if you know how to play with your mind, and enrich it by providing a variety of experiences for yourself.*

Closely tied to your creative force is your imagination. You use imagination to direct the power of your creative force. Imagery, the language of the unconscious mind, is part of the creative process, and a powerful tool for achievement and knowledge. You can use your imagination in two ways. Used in a reflective way, your imagination opens the door to your intuition and you gain insight and wisdom. Or you can use your imagination in an active way to bring about your visions, and create the outcomes you want. Whether you use it to be a better tennis player or a more effective manager, imagery focuses the energy of the mind on a single goal.

## VISIONARY SKILLS: COMMANDING THE FUTURE

A famous saying holds that those who don't know and understand history are bound to repeat it. We must also realize that those who cannot *envision* the future are bound to lose it. We often get so caught up in our immediate crises and short-term goals that we don't see the problems we are creating for ourselves in the future.

Today, when information moves at the speed of light, and technology changes almost as quickly, our ability to clearly see the path of our future becomes more and more critical. In a world where "slow" no longer has much meaning, visionary skills are a necessity, not a luxury. But who are the visionaries?

The great builders, the ones who set out in new directions, are visionaries. They lead social movements, inspire nations, and build industries. They also build communities, counsel others with wisdom, and march to the beat of their own drum. At all levels of society, visionaries have the power to see what others cannot and to bring that vision into being.

We have the power to create the future we want if we master three visionary skills—intuition, reasoning, and decisiveness.

We really don't need to consult an astrologer, or swirl tea leaves in a cup, to gain insight into our future. Our own intuition gives us insight into the cause-and-effect relationships that shape our future. By refining our mind's power of discrimination, we can discern the real consequences of our actions before we commit to an action. When we learn to listen to that small voice within, our true conscience, we make better decisions and fewer mistakes, create fewer disturbances for ourselves and others, and we direct ourselves towards a future that we understand more and more clearly. Think of the times when you could have saved yourself a lot of trouble if only you had listened to yourself.

Insight, however, must be supported with effective reasoning or critical thinking. Many things interfere with our ability to reason clearly— beliefs, memory, emotional disturbances, stress, even our attitudes. Often these are so subtle that we don't recognize them. We rely on logic to minimize mistakes, but even logic can be subverted by beliefs and emotions. Through inner balance and concentration we minimize interference, refine our power of discrimination, and use it along with logic to solve the problems we face.

All of our insight and analysis ends up with us making a decision. Or at least, it *should* end up there. This is where decisiveness, our ability to make the right decisions in time, enters in. Making a decision involves all of the skills we have talked about so far—balance, perceptual sensitivity, creativity, instincts and intuition, even our memory. But often, we don't trust our mind. All sorts of problems interfere—self-doubts, anxieties, fear of making mistakes or of what others may think of us. These create distractions and block our decisions. We hesitate and fail to decide in time. By developing and refining our inner skills, we discover that our mind already knows what to do, and even how to go about doing it. Using these natural abilities of the mind is what *Increasing Executive Productivity* is all about.

## DIRECTING YOUR LEADERSHIP SKILLS

Leaders come in all different styles. Some are democratic, while others are autocratic. Some lead because of their vast experience and knowledge, others because they know how to use someone else's vast experience and knowledge. Regardless of individual style, great leaders exercise personal power through three crucial mind skills—will, unlimited self-confidence, and self-discipline.

To be successful, we must be able to direct the power of our mind. This is called *will*, the ability to carry out what we decide to do. The more we are able to focus all the resources of our mind, both conscious and unconscious, the greater our will, and the more powerful our personality. To do this, we must make our mind one-pointed, free from all distractions. When we allow conflicts, competing desires, and self-doubt to divide our attention, our mind becomes weak and distracted. The more distracted we are, the less able we are to do anything. We enhance our will by refining our concentration and eliminating self-doubts.

Our confidence plays a crucial role in leadership and the exercise of our will. What others often see as courage is actually the expression of unlimited self-confidence. People often remark on how courageous it is for me to talk so easily in front of large audiences. But for me, it isn't courage at all. I'm confident in my knowledge and in my speaking skills. My mind never doubts this skill, so I never worry about doing a good job.

As you will find, this unlimited confidence is a natural part of the most subtle level of the mind. At this level, we are completely free from any conflict. We make a serious mistake when we depend on success to build our confidence. This leads to a chronic insecurity, and actually interferes with our real confidence. We don't really need to build confidence. *We need to stop destroying the genuine confidence that is already a part of who we are.*

Above all, leadership and success require self-discipline. Self-discipline poses a problem for us. We all want to have self-discipline, but no one seems to really like it. It always seems so difficult to achieve. But for those who understand their mind, self-discipline isn't at all difficult. It is simply creating the ability to do what you really want to do. Your mind has an almost infinite capacity to form habits. By taking charge of this capacity, you can consciously build the habits you want, and act in the ways you want to act. When we do this, we seem incredibly self-disciplined to others. But to ourselves, we are only being consistent with our chosen habits.

Productive executives—empowered executives—draw energy from challenges, and find opportunities in obstacles. Lech Walesa, the intrepid leader of Solidarity and a moving force for the freedom movement throughout Eastern Europe, characterizes the self-confidence, will and discipline of an empowered mind. With every setback, with each obstacle placed in his way by the Communist regime in Poland, Walesa found new strength and created opportunities to further his cause. This kind of personal power doesn't come through economic, political or military means, but from unshakable inner strength that will not and cannot be deterred.

## SPIRITUAL SKILLS: VALUES, ETHICS, AND THE HUMAN SPIRIT

When we use our concentration to increase our awareness of harmony, we experience the sovereignty of our human spirit, the finest aspect of our personality. At the heart of our humanity, at the very center of who we are, lies a power that brings freedom from fear and pain, and gives purpose and meaning to our life. Without spiritual fulfillment, all our accomplishments mean very little. Many of us reach a certain level of success only to find out that we're not sure what it all means. Somehow, our success doesn't quite satisfy our human spirit, and we still find ourselves insecure and unhappy, desperately seeking the love and satisfaction that continue to elude us.

Three powerful skills fulfill the spiritual power that is part of every human being: a sense of wholeness and community, humility, and love.

We become empowered when we recognize that we are part of something greater than ourselves—a relationship, a family, a community. Great strength lies in unity. Our ability to act for a greater good or the benefit of others frees our mind from petty emotional distortions. Great leaders become great in part because they could tap this power of community to accomplish their goals.

On the other hand, political and religious demagogues—the Hitlers, the cult leaders—intentionally play upon the fears of their followers, setting one group against the other in order to maintain control and power. When we feel separate and isolated from each other, we become fearful.

You can see the same thing in the workplace. When there is competition for power and position, conflict between management and labor, superiors who are "out for themselves," and corporate policies that don't respect individual needs and concerns, the breakdown of cooperation soon occurs. This leads to isolation rather than community. The result is disloyalty, apathy, and self-serving behavior.

Belonging requires humility, the awe and respect that come when we recognize that we are a small but integral part of something greater and more profound than our own small self. Very few even recognize the power of humility. It is our greatest virtue—and our greatest friend, though we do not experience it as such. Humility provides the foundation for our curiosity and gives us the freedom to learn and to lead others without creating conflict and opposition. We may think of humility as a weakness, but the truth is that only a strong ego has the power of humility.

Our most crucial innate capacity is love. Not the kind of love you might expect—hugging, kissing and emotional attachment—but the ability to give selflessly. Love is what we give, not anything we take. The greater our capacity to give, the less emotional disturbance and unhappiness we experience. And, oddly enough, the greater we can become. If we give respect, we gain respect. If we give power, we gain power. By giving of ourselves, we overcome fear and pain.

The idea that selfless love is a skill you can develop instead of something that just happens to you may seem a bit strange at first. But, as you shall see in this book, the more you practice selfless loving, the more fearless you will become and the greater impact you will have on others.

## THE EMPOWERED MIND: PERSONAL POWER IN ACTION

We all have choices to make. We can do nothing—just take what genetics, culture and chance have given us and hope for the best. Or we can develop our inner capacities and become skilled, responsible human beings. In either case, we will weave the tapestry of our life. It is simply up to us whether we will do it enslaved to whatever unconscious habits and patterns we happen to develop.... or we will take conscious control of our life and create a masterpiece.

To create an Empowered Mind is a life-time journey of self-discovery, a chipping away at self-imposed limits. The wisdom, knowledge and effectiveness that we gain as we explore and develop our capacities are truly endless. We really don't know what the limits of personal power are.

If we think of personal power as something external, something that we must acquire such as financial power, political power, or military power, we already place ourselves in a position of weakness and deprivation. The compulsive need for external power exists because we aren't aware of our inner strength and power. We think that wealth and fame will make us feel secure and lead to happiness. But when we depend on "*things*," all we get is conflict, insecurity and unsatisfied wants and desires. No matter how much we acquire, there will always be more to get, and there will always be the threat of loss.

The successful executive with an Empowered Mind builds on *inner* strength. It is truly "personal power" that emerges from the knowledge and mastery of our own resources. By taking command of our innate capacities, we operate with integrity. Our growing concern with ethics is really a concern about the very best of human behavior. Ethics isn't a question of knowing what to do, but how to be.

In our day-to-day living, we seldom make the connection between ethical behavior, and inner strength, balance and harmony. We believe, mistakenly, that the very best of human qualities and behavior are something to learn, to acquire—something extrinsic, not part of who we are already. The message we fail to hear, or fail to understand when we do hear, is that in being the best possible human being, it is we who benefit the most. When we master our inner resources, we master our life.

In the following chapters, we will explore the ways and means to create an Empowered Mind and increase your executive productivity. The unique program in this book can help you develop the inner skills of vision, leadership and performance. Chapter 2 is a road map for your journey, telling you where to look for the resources you need to develop. Chapters 3 and 4 deal with the knowledge and tools of inner balance and mind control. In Chapter 5, you learn about concentration and how to refine and polish this ultimate skill of your conscious mind. Chapters 6, 7, and 8 show you how to develop and refine the powerful resources of our mind. Chapter 9 focuses on the power of the human spirit and its role in completing the development of an Empowered Mind.

## SUMMARY OF PRINCIPLES

1. The productive executive with an Empowered Mind is one who realizes who he is and who can take command of his inner resources, and achieve the highest levels of personal effectiveness, leadership and fulfillment.

2. Through direct self-awareness, we gain access to the power functions of our personality. Only our conscious mind has the power to direct attention and expand our awareness. Through conscious attention, we gain command over the innate resources of our mind.

3. The ultimate executive skill is concentration. Success in any aspect of our life depends directly on our ability to focus our attention. When we use concentration to achieve awareness of

   - **Balance,** we develop **Health/Wellness Skills**
   - **Sensitivity,** we develop **Performance Skills**
   - **Insight,** we develop **Visionary Skills**
   - **Power,** we develop **Command/Leadership Skills**
   - **Harmony,** we develop **Spiritual Skills**

4. By taking complete responsibility for ourself, our emotions, thoughts and actions, we gain response ability. The more we

blame others, the weaker we become, and the less response
ability we have.

5. The inner skills of an executive with an Empowered Mind are as
follows:

| INNER SKILLS | | |
|---|---|---|
| Category | Skills | Qualities |
| Health/ Wellness | Body/Mind Balance Optimism/Joy Contentment | High level of physical and mental health; a fundamental optimism; zest for life; mental clarity. |
| Performance | Instinct/Creativity/ Decisiveness | Observation without distortion; attunement—sensitive to others and events; knows when to act and when not to act. |
| Visionary | Intuition/Imagination/ Reasoning | Long-term vision, foresight; operates beyond conventional wisdom; uses imagery effectively to tap the power of unconscious mind; reasons clearly and calmly; reflective discrimination. |
| Command/ Leadership | Will/Self-confidence Self-discipline | Turn obstacles into opportunities; commands inner strength; inspires others; can transform atmosphere of any situation; "balance observation, strategy and passion in responsible action." |
| Spiritual | Wholeness/Community/ Humility/Love | Cooperation instead of dominance; builds teams; fearless and unafraid; dedication to service; ethical, acts with integrity; respects others. |

Figure 1:2

# A Map of Personal Power: The Journey Within

**2**

---

*"Do you hear the grasshopper that is at your feet?" asked the old man. "Old Man," said the young boy, "how is it that you hear these things?" "Young man," said the old blind master, "how is it that you do not?"*

*From the movie* Kung Fu

When I learned to really observe my behavior and the behavior of those around me, I began to see how crippling it is when we view the world with pre-conceived opinions. I realized that if I decided that I didn't like the job assigned to me, I wasted a great deal of time and energy complaining and agonizing over it. Consequently, it took longer to do because I never gave it my full attention, and it wasn't done as well as I could have done it. Because of my disturbance, I wasn't able to understand the benefits for myself or the company from doing the job. Now when I am faced with a similar situation, and I recognize my old pattern, I relax, clear my mind, and stop the disturbance. I'm able to concentrate on my work more effectively and finish the job efficiently, all without being upset.

*Joan N., Marketing Manager*

How well you understand yourself determines how well you use the hidden resources of your mind. When you don't pay attention, you can get stuck in habits that aren't very helpful for you. The moment you

23

become aware of who you are, and what you do, you begin to make better choices. The more you know, the more power you exercise, and the more freedom you have.

To discover your resources, you need to know where to look. Imagine what it would be like to travel in a foreign land without a map. You could wander an entire lifetime without reaching your destination. To explore the different levels of your personality, it's helpful to have a map to show you its where's and how's. The diagrams that follow can help you chart the direction you must take in order to develop your innate power and become more successful.

## JOURNEYING THROUGH THE FIVE LEVELS OF SELF-POWER

We often shy away from too much self-analysis, and with good reason. If we constantly analyze ourselves—"Why did I do this?" "Why did I do that?"—we go crazy. We can end up depressed, or neurotic, or both. On the other hand, genuine self-discovery is a journey that makes us aware of our own power. As long as we don't disturb ourselves with negative judgments about what we find, nothing is more fascinating than learning about ourselves.

During my more than twenty years of personal study and professional work in biofeedback, stress management, and executive development, I have found an uncomplicated way of looking at myself and others. It helps me understand my own inner resources, and to help others understand theirs. It begins with the obvious and travels to less known, more subtle levels. In science, the physicist begins by studying matter, but ends up with pure energy in the form of atoms, neutrons, and protons. In this book I will do the same. Exploration of mind and personality begins with matter, our physical body, and proceeds through four more levels to a subtle field of pure intelligence and energy. Each level becomes yet more subtle and powerful than the previous level. These five levels of our personality are shown in Figure 2:1.

Within each level are power functions which provide resources in the form of knowledge and skills. To use them effectively, you must learn what they are. Before you begin to explore them on an intellectual level, however, take an experiential journey through your mind by paying attention to these five levels in the following exercise.

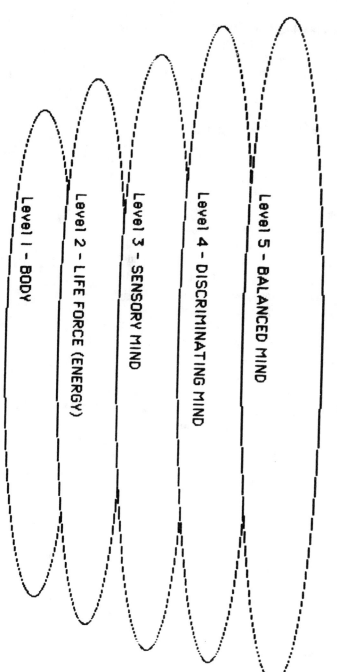

PERSONALITY MAP

Level 1 – BODY

Level 2 – LIFE FORCE (ENERGY)

Level 3 – SENSORY MIND

Level 4 – DISCRIMINATING MIND

Level 5 – BALANCED MIND

Figure 2:1

## A Traveling Exercise

(When doing an exercise, a series of periods [.........] indicates a pause.)

Sit back in your chair, close your eyes, and relax as well as you can........ Let your breath become very smooth and even...... Breathe without any effort on your part........Now direct your awareness to your body..........Where do you feel tension in the body?.........Can you feel your heart beat?...........What else do you feel in your body?............ What do you feel or sense, what do you hear, what do you smell?....... Now bring your attention to your breath...........What does the air feel like as it comes in your body and goes back out?...............Be aware of the lungs as they expand and contract................. Be aware of your level of energy..... Is your energy level low or high?.......Is the quality of the energy calm or tense?............ Now be aware of your thoughts............... Don't try to think about them, just be aware of your mind thinking them for you.............. Notice how they jump from one topic to another.............. Be aware of how some thoughts grab your attention more than others........ Do you notice any relationship between your thoughts and your level of energy?............... What happens when a worry comes to your mind?............. Now go to what seems to be the center of your mind and allow yourself to think of a problem you must solve........... Don't allow your emotions to pull you into the problem, look at the problem as if it were quite separate from you................ Examine the problem as if it had nothing at all to do with you.......... Do you notice anything different about the problem?............ Is there any greater clarity, and do you notice any details that you may have passed over before?....... Now imagine yourself going to the very center of your mind where it is very quiet and still.......... Allow yourself to experience this stillness and quietness for a few moments.......... Notice what happens to the thoughts................. After a few moments, be aware of the thoughts of your mind......Now become aware of your breathing.....Is there any difference in your breathing?................. Now be aware of how your body feels................. Now gently open your eyes.

As you traveled through the five different levels of your personality with your attention, you experienced the different functions of each level—body feelings, the movement of breath, thoughts, objectivity about your thoughts, and quietness. The more you understand and experience these functions, the easier it will be to use them as conscious skills to create an empowered mind that will boost your productivity.

## AN ANALOGY: THE COMPUTER AND YOU

We can use a computer system to help us understand how the five different levels relate to each other. Keep in mind, however, that there isn't a computer built that begins to approach the capabilities of our own mind. Let's draw an analogy between the different parts of the computer and the different levels of our personality:

| Level | Human | Computer |
|-------|-------|----------|
| MAP COMPARISON OF HUMAN PERSONALITY AND COMPUTER SYSTEM | | |
| Level 1 | Body | The shell and hardware of a computer |
| Level 2 | Life Force (Energy) | Electrical energy that runs the computer |
| Level 3 | Sensory Mind | Software programs |
| Level 4 | Discriminating Mind | Computer language |
| Level 5 | Balanced Mind | The potential of the computer language before it's written down as a specific program |

Figure 2:2

When we use a computer, we enter data through a variety of ways, such as a keyboard, modem, or scanner. Inside the computer, the hardware and software work together to manipulate the data and provide some intelligent outcome. We will call these functions "power functions" because they create an intelligent outcome. The more you know how to manipulate these power functions inside the computer, the more creative use you get out of the computer. For instance, if you understand programming, you have greater freedom to develop the power of your system. You can also use your computer without any programming knowledge or skill. But then you are limited to the software packages that you buy.

The same is true of your personality. Each of the levels of your personality has particular power functions. You can use your mind without having much knowledge about how these power functions work, but then you are limited to whatever habits (programs) were created as you grew up. The more you understand about how your personality and, in particular, how your mind functions, the more you will be able to develop and use the power within the system.

## PERSONALITY LEVEL I: BODY—YOUR MOBILE HOME

Your body is like the shell and hardware of a computer. The keyboard and modem represent your senses, the computer screen symbolizes your face, the wiring your nerves, and the boards depict your brain. Of course, this is only a crude analogy. Your body is far more sophisticated, more mobile, and far more interactive with the environment. And like a mobile home, it takes you from here to there, wherever your mind decides to go.

We're all familiar with this level of our personality, but we don't usually realize just what a valuable resource it is. Two power functions of our body play particularly important roles in our personal effectiveness: our capacity for health, and our body's capacity to gather and provide information.

### Health, Performance, and Skill

Your body has amazing resources to maintain a healthy balance. When you interfere with these resources, or don't manage them well, you end up with disease. The relationship between health and performance is simple and direct: when you aren't healthy, you don't function well. It's hard to focus your attention on work when an ulcer hurts, when you have a headache, or when you worry about your blood pressure. Life is no fun when you feel sick.

*The greatest health problem we face is stress.* Stress-related psychosomatic diseases account for 75 to 85 percent of our health problems, depending on which expert you talk to. Stress-related health care costs have become prohibitive. For instance:

- We spend over 11 percent of our Gross National Product on health care.

- In 1988, over 159 million work days were lost due to headaches alone.

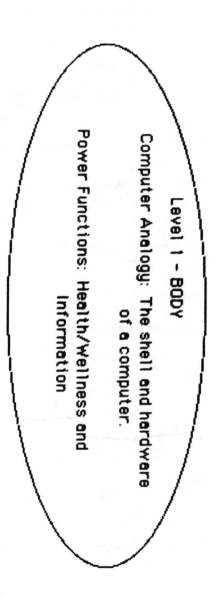

Level 1 – BODY

Computer Analogy: The shell and hardware of a computer.

Power Functions: Health/wellness and Information

THE BODY REPRESENTS THE MOST PRIMITIVE LEVEL OF HUMAN FUNCTIONING; SUBJECT TO DIRECT CONTROL BY THE MIND; PROVIDES VALUABLE INFORMATION ABOUT THE ENVIRONMENT AND UNCONSCIOUS MIND; USEFUL TOOL FOR MOVING ABOUT IN THE WORLD.

Figure 2:3

- Direct medical costs of one heart attack suffered by an executive can cost a corporation over $60,000.

- Corporations which don't have a responsible stress management program for its employees have been held legally liable for stress-related diseases.

- Stress-related disabilities now account for 14 percent of disability payments.

The direct costs are only the tip of the iceberg, of course. We can't even measure the impact that stress has on performance—on our decision-making skills, mental clarity, problem-solving, creativity, and intuition. Stress affects every aspect of our life—our relationships, our work, our ability to enjoy life, even our vacations. The indirect costs of drug abuse, divorce and the disruption of family life are enormous. So are the costs of wrong decisions and low morale. Ultimately, we all pay for these costs, either in higher taxes, higher insurance premiums, or in higher prices for goods.

## Corporate Stress Management

Fortunately, this is one problem we can solve. We can take charge of our health and wellness by learning how to manage our stress. In corporations, stress management is becoming a permanent part of executive training. One of the earliest stress management programs for executives was begun in 1974 by Dewey Balch, a retired FBI agent who was interested in training young "fast track" executives to become more effective managers. In cooperation with Elmer Green of the Menninger Clinic, Dewey created a truly innovative program designed to enhance self-knowledge and self-management skills. The executives stayed for five days at the Menninger Clinic in the Voluntary Controls program, where much of the pioneering work in biofeedback research was done. Here they used biofeedback to learn how to manage their muscle tension, brain waves and blood flow in order to become deeply relaxed. Many of the executives who went through this early program view the experience as a turning point in both their career and their life styles.

In 1975, when I joined the teaching staff of Dewey's program, most executives viewed stress management as "black magic," part of the "feely-touchy psychology stuff" that had little to do with the real world. Today, most executives recognize that to be productive and successful in business, or anything else, you must be able to manage both physical and mental stress.

Effective stress management programs can reduce health care costs, enhance performance and improve morale. But much of the stress management training today is ineffectual and incomplete, and stress-related diseases remain the major source of health care costs. The problem isn't the pressures we face, but *the mismanagement of our own innate resources*. By learning to skillfully manage our inner resources, we can live a life free from the problems of stress.

## The Body as an Information Resource

Your body is a valuable resource for information and knowledge. Like a sophisticated receiver, it picks up and responds to a variety of signals from your environment. It also responds to changes in your mind. If you pay attention to these responses, you understand both the world around you and your inner world—the condition of your health, your emotional states, and your instincts and intuition. These physical responses may be subtle: changes in the pupils of your eyes as you react to something you find disgusting; dramatic, such as a pounding heart as you react to an immediate danger; a tensing of our shoulder muscles as we hear about a new project.

Paying attention to the signals of your body can help you avoid a lot of problems, even disease. We always have early symptoms and warnings of a disease. For example, high blood pressure is most often a symptom of chronic stress. It is a clear signal that we are not handling pressure well. If we are not aware of high blood pressure, it can lead to a disaster, such as a stroke or heart attack. Once we know, we can easily take steps—deep relaxation, proper breathing, and emotional control—to use our resources more effectively and eliminate this problem.

By being sensitive to what our body tells us, we can prevent problems from becoming disasters. For instance, there is absolutely no reason why anyone should suffer from a tension headache. Tension headaches come from chronic muscle tension in the neck and shoulders, the forehead, or in the jaws. Typically, we ignore this tension until we experience pain. Then we take an aspirin or some other pain killer to get rid of the headache. But, in all our medical research and clinical experience, no one has ever described a headache caused by a lack of aspirin in the blood. Taking an aspirin doesn't cure the headache. It only dampens the signal that our muscles have a problem. The next day, we take another aspirin, and continue to ignore the real problem of chronic tension.

It is unnecessary and unhealthy to be so insensitive to changes in our body that we don't notice them until we have a real problem. We can easily prevent tension headaches by relaxing our muscles whenever we feel them becoming tense. The more sensitive we become, the more control we have.

In fact, paying attention to muscle tension is one of the easiest ways to learn how to use our body as an information resource. When you pay attention, you become more sensitive to the deeper, more subtle signals of your body, such as the changes that signal your instincts and intuition. The following simple exercise helps develop your sensitivity to the information and knowledge provided by your body.

### Body Check Exercise

Take a few moments to sensitize yourself to what your body is feeling at this moment. Close your eyes, and be aware of any tension you feel in your face—forehead, eyes, mouth, jaws. Then scan the rest of your body for tension. Are your shoulders tight? The back of your neck? Stomach muscles tense? How about your legs? Wherever you feel any tension, try to relax those muscles by picturing them as warm, heavy and loose. Be aware of your breathing. Is it uneven, jerky or rapid? Try to slow your breath down, and make it very smooth and even. What happens when you do that? What do you feel inside when your breath becomes slow and even? Then be aware of your heart beat. Don't be alarmed if it sounds too loud or hard. Even try to feel the pulse as it flows throughout the body. Don't judge anything you find as good or bad, simply practice observing and developing sensitivity to what your body is telling you.

Do this exercise at home several times. Then as you gain more experience, do it at work and in different settings to become more sensitive to what you are feeling at these different times and places.

### Tuning In to Knowledge

We are often astonished at the sensory acuity of the blind. They seem to develop amazing powers of smell, touch and hearing, and are sensitive to environmental changes which we do not notice. Yet, except for vision, the blind have the same sensory equipment as the sighted. Because they can't use their vision, they learn to use their other senses more effectively.

Also, they really pay attention, while we ignore staggering amounts of information.

We have access to an almost endless amount of information about people and situations. We can hear sounds, such as changes in voice timbre and tone, we can feel kinesthetic changes in the room as tension increases and decreases, and we can smell all kinds of smells. The blind pay attention to all of it. *So can those of us who are sighted.* We can also see subtle visual cues, like changes in the fine muscles around the lips, changes in the pupils of the eyes, even on-going changes in skin coloration. When we use this information, we understand others more completely, make better decisions, and communicate more effectively.

Top sales people are very sensitive to the nuances of feeling that go on during the sales approach. They may not be able to tell you why, but they have an uncanny ability to know when to press forward, when to pause, and when to retreat gracefully. Kenny Rogers's song about the old gambler who knew there's a time to "hold 'em, a time to fold em, a time to walk away, and a time to run" is a classic statement of instinct.

The key to this perceptual sensitivity is knowing how to pay attention. Try the following brief exercise. It will give you an idea of how much information you can gain by paying attention.

### Sensitivity Exercise

Take a few moments to stand in front of a mirror and look closely at your face. Pay attention to the skin tone and the colors that seem to constantly shift. See how many different colors you can observe in your face. Then watch the subtle changes occurring in the fine muscles around your eyes and your mouth. Allow your mind to think about different things going on at work or at home. Think about problems, accomplishments, arguments, enjoyable activities—whatever comes to your mind. Watch carefully for the subtle changes in your face as your mind moves from one topic to another. Once you begin to notice these in your own face, try watching the faces of others. These constant and subtle changes provide a rich source of information about what others think and feel.

### Accessing the Unconscious Mind Through Sensitivity

When you turn this sensitivity inward, you access the knowledge in your unconscious mind. Every emotion, thought or image that goes on in your mind has some impact on your body, even if you are not aware of it. In many ways, your body is a semi-frozen picture of your mind. Because of this extremely close relationship between the body and mind, you can use your body as a doorway to the subtle unconscious levels of your mind. In fact, it's often the subtle changes we feel in our body that alert us to an intuition. Remember the time when you were working on a project and something just didn't feel right? You could not tell what it was, but you had a sense that something didn't fit. You might have even said to your colleague "Something smells funny." Sure enough, a few days later, the project fell apart and you had to take a different direction.

These subtle feelings give us a direct line to our unconscious intuitive knowledge. For example, I can always tell several days in advance whenever I'm about to get some very bad news. I get a certain apprehension, a feeling of danger that is quite different from what I feel when I worry. Recently, I was prepared for a major training program that was to begin in two weeks. We had spent three months in finalizing the program, scheduling the training, and preparing the materials. Everything was ready to go. Then I decided it was time to buy a new car. As I negotiated the financial arrangements, I had a sense that I was going to lose the income I was counting on. Both my logical mind and my emotions argued that everything was fine. After all, nothing could go wrong—I was prepared for a delay of a few weeks, or even a few months.

Sure enough, two days after I bought the car, the training contract was canceled. Fortunately, I had listened to that sense of "something's not quite right here," and I had taken some extra steps to protect myself financially. Even though I couldn't identify the problem, my intuition told me that one was coming, and I had better prepare for it.

Of course, not everything we sense or feel is helpful or true. Emotional patterns, such as fear, worry or desire, also create feelings in our body. We've all been fooled by feeling absolutely sure of a job we were going to get, or a lottery we were certain to win—only to find out later it was wishful thinking, and had nothing to do with reality at all. But once we develop our perceptual sensitivity, we can easily recognize the difference between useful feelings and sensations, and ones that should best be ignored. After years of paying attention to my body's messages from the unconscious, I can easily tell the difference between worries or desires and instinct or intuition.

But let's go a little deeper into our personality. There are more powerful resources available to us in the next level, the level of energy.

## PERSONALITY LEVEL II:
## ENERGY—MIND/BODY CONNECTION

Our life force, the second level, is like the electricity that allows the computer to run. If we cut off the electricity, the computer doesn't work. If we lose our life force, we don't work. But there is at least one critical difference between a machine and a living human being. The physics of a machine are self-contained. You can turn the electricity on and off as many times as you wish, and the machine still functions. That doesn't work with our life force. Once it is gone, so are we.

It's an interesting phenomenon that for a few moments after death, the physics of the body do not change. You can pass electrical current through the nervous system, keep the organs functioning, and maintain the system for some time. But the body is not alive, and the person never returns. Literally, no one is at home in that body.

We experience our life force as energy. At times we feel energized, ready to take on the world. At other times, we feel very low on energy, maybe even feel depressed, and barely able to function. When we take control of the life force level, we enhance and maintain our energy. At this level, the power function to manage is our breath, the critical source of energy. We can go without food for several days, and almost as long without water, but we can live only a few moments without breathing.

Breathing is so much a part of us that as long as we aren't deprived, we pay little attention to it. We don't realize that the *way* we breathe can either lead to chronic stress or create a state of inner balance and harmony. Unfortunately, most of us have a habit of breathing that creates more work for our heart, leads to chronic stress, and often to hypertension. By taking control of our breathing habits, we can balance our system, take the pressure off the heart, and calm our mind.

On a physical level, both diet and exercise play vital roles in regulating our energy. When we do not eat properly, we do not supply the fuel necessary to maintain stable energy levels. A poor diet leads to poor overall health and disease that deplete our energy reserves. This has a direct impact on our mind. We do not think as clearly, solve problems as easily, or enjoy life as completely.

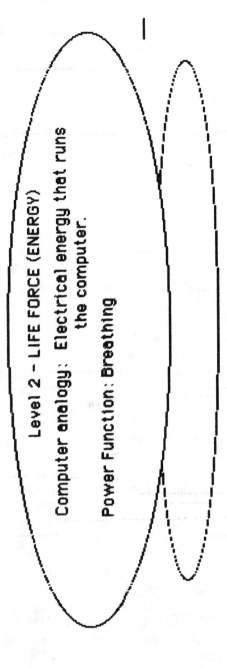

Level 2 – LIFE FORCE (ENERGY)

Computer analogy: Electrical energy that runs
the computer.

Power Function: Breathing

THE LIFE FORCE IS THE INTERACTIVE LEVEL BETWEEN THE
BODY AND THE MIND; IT IS THE ATOMIC/SUB-ATOMIC LEVEL
OF HUMAN FUNCTIONING; THE MAJOR VEHICLE FOR ENERGY
INTO THE SYSTEM IS THE BREATH.

Figure 2:4

The same is true of exercise. When we exercise consistently, we feel better, more energized and more alert. On the other hand, if we sit like couch potatoes in front of the TV for hours at a time, and don't exercise regularly, our level of energy drops. We become lethargic, and our mind becomes as lazy as our body. Even our posture can affect how we feel and think by creating a negative or positive energy field. Try the following exercise to see how your body can affect your mood states.

**Body-Energy-Mind Exercise**

Some morning when you wake up feeling good, walk as if you were depressed—your shoulders slumped, back bent over slightly, eyes downcast. After a brief period of time in this posture, be aware of what happens to your mood and your thoughts. Then correct your posture. Sit and walk erect, but without tension, as if you owned everything that you saw —head up, eyes forward, and your carriage proud. Watch the impact on your emotions and thinking. When you wake up in a bad or depressed mood, try walking in this erect posture and see how it affects you.

**Mind and Energy Level**

Although not as obvious, your mind plays an even more critical role in determining your level of energy. Look how energized you feel when you think about a new and exciting project, or about someone you really like. On the other hand, worries, anxieties, or remembering all your past mistakes, deplete your energy, and you feel worn out, bored or restless. *Depending on how you channel your emotional energy, you create either health or disease for your body.*

As crucial as energy is to our health and performance, we seldom think or talk about ourselves as complex patterns of energy. Yet, energy is the basis of our physical existence, and serves as the crucial connecting link between our body and mind. Mismanaged energy can cause stress, emotional disturbances, and cloudy thinking. Once we understand and manage our energy level skillfully, however, stress ceases to be a problem. We can then increase our power of concentration, and gain powerful tools to regulate and direct our emotional energy.

**The Mind—Our Ultimate Resource**

Now our journey brings us to the fascinating realm of our mind, the three inner levels of our personality. Our mind is the instrument we use to understand the world around us. Its sole purpose is to create knowledge. Our mind is a field of intelligent energy, that is modified or altered by its interaction with the world. We experience these changes as knowledge.

You should not confuse your mind with your brain. These are two very different realities. The brain is a physical organ, part of the body, which serves as the control room for the mind. In a sense, the brain operates as a transducer, changing the subtle energy modifications of the mind into biochemical and neurological events that move the body. Although the body can influence the mind, the real power lies in the mind.

Using our computer analogy, your mind is like software—both the programs (the patterned electromagnetic fields) and language that uses the hardware. The hardware of the computer is really there to allow the software to do its job. This also defines the relationship of your brain to your mind. Your brain (hardware) is the structure which your mind (software) uses to express itself.

Within each of the three levels of your mind (sensory, discriminating, and balanced mind) lie powerful resources. The greater your ability to understand, access and use these inner resources as conscious skills, the more empowered you become.

## LEVEL III: SENSORY MIND—MAKING SENSE OF THE WORLD

The Sensory Mind is a busy, noisy place, filled with sensory stimulation, emotions, wants and desires, habits and feelings. Out of all this, we try to make some kind of sense of the world around us. Your sensory mind is like the software programs in a computer that take input and organize it into meaningful patterns. Your sensory mind takes information from the environment and organizes it along the habit patterns formed by your past experiences. Then, like the software, it sends a response back to the body and the environment.

If you enter accurate data into a computer, and there are no bugs or virus in the program, you get intelligent, useful output. On the other hand, if you put the wrong data in, or if there are bugs or a virus in the program, you get the wrong answers. If you have "garbage" coming in, such as emotional stress, pollution, or bad food, you get "garbage" coming out—emotional disturbances, stress diseases, fuzzy thinking, and ineffectual behavior.

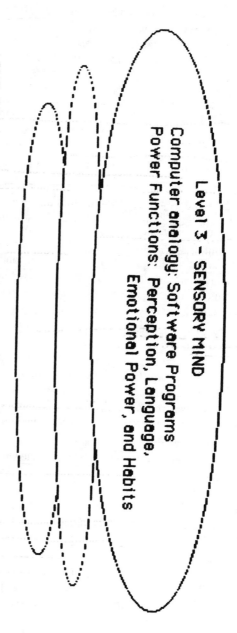

**Level 3 – SENSORY MIND**

Computer analogy: Software Programs

Power Functions: Perception, Language,
Emotional Power, and Habits

OUR SENSORY MIND ORGANIZES SENSORY DATA; CREATES
MEANING THROUGH LANGUAGE; CHANNELS EMOTIONAL ENERGY
AND OPERATES THROUGH HABITS.

Figure 2:5

Fortunately, we are far more sensitive, flexible, and adaptive than even the most sophisticated computer. We can change our programming, and create entirely new ways to respond to our environment. But if we don't know how to manage our sensory mind, we lose this advantage. Our habits control us, and we end up being abused by our own programming.

## Facts and Instincts: Two Kinds of Knowledge

To understand the world around us, we use our mind to create three different forms of knowledge. Two of these, sensory knowledge and instinct, are found in the sensory mind.

Our sensory mind creates the context in which we view the world. When we organize our perceptions into a consistent form, we have facts and beliefs, which we accept as the truth. But the mind does not always tell us the truth. Facts change, and so do our beliefs. As we gain wisdom, expand our experience, and change the context in which we view the world, our sensory knowledge also changes. At one time, it was self-evident that the world was flat. All the scholars and scientists agreed. But then a few visionary and courageous souls, like Magellen, Columbus, and Copernicus, refused to accept "common knowledge," and the facts changed to fit our new perceptions.

Sensory knowledge is the most common knowledge. It is also the *least* reliable. The quality of sensory knowledge depends on how well we manage our sensory mind, and how sophisticated our concepts are. Emotions, memory, lack of attention, strong beliefs, attitudes—all of these limit the usefulness of sensory knowledge. Logic may help us think in a consistent manner, but it does not guarantee the right answer, especially if the information in our data base is inaccurate.

Our sensory mind is also the level of our instinct, the second knowledge state of our mind. Instinct is an awareness of events or things in the world that directly affect our self-preservation. It concerns our personal well-being, or the well-being of whom or whatever we emotionally identify with, such as our children, our jobs, or our financial status. Our instincts tell us about the world as it is at this moment, and instinctual knowledge is much more reliable than facts and beliefs of sensory knowledge.

As an energy field, our mind is sensitive to subtle changes in the energy fields that surround us. These may be physical events, such as changes in barometric pressure, in the electromagnetic spectrum, or even in sunlight. More often, they will be changes in the emotional states of the people around us. Most of us have had the experience of walking into a room full of people and suddenly feeling that "something is wrong." Or we walk into a room where the tension is so thick we could cut it with a knife. No instrument in physics can measure these changes, but we know them instantly and accurately.

Instinctual knowledge is emotionally based. It bypasses the intellect. It is direct, and in a sense, more honest than sensory knowledge because it doesn't require a conceptual framework. However, this doesn't mean that you cannot make a mistake. We often confuse our emotional needs, desires and disturbances with instinct. We must develop our perceptual sensitivity and understand our emotional states in order to take full advantage of our instincts.

To develop the resources of our sensory mind, we must take control of four power functions:

1. Perception;

2. Language;

3. Emotional Power;

4. Habits.

**Perception: Creating Personal Reality**

The process of perception is our basic reality generator. We collect information through our senses, and organize it into a meaningful reality for ourselves. In this process our emotions, memory, beliefs, expectations, as well as our constitution, genetic factors, state of health, and stress all act as filters which shape and color our perceptions, and determine the quality of our experience. These factors also lead to a unique reality for each individual. Two people sitting in the same room, having the same experience, will interpret that experience in their own unique way, not always agreeing as to what really happened. We each experience the same reality, but we interpret that reality in very unique ways.

If we understand that our reality depends on the quality and nature of our perceptual process, we can easily accommodate each other, and find common ground and common definition. But when our perceptions become too influenced or distorted by our emotions, beliefs, attitudes, or any of the factors which influence the perceptual process, finding agreement with others becomes much harder. Just think of the last disagreement you had with someone close to you. How much of a role did a different perspective play in that disagreement? How much did you each insist that the way you see things is "the truth"?

Two powerful events of our sensory mind play a critical role in how and what we perceive: (1) our experience of pain and pleasure; and (2) our experience of time and space. Without these two, sensory experience would be a meaningless jumble of sensations.

Pain and pleasure shape our emotions and strongly influence our thoughts. Just as powerful is our experience of time and space, which depends on sensory experience. Even when scientists use the most sophisticated atomic clock, the infinitely subtle measurement of decaying atoms, they read that clock through sensory experience. The experience of pleasure/pain and time/space help define our personal reality, but they also impose powerful limits on our understanding of reality.

The act of perception is a creative process. Of course, the world is really there, but in the process of organizing our sensory input, *we create reality as we understand it*. Our skill in directing and using this creative process determines the usefulness and richness of our reality. Language, the second power function, is the means through which this happens.

## Language: The Power to Define Reality

> In the clubhouse, three umpires were discussing the pending World Series game. The youngest, proud of being selected to participate in the World Series, bragged to his colleagues: "I never worry about mistakes. I call 'em as I see 'em."
>
> The other two umpires started laughing, and the middle-aged umpire retorted: "Well, you're still a little wet behind the ears. I call them as they are!"
>
> The old umpire smiled and looked out the window.
>
> "What are you smiling at?" the middle-aged umpire finally asked his elder.
>
> "Well," said the old wise one. "It seems as if there are two here who are still a little wet behind the ears. They are what I call them."

Our life, too, is what we call it. A particular event in our life is either good or bad, exciting or dull, awful or wonderful. We are not really describing the actual event, but what that event *means* to us. Our personal reality is not the event itself, but the *meaning* that we give the event. Once our mind assigns words to describe the event, these words, and not the event, become the reality to which we react.

As long as we remain unaware of this relationship between personal reality and language, we forfeit a significant power. Worse, we get stuck with the consequences of our interpretations. Unknowingly we use language to create limits, stress and ineffectiveness for ourselves.

Kate, an attractive young government lawyer, was stuck in a position that was far below her capabilities. She was sophisticated, intelligent, and had excellent communication skills. We talked about her desire to find more productive and satisfying work. During our conversation, I noticed that as soon as she began to talk about a different possibility, she would quickly list all the reasons she couldn't do it. It wasn't as if she had tried these possibilities and failed. She was already failing in her mind by using such phrases as "This will never work" and "I probably couldn't do that." The only obstacle preventing her from moving forward was her own thoughts. She literally trapped herself with her own language. By changing her language, she began to focus on what she could do. Within a week, she was exploring a number of new offers and exciting possibilities. These opportunities were always there, but her language and perceptual set wouldn't allow her to see them.

When you allow your language to take the form of self-doubts, such as "Oh, I can't do that" or "I never do things right," you create a limiting and destructive reality. If you tell yourself that you cannot do something, then sure enough, you don't. By taking control of this power function, you can alter your perceptions and create a more productive reality for yourself.

**Emotional Power**

Our emotional energy, managed properly, gives us the power to accomplish what we want. We can become impassioned and inspired; we can maintain our effort over a long period of time; we can become intensely involved—all with the help of emotional energy. The better we manage our emotional energy, the more effective and productive we are. When we misdirect or frustrate this energy, we create emotional problems which color and distort the entire sensory mind. We can't think clearly, we act in rigid and inflexible ways, we diminish our creativity and output, inhibit our instincts and intuition, and suffer imbalance and stress in our body.

When we create a strong, positive emotional state, we enhance our possibilities for success. A good coach emotionally charges his players so that they are up for the game. A good manager motivates his staff by creating a positive emotional atmosphere. On the other hand, we also *conditioned by habits and attachments*

know the power of emotions to create misperceptions and distortions. Who hasn't made a decision or taken an action in the heat of an emotion only to realize later what a lousy choice it was?

Whether we use emotional energy to achieve our goal or to create problems for ourselves depends on how skillfully we manage our sensory mind. This involves the fourth power function of our sensory mind, its ability to form habits.

## The Power of Habit

We could easily call sensory mind the habitual mind. We express our entire personality through *habits*. Habits regulate every aspect of our life, from the most trivial, like our taste in desserts, to the most vital, such as the skills exhibited by a neuro-surgeon.

**Definition:** A habit is an unconscious organization of a repetitive pattern of behavior. In other words, a habit is whatever we do over and over without thinking about it.

Habits dominate the three outer levels of our personality—sensory mind, energy, and our body. They regulate our behavior, such as driving habits or the way we walk and talk; physiological activities, such as blood flow or muscle tension; emotional and mental activities, such as our emotional reactions and the ways we think and perceive.

The process of forming habits is called *conditioning*. By the time we are five or six years old, the basic patterns (programs) of our personality have pretty well formed within our sensory mind. Because of these programs, we interpret events along the lines of our past experience. If we grow up as an American, we look at the world with the perspective of an American. As long as we aren't aware of the effects of this conditioning, we don't have any way to counteract this built-in bias.

Habits get us through the day with a minimum expenditure of energy and effort. They help the mind conserve energy, and work more efficiently to accomplish its task. When we do something with ease, it is because it is part of our habit patterns. When something seems hard or difficult, it's usually because the task is not part of our habit patterns. Remember the first time you drove a car? You were aware of every button, every change in pressure necessary to speed up, slow down, or change direction. Now you hardly are aware that you are driving. Your driving habits control the operation of the car with ease and facility.

## An Exercise in Habit Sensitivity

It's easy to see how pervasive habits are in your life. Fold your hands together in front of you, on your lap or on the desk, wherever they are comfortable. Now, look at your hands. Notice the position of your thumbs. Now, switch your thumb position. Doesn't that feel odd? You can even shift the interlocking positions of your fingers. It still feels odd. The slight discomfort you feel is because you changed a habit of the body. Try another one tomorrow morning when you get dressed. As you put on your slacks, stop, and put the other leg in first. Most people almost fall over as they alter this simple, almost meaningless pattern of behavior.

## Habits and Energy

Our most powerful habits involve emotional energy. If we have built "good habits," they channel emotional energy in ways that allow us to accomplish whatever we set out to do. But if we have "bad habits," they channel energy in destructive patterns, distorting our perceptions and thoughts in ways that we aren't even aware of. For instance, the manager who unconsciously fears that someone will look better than himself constantly stifles the initiative of his staff. As long as he isn't aware of his unconscious emotional habit of fear, his productivity as a manager suffers.

Our habits give consistency to our perceptions, which, in turn, provide stability for us. But habits can become too stable, preventing us from finding new ways to solve old problems, or locking us into emotional patterns that are counterproductive. We have all found ourselves at one time or the other unable to find any new solutions to persistent problems. We come up with the same old answers over and over again. When habits become too powerful, our mind loses its flexibility.

Our sensory mind's capacity to form habits is a powerful tool if we use it consciously and intelligently. With this power, we can create whatever habits we want. This is what skills training is all about. We don't have to limit our ideas of skills simply to playing tennis or public speaking, or to job-related tasks. Taking control of this power function, we can build powerful habits involving:

- stress management and self-discipline;
- emotional control and the constructive use of emotional energy to power our will;
- creativity and problem solving abilities;
- perceptual sensitivity to enhance instinct and intuition;

To direct the power functions of our sensory mind effectively, we must turn to the next level of our mind where we find the most powerful tool of the mind, called discrimination.

## PERSONALITY LEVEL IV: DISCRIMINATING MIND— DECISION AND INTUITION

Deep within every mind is the capacity to know the truth, to understand reality for what it actually is, not just what we think it is. We call the fourth level of our personality the Discriminating Mind. To discriminate means to distinguish between things, to differentiate. At this subtle level, our mind has the power to distinguish between what is real and what the habits of our sensory mind tell us is real. It is the sudden realization that the person you made the appointment with for next week won't be able to keep it even though everything now appears in order. The power of discrimination lies in direct awareness, free from the limits imposed by habit, memory, emotions, pain and pleasure, and time and space—all of which shape the less powerful sensory mind.

Just as computer language determines what the software program will be, our discriminating mind tells us what is real and what isn't. There are two vital power functions of discriminating mind:

### 1. Analysis and Thinking:

When we use our power of discrimination in conjunction with our sensory mind, we have the capacity for reasoning and critical thought. We analyze, use logic and reason to make decisions based on information rather than emotions or habit.

We have a strong tendency to use our discrimination to avoid pain and seek out pleasure, or to use our intellect to rationalize our actions. Unfortunately, this only leads to less effective action and greater problems. We all know someone who has an answer to everything, and is unable to explore other alternatives. These individuals are not only difficult to work with, they are difficult to live with as well.

By staying balanced and developing inner awareness, we can learn to use our power of discrimination to think things through, make decisions based on logic, and use our common sense. We still use our sensory mind, but we don't let it dominate the action. Our instinct and emotions serve the intellect, and our will determines our behavior. Instead of reacting emotionally to a problem, we calmly reflect on the choices we have. In

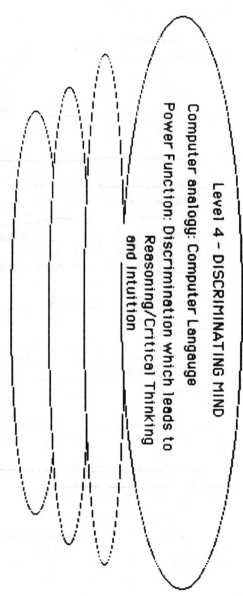

## Level 4 – DISCRIMINATING MIND

Computer analogy: Computer Langauge

Power Function: Discrimination which leads to
Reasoning/Critical Thinking
and Intuition

OUR SENSORY MIND HAS THE POWER OF DISCRIMINATION, THE
DIRECT DISCERNMENT OF CAUSE/EFFECT RELATIONSHIPS; NOT
LIMITED BY TIME/SPACE CONSTRAINTS OR PAIN/PLEASURE OF
SENSORY INPUT. IT IS THE LEVEL OF INTUITIVE KNOWLEDGE AND
FREE OF ANY IMBALANCE.

Figure 2:6

this way, we refine sensory knowledge, making it more accurate and powerful.

## 2. Intuition—Direct Awareness Of Cause/Effect Relationships:

When we gain insight into the real consequences of our actions, we call that experience "intuition". It's that sudden realization that what you are doing is not going to give you the results that you want. You may not always listen to that insight, but your mind does provide it for you. Intuition forms the third and purest form of knowledge formed by your mind. Four critical factors define intuitive knowledge:

- Intuition is pure awareness of cause/effect relationships. It does not depend on analysis, logic or intelligent guessing. Thinking may either facilitate or interfere with intuitive insight, but we do not need to think to have an intuition. Just as mathematics is pure conceptualization, intuition is pure awareness.

- Intuition is free from time/space restrictions. It is not fortune telling, but direct awareness of cause/effect relationships as they exist now or in the future. As these relationships change, intuitive knowledge changes.

- Intuition is free of sensory pleasure or pain. As a consequence, emotions neither influence nor distort intuitive knowledge.

- Intuitive knowledge is unconditioned knowledge. This means it uses experience without being limited by it. It remains totally spontaneous, in tune with reality as it is, not as we have learned to see it.

The difficulty is that our discriminating mind is very subtle and quiet, easily buried beneath the noisy activity of the sensory mind. Our noisy emotional reactions and habits distract us, and we don't use our intuitive power. Intuition depends on our capacity to concentrate, and our level of inner awareness. Because intuition is so subtle, it takes a great deal of skill to use effectively. Without training, we can easily confuse intuition with hunches, desires, fears, or we can simply fail to recognize it.

When we direct our power of discrimination outward, we gain insight about our environment. When we direct this power inward, it leads to inner strength and spiritual insight. Through discrimination, we gain access to the fifth level of our personality, the Balanced Mind.

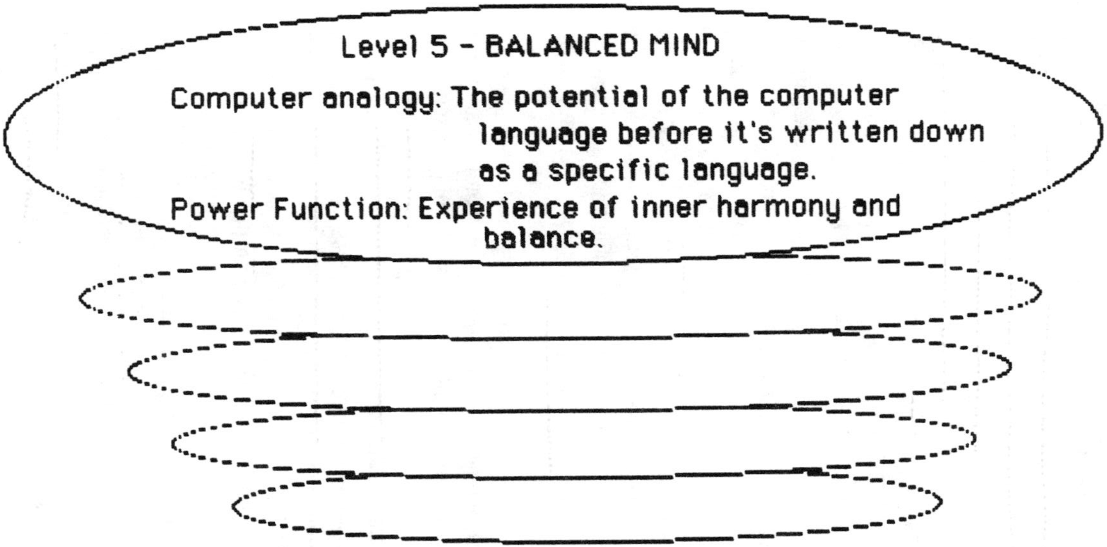

## Level 5 - BALANCED MIND

Computer analogy: The potential of the computer
language before it's written down
as a specific language.

Power Function: Experience of inner harmony and
balance.

MIND IS IN A STATE OF PURE ENERGY, NO MODIFICATION OF MIND
ENERGY INTO KNOWLEDGE; THE ABSENCE OF ANY STRESS OR
CONFLICT; FEELINGS OF HARMONY, BALANCE; SOURCE OF INNER
STRENGTH AND ABSOLUTE SELF-CONFIDENCE.

Figure 2:7

## PERSONALITY LEVEL V: BALANCED MIND— SOURCE OF INNER STRENGTH

At the center of our personality lies the fifth and most subtle level, our *balanced* state. This fifth level corresponds to the potential of a computer language before it is written into specific instructions. At this level, our mind's energy is in a state of pure harmony, not yet modified into the thoughts, images and sensations of information and knowledge. This level is unaffected by sensory input, and free of any emotions.

When we become aware of this inner balance, we experience a profound peace and harmony. This peace and harmony does not have anything to do with happiness or pleasure. It is the complete freedom from all conflicts, compulsions, needs, and anxieties. At that moment, we are entirely at peace with ourselves and the world. The critical power function of this level of our personality is the experience of inner harmony and balance.

Inner harmony is not strange or unusual. We have all had this experience at one time or another. Remember the time when you were out for a walk on a beautiful day up in the mountains, or along the beach, and all of a sudden, you felt complete contentment? It was the feeling that "God was in the heavens, and all is right with the world." The experience did not last much longer than a few moments, but for that brief time, you were completely free of worry or compulsion of any kind. You felt absolutely wonderful, free and content.

*Nothing* had changed in your life. You still had the same job, the same spouse, the same bills and problems to solve. But those few moments had a profound impact, and you went home refreshed, ready to tackle the world again.

You did not take drugs to have this experience, nor did it come from someone stroking your ego. The magic was all you. You did it by relaxing, getting away from the noisy chatter of your sensory mind, and by not trying to figure things out. You simply allowed yourself to become conscious of your own calm center, which was always there. Our Balanced Mind is the source of strength for our personality. It provides the inner strength we need for unshakable self-confidence and fearlessness.

What if you could access this balance any time you needed? What if you could create this experience right in the middle of a hectic schedule, or a conflict situation at work? How do you think this experience would affect your self-confidence and executive productivity?

## THE CENTER OF CONTROL

One final level applies to both the computer system and to our human personality. It is the owner/operator, a force independent of the computer, who decides how to use the computer. This is also true of the personality. The mind/body complex has tremendous resources, but the final power lies in that Self, the owner/operator, which uses the personality as a tool. This higher power goes by various names, depending on one's perspective and beliefs. We will call this ultimate decision-maker the Center of Consciousness (with a capital C) or Self (with a capital S).

Just as the language and programs run the computer, our mind is the control mechanism of our personality. But what guides the mind is our own unfailing human spirit. This spirit, or Self, is our most powerful resource. When we gain awareness of our Center of Consciousness, we find both purpose and fulfillment in our life.

## BEING HUMAN: MORE THAN A MACHINE

We have compared the levels of our personality with the different functions of a computer to help simplify its enormous complexity. But even the most sophisticated computer cannot begin to approach the power and capacity of our mind. We build computers, piece by piece, chip by chip. But we can never add up parts and pieces to get a human being.

We come as a complete package. Any action we take involves all levels of our personality. We do not make decisions without our memory playing a role, nor do we play handball without our liver functioning. Just as teamwork makes a world-class team, it's teamwork within the personality that makes a world-class human being.

When we act as if the different aspects of our life are separate from each other, we lose part of our human power. For example, when the cardiologist treats high blood pressure with medication and ignores the role of diet, exercise, emotions, family and work life, he treats the patient as a machine. When we ignore our intuitive knowledge, deny our emo-

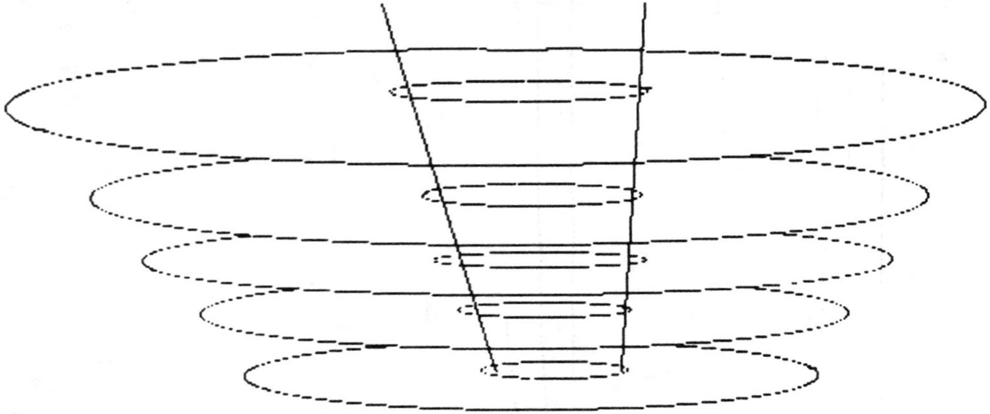

# Center of Consciousness

Computer Analogy: Owner/Operator
Power Functions: Spiritual Awareness and Skills:
Love (Compassion)
Humility
Cooperation

THE FINAL POWER RESTS IN OUR UNFAILING HUMAN SPIRIT,
OUR MOST POWERFUL RESOURCE, WHICH USES THE PERSONALITY
AS A TOOL.

Figure 2:8

tions and rely solely on so-called "logic," we act as if *we* are a machine. When we separate work life from family life, corporate decisions from ethical standards, or ignore the value contribution of clean air and water when making accounting decisions, we are treating ourselves as machines.

Imbalance or disturbance anywhere in the system interferes with our ability to act powerfully and effectively. Stress interferes with our ability to think clearly and respond appropriately. Emotional reactions color our perceptions so that we fail to understand the situation, or we take actions we later regret. If we are afraid of what others think of us, we won't take risks, put forward new ideas, or try new ways to solve problems.

We not only react to our environment, we constantly interact and change it. We are influenced and changed by our environment which, in turn, changes the way we interact with it.

For example, we influence the people we work with, and they, in turn, influence us. Our personality has an impact on the family, and the family has an impact on our personality. Our emotions influence both the quality and the depth of our intellectual insight, and our intellect influences where we direct our emotional energy. The levels of our personality constantly coordinate information and function to give us an understanding of the world around us.

## INTEGRATION, BALANCE AND POWER

Turn back to the beginning of this chapter and go through the Traveling Exercise again. This time, be aware of the different power functions at each level. Don't try to change them, or use them in any particular way. Just pay attention and become more familiar with how they operate within your system.

Your success depends on how skillfully you integrate and manage the various levels and functions of your personality. For instance, most people rely primarily on sensory information to make decisions. An Empowered Mind skillfully uses all three knowledge states—sensory, instinct and intuition. Using my intuition, I have a sense that a project which looks bad on paper is really a sleeper, and I should invest heavily in its completion. My instincts tell me whom to trust—and whom not to trust—to work with me on this super-secret development. My sensory

2

knowledge solves the practical problems I face in moving equipment and arranging finances to successfully carry out the project. By using all my resources, I maximize my opportunities for success.

Our inner resources give us the ability to reach our goals through a variety of ways and means. In more colloquial terms, we have many ways to skin a cat. A computer is rigidly limited to its operating instructions and logic. But our mind has unlimited creative capacity to structure knowledge, insights and creative expression. There is no technology or instrument that can match human creativity, adaptability and flexibility.

For instance, we may cure disease by altering our emotional condition, by stimulating our immune system through imagery, by taking herbs and natural medicines, or by using synthetic medicines. Similarly, we can solve problems in a variety of ways. We may draw upon our past experience, base our decision on instinct, use intuitive knowledge, rely on logic and intellect, or a combination of these methods. We see this principle reflected in the wide variety of leadership and management styles. One manager successfully uses a democratic approach; another uses management by objectives; still a third may be autocratic. An Empowered Mind is vastly capable of solving problems in many ways, using a variety of resources.

We also have an inherent ability to maintain inner balance which allows us to function efficiently and effectively. An excellent example is the resting heart beat. The heart pumps blood and performs its duties, but does so in a state of balance. No one dies from a resting heart beat. We die when we mismanage our inner resources and create stress. Then our heart overworks, becomes unstable, and we suffer irregular heartbeats.

In society, balance and harmony are just as critical. Our actions today may affect someone on the other side of the planet, and vice-versa. The problems we face are seldom local, whether air pollution, hunger and homelessness, or international competition. We no longer live regionally. Like it or not, we are discovering our interdependency with the rest of the world. Our ability to adjust to that reality will determine our survival.

Successful people are successful, in part, because they understand the necessity for balance and harmony between the different areas of their life. We are complex. We function simultaneously on many levels both personally and within the world community. When we understand and take command of our inner resources, we maximize our power and effectiveness.

Each of us, whether we are executives, managers, artists, truck drivers, students or housewives, play some role. We execute actions, make decisions, and interact with others. We succeed or fail according to our ability to use our resources. We have an obligation to ourselves to become all that we can. To do so requires an immense discipline, but that too is part of our project, and well within our capabilities. To this end, we turn now to the specific skills and qualities that comprise an Empowered Mind.

## SUMMARY OF PRINCIPLES

1. Our personality is a complex organization which functions simultaneously on five levels—body, energy, sensory mind, discriminating mind, and the balanced mind.

2. Within each level of our personality, we find power functions that determine our personal effectiveness and fulfillment:

Figure 2:9

| PERSONAL EFFECTIVENESS AND FULFILLMENT | | |
|---|---|---|
| Level | Name | Power Function |
| I | Body | Balance and Health Information Resource |
| II | Energy | Breath |
| III | Sensory Mind | Perception Language Emotions Habit |
| IV | Discriminating Mind | Discrimination |
| V | Balanced Mind | Experience of harmony/peace |
| | The SELF | Human Spirit |

3. As long as we remain unaware of these power functions, the mind skills they provide remain undeveloped.

4. Our mind (personality levels III, IV, and V), the instrument we use to understand the world around us, is our finest resource. Our mind is a subtle field of intelligent energy, distinct from, and superior to, the brain and body.

5. Our mind forms three different knowledge states—sensory,

instinctual and intuitive—each unique in structure and function. We rely on sensory knowledge only because we are not trained in the access and use of instinct and intuition. With training, we can utilize the power and wisdom found in these two resources.

6. Personal effectiveness depends on our ability to integrate and manage the various levels, power functions and knowledge inherent in our personality.

7. In everything we do, all levels and functions of our personality act together. We *always* function as a total unit, not as pieces of a machine.

8. We are capable of solving problems in a variety of ways, using a variety of resources.

9. We have an inherent ability to maintain balance and harmony, regardless of what we are doing.

# The Balance Factor: Productivity and
**3** Stress Management

*He who is of a calm and happy nature will hardly feel the pressures of age, but to him who is of an opposite disposition youth and age are equally a burden.*

*—Plato*

When I first started this project, the challenge was wonderful. I woke up every day excited about going to work. I couldn't wait to sink my teeth into the problems that we faced. We all worked pretty hard, but we were pulling together, and we all took whatever time we needed to rest. Then they changed the rules on us, put on a new VP that couldn't care less about the people in the project, and he just wanted results. After about three months of 70 hour weeks, my feelings about work began to change. I started waking up with tension headaches, I began to hate Mondays, and I felt tired most of the time. That sure didn't help my family life. Instead of coming home excited, I would drag my poor body through the door, and hardly had anything left to give to the kids, or a kind word for my wife. I hate to say it, but my productivity went down just like everyone else's. Finally, they called an end to the project entirely, but I still get headaches, and I don't have the same excitement about going to work that I started with.

*Dave D., Project Manager*

The first, and most important, step to an Empowered Mind, is to establish a healthy, balanced personality. The initial obstacle to empowerment is stress. The more stress we have, the more difficult it becomes to develop our inner skills. Tragically, we accept stress as a necessary part of life when we have all the resources we need to free ourselves from this self-imposed disease.

We all know about the problems that stress causes: disease, drug abuse, poor performance, breakdown of family structures, child abuse, anxiety, depression—the list could go on and on. In 1970, medical researchers at Cornell University declared stress to be the number one medical and social disease in our country. Eighteen years later, *Newsweek* (April, 1988) ran a four-page spread entitled "Stress: The Test Americans Are Failing." With all the programs, stress consultants, and books in the past twenty-plus years, we still have not solved the problem. If anything, stress has increased. Information technology, geopolitical changes, global pollution, AIDS—the pressures and problems we face have grown in scope and complexity. Meanwhile, our ability to cope seems to be diminishing

## STRESS: MISMANAGED RESOURCES

We do a lousy job in managing stress because we do not understand the nature of the problem. *Stress is the product of an untrained mind, a mind that can't manage its own resources.* And if we can't manage our own inner resources effectively, how can we expect to manage the resources of others, such as the family, or the corporation?

There are only two reasons why stress continues to be a problem for us:

1. We do not understand the nature of stress, and so our solutions are ineffectual;

2. We do not understand how to use our inner resources, so we lack the skills necessary to live without stress.

Stress is the result of ignorance and mismanagement. When we solve these two problems, we solve the problem of stress.

## STRESS: THE MYTH AND THE REALITY

Three myths about stress create confusion and limit our efforts to free ourselves from it. These myths are repeated as gospel in our society, even though they are illogical, do not fit the facts of human functioning, and create disaster for us.

### Myth Number 1: There Is Good Stress and Bad Stress

The "good stress–bad stress" myth is like saying there are good heart attacks and bad heart attacks. For instance, you take a jog in the park and come back feeling refreshed and energized. Someone says to you, "That's good stress," and you think, "Ahhh, good stress." The next day you're out in the park jogging, and you have a heart attack. While you are lying in the grass, that same person comes up to you and says, "That's bad stress." You have "good stress" when good things happen and "bad stress" when bad things happen. Unfortunately, you can't tell the difference until after you've suffered a heart attack, an ulcer, an anxiety attack, or the consequences of poor decisions.

If you only know the difference after you've had the heart attack, that's a little too late to be of any help. Some people say that it's a question of too much or too little stress. But how do you distinguish between enough and too much? Only after you have created a problem for yourself. "After the fact" has little practical value for us.

## Myth Number 2: Stress Is Something That Happens to You

You are really an innocent victim, just walking through life, when all of a sudden, this monster of many disguises called stress leaps out of the bushes, and bang, he gets you.

Nothing could be further from the truth. You cannot point to a thing, situation, or person in any place and say to me, "Now, that's stress!" Contrary to what you may think about your boss, your spouse, or even the streets of New York City, they are not stress. Stress exists in only one place in the world: the space between your ears. *Stress* never *happens* to you; stress is *your reaction* to the things that happen to you. *You* are the source of your own stress.

We can't control the world around us. No matter how much insurance we buy, how many contracts we sign, how long we have been married, we cannot protect ourselves from change. That does not mean we have to be victims, however. We *can* learn to control our reactions to the world. By managing our innate capacity for balance, we can take charge of our reactions and manage—even eliminate—stress.

## Myth Number 3: To Excel, to Really Produce, We Need Stress

This myth stems from confusing stress with arousal. Not all arousal is stressful. The arousal or excitement we feel when we are challenged is balanced, and does not create stress. We need challenge in our life to test us, and make us reach heights that we normally would not reach. This arousal is very healthy for us. But if we become fearful, the arousal we experience is unbalanced, and destructive. It clouds our mind and distorts our thinking. The more fear we have, the more unbalanced we become, and the more stress we have.

The myth that we *need* stress leads to statements like "I need to put my people under stress so they produce." No doubt! If you put the fear of God into people, they start producing. But what happens tomorrow? All the research on motivation and behavior leads to the same conclusion. Fear causes an immediate increase in productivity, followed by an even greater decrease. A fearful employee soon becomes worried, resentful, and angry, which diminishes his effectiveness and productivity. The rapid increase in productivity is short-lived, but the anger and resentment are long-term. It's amazing how many managers, supervisors, and executives manage by fear, with no awareness of the negative long-term consequences. When I hear a supervisor, manager or executive talk about putting their people under pressure, I know that the long-term prospects for this department or organization are very bleak. *No one wins through intimidation!*

## STRESS: A QUESTION OF BALANCE

We cannot solve the problem of stress if we do not understand what it is, or what happens in our mind and body to create it. Actually, stress only happens in the three outer levels of our personality—body, energy and sensory mind. At the deeper levels of our personality, we are entirely free of it. So let us focus first on the body where we experience most of the symptoms of stress.

Recall a time when you were under stress. For example, remember the last time you were in your car, and you came within a paint job of having a very serious accident. You probably felt:

- your heart beat faster and your blood pressure go up;
- muscle tension throughout your body;
- emotional changes, such as fear or anger;
- changes in your breathing patterns;
- changes in perception, such as everything happening in slow motion;
- spasms in your gastro-intestinal tract;
- a cold sweat.

These are just a few of the symptoms that come from dramatic changes in your biochemistry and your nervous system. The control mechanism for most of these changes is the autonomic nervous system. To understand and take control of stress, you need to know a few simple principles about this important control system.

The autonomic nervous system directs the function of our organ systems, such as our digestive system, heart and lungs. It consists of two interdependent systems called the sympathetic and parasympathetic nervous systems. These two work together to ensure that our organ systems work smoothly. We can picture these two systems as a balancing act. The sympathetic system creates arousal in the body. It does things like speed your heart up and cause your liver to release fuel for the muscles. The parasympathetic system does just the opposite. It creates inhibition, or rest, in the body. It slows your heart down and makes the liver store fuel. These two systems are supposed to work together like your right and left hand work together.

The sympathetic system allows us to have instant arousal throughout the entire body. So when something startles us, our whole body reacts. The parasympathetic controls each organ system independently from all the others. As a result, we can be tense and uptight, with almost all systems overproducing, and still have one or two organ systems underproducing because of parasympathetic influence. For instance, ulcers are a parasympathetic disease, but tension exacerbates the problem. Because these two systems work a little differently, we have a great variety of possible combinations between arousal and inhibition. This flexibility in our control system gives the body a variety of ways to carry out the directives coming from the mind.

## FIGHT-OR-FLIGHT: ONLY HALFWAY THERE

Most of us think of stress as the arousal that we experienced during the close call in our automobile—being wound up too tight. This is called the "Fight or Flight" alarm response and is created by the sympathetic nervous system. Whenever we think something is going to hurt us either physically, emotionally, financially, or socially, this alarm goes off. It also goes off whenever we think someone or something that we care about is going to be hurt, such as our family, our car, our position in society, a friend, our reputation, or even our favorite football team.

This alarm reaction depends on our perceptions. If we don't see any danger, we don't react even if the danger is really there. On the other hand, if we perceive danger, even if it really is not there, we react as though it is. The greater we think the danger or threat is, the greater our alarm reaction. Little threats, such as day-to-day worries, set off a limited reaction. Large threats, such as your boss threatening to fire you, can set off a reaction that could last for several days, even weeks.

Whenever you react to a threat with a Fight or Flight response, you go through four stages, as follows:

**The Alarm Stage:** Our body prepares to protect itself by either confrontation or flight. This is what you felt when you came close to having that automobile accident. You can have the same response when you see your child in danger, or to a lesser degree when you hear that your project is cancelled, and to an even lesser degree when you hear someone talking about you in a negative way.

**The Calming Stage:** Your body adjusts to its initial arousal by returning back to normal as quickly as possible. But you usually don't get quite as relaxed after the threat as you were before. Even after a threat is resolved, a subtle residual alertness remains in your unconscious mind, keeping the body from becoming completely relaxed. This leads to chronic stress as you become used to higher and higher levels of alertness and tension in the body.

**The Fatigue Stage:** Since every threat, large and small, sets off your fight or flight, it isn't long before you begin to wear out. You over-utilize your resources, exhaust yourself, and reach a state of fatigue. You go to your office and work harder and harder to get the same amount of work done. Or you are so tired that you can only shuffle papers around. When fatigue becomes chronic, we call it "burn-out."

**The "Goodbye" Stage:** The world seldom lets you rest just because you are fatigued. But if you continue to drive yourself, you suffer the consequences: your health breaks down, you suffer from a disease, and you can even die. You literally burn yourself out, and you end up with high blood pressure, a heart attack, or some other serious condition.

Because the fight-or-flight alarm is a condition of arousal, many experts began to think of all arousal as stress. And we need arousal if we want to exercise, work hard, or go dancing. So they called arousal that led to harmful consequences "Distress" and called helpful arousal "Eustress," perpetuating the myth of good and bad stress. Unfortunately, if you can't tell the difference before you have the heart attack, adding new words doesn't clarify the picture.

The fight or flight response is only half the problem. Getting aroused and becoming tense isn't the only way we react to threats and danger. Many of us react in a way that involves a completely different pattern controlled by the parasympathetic nervous system instead of the sympathetic nervous system.

# THE POSSUM RESPONSE: THE OTHER HALF OF STRESS

We *never* function with just half of our nervous system. While many of us react with a fight or flight arousal response, a great many of us do just the opposite. Just as a possum rolls over and plays dead when threatened, some people, when faced with a threat, withdraw, become passive, and feel depressed. Instead of getting uptight, the people who react with the "Possum Response" turn everything off by going home and going to bed.

When we react to a threat with a possum response, we also go through four stages:

**The Alarm Stage:**  Our body tries to protect itself by withdrawing, and closing down. In the Possum Response, the individual withdraws, is depressed, and/or feels chronically fatigued. Just like the possum, some people "play dead" by shutting down and sleeping ten hours a day, or watching T.V. for endless hours. Instead of being wound up too tight, these people aren't wound up tight enough.

**The Activation Stage:**  Possum responders have turned their systems on low as a way to protect themselves. To re-balance, they speed up, getting their systems back into gear and running properly. Solving the problems of a possum response requires an approach quite different from that for the problems created by too much fight or flight arousal. For example, if you have high blood pressure, a symptom of too much inner tension, you should practice deep relaxation in order to reduce the pressure on your vascular system. On the other hand, deep relaxation therapy for a depressed "possum responder" can deepen the depression, and even increase the potential for suicide. For this person, intense aerobic exercise and regulated sleep become part of the treatment regime in order to shift the balance back towards a more active state.

**The Atrophication Stage:** Fight-or-flight reactors burn themselves out. But it's very difficult to over-utilize your body's resources when you sleep ten to twelve hours a day. A possum responder feels chronic fatigue not because they over-utilize their resources or burn out, but just the opposite. They under-utilize their systems by constantly turning them on low. Eventually, their systems lose their capacity to function. The same thing happens when someone breaks an arm or leg, and wears a cast for six months. The muscles aren't exercised, so they begin to atrophy. When we don't use our organ systems appropriately, they lose their ability to function. That's why aerobic exercise is so important for the heart muscle. If we don't make a habit of urinating more than once a day, by the time we are sixty, we may lose the voluntary use of our bladder. If we don't use it, we lose it.

**The Goodbye Stage:** The consequences of a possum response are just as deadly as the fight or flight response. When we constantly reduce functioning in our organ systems, the end result may well be breakdown, disease and/or death. One example is the strong relationship between depression and certain forms of cancer, particularly breast cancer. Although some physicians still argue the point, the research is clear that chronic or severe depression can contribute to the onset of cancer.

## THE WORST OF BOTH WORLDS

Because the two systems work a little differently, we don't have to be limited to having either a fight-or-flight or the possum response. We often mix them up quite nicely, creating problems that involve extremes in both systems. For instance, we can be depressed and still feel tense and anxious. This mixed imbalance characterizes many diseases, such as asthma, Krone's disease and ulcers. The different alarm reactions are summarized in the following table. Once we see that we create stress from fight-or-flight, or the possum response, or a complicated mix of the two, the question "What is stress?" becomes much easier to answer.

## STRESS: THE ANSWER IS BALANCE

The sympathetic and parasympathetic systems are designed to work in harmony and balance. When we disturb our inner balance by too much arousal or too much inhibition, or a combination of both, we create

# Stress Reaction Stages
## Fight or Flight and the Possum Response

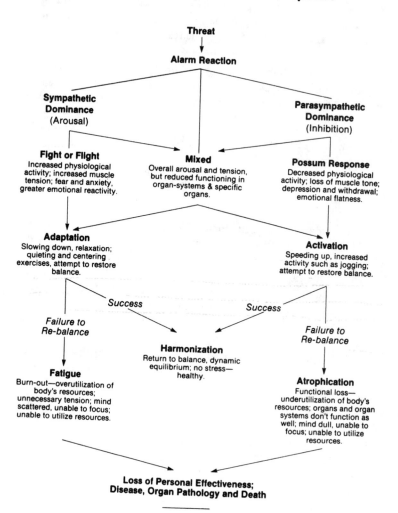

**Threat**

↓

**Alarm Reaction**

**Sympathetic Dominance**
(Arousal)

**Parasympathetic Dominance**
(Inhibition)

**Fight or Flight**
Increased physiological activity; increased muscle tension; fear and anxiety, greater emotional reactivity.

**Mixed**
Overall arousal and tension, but reduced functioning in organ-systems & specific organs.

**Possum Response**
Decreased physiological activity; loss of muscle tone; depression and withdrawal; emotional flatness.

**Adaptation**
Slowing down, relaxation; quieting and centering exercises, attempt to restore balance.

**Activation**
Speeding up, increased activity such as jogging; attempt to restore balance.

*Success*

*Success*

*Failure to Re-balance*

*Failure to Re-balance*

**Harmonization**
Return to balance, dynamic equilibrium; no stress— healthy.

**Fatigue**
Burn-out—overutilization of body's resources; unnecessary tension; mind scattered, unable to focus; unable to utilize resources.

**Atrophication**
Functional loss— underutilization of body's resources; organs and organ systems don't function as well; mind dull, unable to focus; unable to utilize resources.

**Loss of Personal Effectiveness;
Disease, Organ Pathology and Death**

Figure 3:1

*dis-ease*, or stress. *Stress specifically means autonomic disharmony or imbalance*. The moment we become unbalanced, we create changes in our body that lead to disease and inhibit the resources of our mind. Stress is *not*, and never has been, good for us.

If we stay balanced, we can do anything—work, play, relax—and we stay free of stress. On the other hand, whenever we become unbalanced, we have stress no matter what we do. There are two forms of balance:

**1. Balance may be dynamic,** shifting back and forth between arousal and rest. For example, we can work hard for periods of time, and if we balance these with periods of rest and relaxation, we avoid stress. But too much of one without the other creates imbalance, and we experience stress.

**2. Balance may also take the form of harmony**—a dynamic equilibrium between sympathetic and parasympathetic activity. In this state, work seems almost effortless, like a resting heart beat. Another example of dynamic equilibrium is task absorption. We become so focused on what we are doing that we forget about everything else. Even time seems to stop. In this state of complete concentration, body and mind are coordinated. We work totally relaxed, using only the energy necessary to do the work.

The autonomic nervous system is a very sophisticated energy system that works as a unit to maintain balance and harmony in our body. Although anatomically the two systems are very distinct from each other, whatever the sympathetic system does influences the parasympathetic, and vice-versa. The same is true of all our organ systems. If one organ system becomes diseased, it affects the entire nervous system to some degree. Conversely, if the overall personality is balanced, the individual systems within the personality become more balanced and healthier. As long as we maintain balance and harmony, we stay free of stress. The crucial question is "How do I create and maintain balance?"

To answer, we turn to our own innate capacities for mental and physical balance. To utilize these capacities, we must master three categories of inner skill:

1. Neurological self-management to maintain autonomic balance;

2. Relaxation;

3. Managing the chatter of our sensory mind.

## TAKING CHARGE OF OUR CONTROLS

The idea that we can consciously direct any part of our nervous system seems a bit far-fetched. After all, didn't we learn in high school health class that we can't control our involuntary nervous system and the functioning of our organs? This is one of the great scientific and medical myths of all time. If we do not control our body, who or what else does? By going to a more subtle level of our personality, we often can find the tools we need to manage the level with which we are concerned. The key is to become aware of these controls and become skilled at using them.

Take your fingers and find a place where you can feel your own pulse, either on the inside of your wrists, or in your neck. Pay attention to your pulse for a few moments. Notice that your pulse doesn't tick like a clock. Instead, it fluctuates slightly. There is a slight slowing and speeding up of your pulse. This gentle rhythm is related to another process going on in your body.

As you keep track of your pulse, pay attention to your breath. As you inhale, notice how your pulse begins to speed up, and as you exhale, your pulse begins to slow down. This is called sinus arrhythmia, and is a healthy and natural rhythm or fluctuation in your pulse. Your pulse is controlled by the autonomic nervous system. The fluctuation in the pulse reflects the influence of your breath on the autonomic nervous system. Your inhalation reflects and stimulates sympathetic activity, while your exhalation reflects and stimulates parasympathetic activity. This influence is so strong that you can use your breath to regulate autonomic balance. Taking charge of your breath is the crucial "first step" to managing stress.

The key word here is "regulate." Control of the autonomic system lies in the limbic center—specialized neural and glandular tissue which lies in the center part of our brain. We cannot control the autonomic nervous system with our breath, but we can influence or regulate it enough to bring balance to it.

Our breath is part of both the sensory-motor nervous system and the autonomic system. We can either consciously control the way we breathe, or we can let it run on automatic. We can use this dual connection to influence the autonomic system. But like everything else, we develop habits in our breathing patterns. And some of these breathing habits can be harmful.

# WHEN NORMAL MEANS STRESSED

Take the following short breathing test to see if you breathe normally. Count the number of times you breathe in one minute—an inhalation and exhalation together counts as one breath. If you breathe normally, your respiration rate will be anywhere from sixteen–twenty times a minute. If you are sitting quietly, it may go as low as twelve. Or it may be as high as twenty-four times a minute, and still be considered normal. Most people breathe within this range. Did you check? Chances are you breathe normally, and that you breathe with your *chest*, which is also considered to be normal. If your breathing is "normal," then it's about 90 percent certain that you are suffering from a chronic level of stress.

The term "normal" is a statistical term which refers to what "most" people do. It does not mean that they have healthy breathing patterns. Most people breathe predominantly with their chest, or thoracic mechanism. Chest breathing is emergency breathing. When we use it as our habitual moment-to-moment breathing mechanism, it leads to a chronic imbalance in the autonomic nervous system. Although this imbalance is very slight, over a period of time it leads to some serious health problems.

The *natural* mechanism for moment-to-moment breathing is the diaphragm. The diaphragm is the large muscle that separates the chest cavity from the abdominal cavity. If you want to see how your body was designed to breathe before you developed the bad habit of chest breathing, watch an infant breathe. You will see their stomach move up and down as their diaphragm contracts and relaxes. You never see their chest move. But as we grow up, many influences lead to chest breathing—tight clothing, poor posture, cultural preferences for flat stomachs, and emotional trauma which contracts our stomach muscles and forces chest breathing. By the time most of us graduate from high school, we have developed the harmful habit of chest breathing.

People who must control their breath—singers, musicians who play wind instruments, and some athletes—know the value of diaphragmatic breathing. Only diaphragmatic breathing gives them the depth and control they need. If you want to re-establish the body's natural balance, you must breathe with the diaphragm. Diaphragmatic breathing offers us these advantages:

**1. Efficiency:** We must have oxygen in our blood in order to stay alive. Oxygen entering the blood stream is called ventilation perfusion. When we breathe with the chest, we bring air into the upper two-thirds portion of the lungs. When we breathe with the diaphragm, we bring air into the lower two-thirds portion. Because of gravity and the way we are built, most of the blood necessary for ventilation perfusion collects in the lower two-thirds portion of our lungs.

You can see the blood distribution in the lungs in Figure 3:2. Diaphragmatic breathing pulls air into the blood-rich lower lobes, resulting in more efficient ventilation perfusion (2a). A person who breathes habitually with the diaphragm typically breathes six–nine, ten times a minute, or 9,000–11,000 breaths a day. On the other hand, chest breathing pulls air into the upper lobes where less blood is available for ventilation perfusion to take place (2b). Consequently, a chest breather must breathe sixteen–twenty times a minute, or approximately 22,000–25,000 times a day in order to get sufficient ventilation perfusion. What a difference in the amount of work done by the body! In order to use the *natural* efficiency of our body, we must breathe with the diaphragm.

**2. Autonomic Balance.** Two key neural systems are directly influenced by the way we breathe. The first, the tenth cranial nerve, called the vagus nerve, separates into two paths and passes through the left and right chest cavity. This nerve constitutes about 85 percent of the parasympathetic nervous system. The motion of the lungs has a direct impact on how this nerve functions. The second, the Herring-Breuer reflex, consists of nerve receptors scattered throughout the lungs. These receptors send signals directly back to the limbic system in the brain indicating the exact motion of the lungs. The limbic system is that part of our brain that controls the autonomic nervous system.

When we breathe with our chest, we send a signal to both the limbic system and the autonomic system that says "Get ready! Something out there requires you to take some kind of protective action!" *Chest breathing is emergency breathing.* It stimulates the fight-or-flight alarm response. Yet we rarely need to put ourselves on alert or in a state of emergency preparedness. If you chest breathe while reading this book, you may think you are calm and relaxed, but your breathing is sending a different message to your nervous system.

On the other hand, diaphragmatic breathing sends a message that says "Everything is calm, stay relaxed, all is well, you are in control." Smooth, even diaphragmatic breathing brings balance to the autonomic system, and we feel calm and relaxed. To achieve balance, our diaphragmatic pattern must be smooth and even. If our breath is jerky, full of stops and pauses, it destabilizes our inner balance. For instance, watch someone

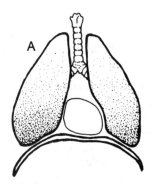

**BLOOD DISTRIBUTION**

The darker the area, the greater is the concentration of blood available for gas exchange.

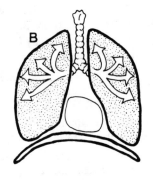

**AIR FLOW INTO LUNGS DURING CHEST BREATHING**

Chest wall expands, pulling lungs outward, creating a partial vacuum.

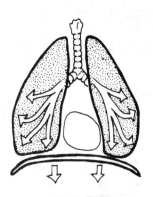

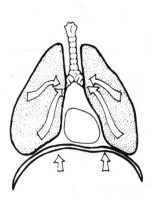

**AIR FLOW INTO LUNGS DURING DIAPHRAGMATIC BREATHING**

Diaphragm contracts and is pulled downwards (flat) creating a more complete vacuum, pulling air down into lowest lobes.

In exhalation, the diaphragm relaxes and is pushed back into a dome-shape, forcing air out of the lungs.

Figure 3:2

who is angry. The moment they hold their breath, they become even more angry. Or, whenever a depressed person sighs loudly, and then pauses before the inhalation, they become even more depressed. The moment we hold our breath, it intensifies whatever emotional state we are in.

Certain breathing patterns can become quite dangerous. One, a disease called apnea, involves an involuntary pause lasting three or more seconds after each inhalation or exhalation. When this happens at night, it's called sleep apnea, and is characterized by loud, open-mouthed snoring with periodic silences between the snores. Sleep apnea is considered to be a central nervous system disease, and is a major reason why people suffer heart attacks at night.

**3. Healthy Coronary Functioning:** According to University of Chicago cardiologist Dr. D.S. Das Gupta, when we breathe with our chest, we can create problems for our heart in at least four ways:

**Heart Rhythm:** The heart creates its own electrical impulse through a sodium chloride/potassium chloride ion exchange in the pacemaker cells of the heart. This ion exchange is regulated by the autonomic nervous system. If autonomic balance is disturbed by sleep apnea, it can lead to severe rhythmic dysfunctions in the heart beat, such as atrial fibrillation, and then ventricular fibrillation. Once ventricular fibrillation begins, survival becomes problematic. For those already suffering heart damage, sleep apnea is a grave danger.

**Chronic Arousal:** Chest breathing, our emergency breathing pattern, stimulates sympathetic arousal. As part of the arousal response, the peripheral blood vessels constrict, sending more blood to the center of the body. This constriction can contribute to higher blood pressure levels.

**Coronary Effort:** Chest breathing exerts pressure on the heart cavity which increases the amount of blood that enters the heart, which is called *Preload.* The more blood that enters the heart, the harder the heart muscle must work to pump the blood out. This effort is called *Afterload.* Higher levels of Preload and Afterload lead to higher levels of blood pressure.

**Carbon Dioxide Cleansing:** Carbon dioxide is a waste product that is eliminated through exhalation. During chest breathing, the lower lobes of the lungs are not properly cleansed, resulting in a build-up of carbon dioxide. This carbon dioxide re-enters the blood stream, and elevates the level of carbonic acid in the blood. This can change the acid/base balance of the body and may eventually disturb the inner linings of the blood vessels, which can lead to hardening of the arteries.

Dr. Alan Hymes, a thoracic surgeon, notes that only chest breathers seem to develop essential hypertension. Very few people who breathe with their diaphragm ever develop essential hypertension. Chest breathing increases your risk of high blood pressure in several ways. By breathing with the diaphragm, you maintain internal balance and reduce pressure on the vascular system, which helps prevent high blood pressure.

## LEARNING DIAPHRAGMATIC BREATHING

Re-learning how to breathe with the diaphragm is quite simple. Your body wants to work efficiently. It takes a few weeks of practice, but soon you'll begin to notice changes in your breathing patterns. You will also have more energy at work, feel calmer during the day, and be less tired at the end of the day.

### Step 1. The Relaxation Posture

Use this basic posture to practice breathing and to develop skills in deep relaxation. Lie on your back on a pad or carpeted floor. Place your feet about twelve to eighteen inches apart, and your arms and hands slightly away from the body, palms facing up. Use a small pillow under your head to support the curve of your neck. This posture is called the *relaxation posture* because every muscle in your body has an opportunity to relax. In any other posture, the posture itself creates some tension.

### Step 2. Diaphragmatic Breathing

To re-establish the habit of diaphragmatic breathing, lie in the relaxation posture and practice diaphragmatic breathing for at least 10 to 15 minutes twice a day. You can do this easily if you practice when you go to sleep at night, and after you wake up in the morning. Lie in the relaxation posture. Place your right hand on your stomach, your little finger over the navel, and the other fingers stretching up towards your chest. Place your left hand on the upper part of your chest. When the diaphragm contracts, it flattens out and pushes against the internal organs in the abdominal cavity. Instead of the chest going up and down, the stomach moves out and in as if there were a small balloon inside your stomach. Now breathe as if you are filling this small balloon in your stomach. Your stomach and right hand will rise with the inhalation and fall with the exhalation. This should be very gentle, no effort or work required. Don't try to completely fill or empty your lungs. Let your body decide how much air it needs. There should be no movement at all in the left hand.

Let the breath become very even and steady, with no jerkiness, stops or pauses. The inhalation and the exhalation should be the same length, and the pressure should be the same throughout the inhalation and exhalation. The evenness and balance of the breath will balance the nervous system. To strengthen the diaphragm, place an eight to ten lb. pliable weight, such as wrist or ankle weights, a sand bag, or a sack of beans, across the upper abdomen when you practice. This strengthens the diaphragm, and establishes diaphragmatic breathing more quickly as your moment-to-moment breathing response.

## Step 3: Balanced Diaphragmatic 2:1 Breathing

Once the breath is balanced and even, and has become very smooth with no jerkiness, stops or pauses, gently slow the rate of exhalation until you exhale about twice as long as you inhale. We call this *2:1 breathing*. The exhalation stimulates the parasympathetic system twice as long as the inhalation stimulates the sympathetic system. This rhythm greatly reduces tension and creates a deeper state of rest for your heart and vascular system. You can practice 2:1 breathing anytime after balancing the breath with even, diaphragmatic breathing.

Do not reverse the rhythm, however, and inhale twice as long as you exhale. This reversed pattern can make you tense and nervous. Do not practice 2:1 breathing if you suffer from chronic depression. In chronic depression, the parasympathetic system is already too dominant, and you don't want to emphasize its dominance with long exhalations. For depression and low energy states, balanced breathing is much better.

## Step 4: The Two-Minute Breath Break

During the day, every hour on the hour, or as often as you can remember, take a two minute breath break. Close your eyes and concentrate on either even diaphragmatic breathing or 2:1 breathing, for two minutes. This important practice clears your mind and breaks the daily tension habits that can lead to headaches and high blood pressure. Make sure to breathe through your nose and not your mouth.

You can easily check to see if you are breathing properly with your diaphragm while sitting or standing by using a wide belt or piece of cloth. Put the belt around your lower rib cage. When you inhale, the lower rib cage and upper abdominal area should expand, using more of the belt to encircle you. When you exhale, the lower rib cage and upper abdominal area contract, and the belt can be tightened. Remember, don't try to fill the lungs completely, or exhale completely. The breath should be effortless, rhythmic and diaphragmatic, with no movement in the upper chest.

## DEEP RELAXATION—A CRUCIAL SKILL

After re-establishing diaphragmatic breathing, the next crucial skill is *deep relaxation*. Much more than a stress management technique, deep relaxation opens the gateway to your inner resources. Relaxed people think more clearly and creatively, feel better physically and emotionally, and access their instinctual and intuitive knowledge more easily.

There is some confusion about the word "relaxed." To be relaxed means *no excess tension*, a state of complete efficiency, both physically and mentally. We do our best work, play, or anything else when we relax and eliminate any excess physical or mental tension.

Most of us confuse being relaxed with deep relaxation. When we hear the term "relaxed," we see ourselves as completely limp and lethargic, unable or unwilling to move. While this can happen in the first level of deep relaxation, the second and third levels leave you feeling relaxed but very alert. In *deep* relaxation, we eliminate all tension from the body, and minimize any activity of our organ systems. Practicing deep relaxation eliminates chronic tension, strengthens our immune system, and helps us be more calm and focused during daily activities.

Just like any skill, relaxation requires a consistent practice of systematic techniques. It's really too bad that so few of us take the time to develop this crucial skill. The benefits we gain from such a practice far outweigh the small amount of time it takes. A minimum investment of effort and time provides enormous benefits in return. The practice of relaxation is one of life's few genuine bargains. Just a few of the benefits include:

- stronger immune system; greater physical and psychological health;

- fewer psychosomatic diseases such as essential hypertension, tension headaches, and anxiety;

- higher tolerance for pain;

- control over the relaxation response, able to completely relax within two breaths;
- greater access to intuitive knowledge;
- more creative, greater use of imagery;
- feel better, get along better with family and friends.

## THE THREE LEVELS OF RELAXATION

We can experience three different levels of deep relaxation. Each requires a different approach. The deeper the level, the more complete and powerful the effects.

### Structural Relaxation

The most common relaxation techniques focus on muscle relaxation. A variety of different techniques lead to deep states of structural relaxation. These techniques focus on relaxing muscle groups, either by tensing and releasing, or through imagery. When done successfully, muscle relaxation leaves the body feeling very heavy and warm, as if you were encased in a sheet of lead. Your mind feels lethargic, and you feel reluctant to do any work or make any effort.

When we first learn deep relaxation, we begin with muscle relaxation. Some of the benefits of muscle relaxation include:

- an easy first step to learn the skill of deep relaxation.
- reduction of chronic levels of stress.
- elimination of chronic muscle tension in target groups like the neck, the shoulders, and the lower back where chronic tension creates a variety of aches and pains.

For best results, practice all relaxation exercises in the relaxation posture. If you have a lower back problem, lift your knees off the floor until your feet are flat on the floor. Then place pillows under your knees for support so that you don't have to use muscle tension to keep your legs up.

The best time to practice is when no one will disturb you for at least fifteen minutes. Right when you come home from work is an excellent time. Take fifteen minutes to clear your mind and body of stress and tension, and you'll feel refreshed, calmer and more content. And, your interaction with your family and friends will be much better.

Obviously, the more you practice, the more skillful you will become. Start out by practicing for fifteen minutes. The more skill you gain, the less time it takes to become, and stay, relaxed. You can become so skillful that it only takes few focused breaths to become completely relaxed. After you have built your skill, do not spend any longer than five minutes doing relaxation. The rest of the time is much better spent making your mind stronger with concentration exercises, developing your creativity, or working with your intuition.

The best way to learn relaxation exercises is to use an audio cassette tape until you have memorized the exercise. The tape allows you to listen and follow directions without getting actively involved. The key to learning relaxation is passive volition, or effortless effort. Relaxation is like floating—simply lie back in the relaxation posture and let it happen to you. The more you try to make yourself relax, the more tense you become. Just pay attention and let your mind form the images suggested by the instructions on the tape.

You can purchase tapes commercially, or make your own. Below are instructions for an effective muscle relaxation exercise. Read through the entire exercise and make sure you understand the systematic approach. Then slowly read the instructions while recording them on a cassette tape. The periods between the sentences indicate a few seconds pause. After you have taped the exercise, lie down in the relaxation posture and listen to it. Practice this exercise until your muscles feel so relaxed and heavy that it feels like you can't move.

### A Muscle Relaxation Exercise

Close your eyes and focus your attention on your breath...Breathe easily and gently with the diaphragm, with no jerkiness, stops or pauses...Let your breath be very smooth and even, without any effort on your part... Picture yourself breathing in relaxation and exhaling all the tension out of your body...Let your breath be very easy and gentle, with no strain or effort...You are breathing in peacefulness and quietness, exhaling all thoughts of the past, all concerns for the future...Just bring all of your attention to your breath as it flows in and out of your body...Now picture your forehead as smooth as a piece of silk...as if you are looking into the mirror of your mind and seeing all the bumps and wrinkles melting away in your forehead...You can feel the muscles in your forehead relaxing down into your face, relaxing your eyebrows and your eyes... relaxing your cheeks...the corners of your mouth, your lips and even your tongue...relax your lower jaws and your ears...and relax your neck muscles, front and back...Picture the muscles in your neck as being very warm, very heavy and so loose they can't even hold your head up....

Again, bring your attention back to your breath, breathing in relaxation and exhaling tension...easily, gently, no strain or effort...Let your body do all the breathing for you...Relax your shoulders, letting go of all tension from your shoulders...Relax your upper arms and your forearms, picturing the muscles in your arms as being very warm and heavy...Relax your hands, your fingers and even your fingertips...Again bring your attention back to your breath, and imagine yourself inhaling down into your fingertips and exhaling all the tension out of your arms...Very easy, very gentle, no effort...Letting your body do all the breathing for you...Relax your fingertips, fingers and hands...Relax your forearms and your upper arms, picturing the muscles as being very warm and heavy...And relax your shoulders...Again, bring your attention back to your breath...Let the inhalation merge into the exhalation merge into the inhalation...smooth and even, the breath is like a large wheel moving effortlessly through the body...Relax your chest muscles...Relax your stomach and your abdominal muscles...Relax your hips...Relax your thighs, picturing the muscles as being very warm and heavy...Relax your calves...Your feet, toes and even the tips of your toes...

Again, bring your attention back to your breath...Imagine your body to be like a hollow reed, and you are breathing in through your toes, inhaling to the top of your head, filling the body with breath...then exhaling from the top of your head to your toes, completely emptying the body of breath...all very easily and gently, and without any effort...you are only the witness, allow the body to do all the work...In your mind you can feel the entire body breathing in and breathing out...expanding on the inhalation and contracting on the exhalation...

Relax your toes and your feet...relax your calves and thighs, picturing the muscles in your legs as being very warm and heavy...Relax your hips...Relax your abdominal muscles and your stomach...Relax your chest muscles...And relax your shoulders...Give up all control over the body, and trust that the floor will support you completely, let your whole body become very warm and heavy...Again, bring your attention back to the breath...Let the inhalation merge into the exhalation merge into the inhalation...Very easy, very gently...breathing in and out very smoothly, without any effort on your part...

Relax your neck muscles, front and back...Relax your lower jaws and your ears...Relax your lips, the corners of your mouth, and even your tongue...Relax your cheeks...And your eyes...Now picture your forehead as smooth as a piece of silk...Now right in the center of your mind, where all your thoughts seem to begin, on your next exhalation, relax that mind center...

After you finish this exercise, try to remain as relaxed as you can throughout the day. During the day, take a few moments to picture your forehead becoming very smooth and even. This will help you stay more relaxed. Don't forget to use diaphragmatic breathing to also keep you more balanced. The greater your skill at muscle relaxation, the more relaxed you stay throughout the day.

## Autonomic Relaxation

We achieve the second level of relaxation, *autonomic relaxation,* by using our breath to shift the balance in our autonomic nervous system. By changing the motion and rhythm of our breath, we increase parasympathetic activity and create a deeper state of rest in the body. Autonomic relaxation provides a different kind of experience than muscle relaxation. Instead of feeling heavy and lethargic, our body feels light, and our mind becomes clear and alert.

We can breathe in a number of different ways to create progressively deeper states of relaxation. The simplest is the 2:1 breathing discussed above. It stimulates the parasympathetic system, and creates a deeper state of balanced rest. One of the most effective breath relaxation exercises is also the most simple:

### *Sweeping Breath Exercise*

Visualize the body as a hollow reed. Then breathe in as if inhaling through the toes and filling the body with breath to the crown of the head. Exhale as if you are breathing back down the body and out the toes. Breathe easily and gently, without any effort. Do not try to force your breathing, let your body decide how much air you need. Focus your concentration on feeling the entire body breathe, and imagine every cell and pore in the body breathing in and out. It's as if you are feeling your entire body expanding on the inhalation and contracting on the exhalation. After a few moments, visualize the breath like a wave washing upon the shore on the inhalation and receding back into the sea on the exhalation.

A few minutes of concentration on the sweeping breath brings on a deep, restful state. Use this exercise as a preliminary exercise for the "61 Points" concentration exercise given in Chapter 5, or as a finishing exercise to other relaxation techniques.

One of the most sophisticated breath relaxation techniques is called Deep-State Breath relaxation. In this exercise, you will systematically alter the motion of the lungs, moving from very deep and slow breathing to very shallow, rapid breathing, and then returning to very deep, slow breathing. The effectiveness of this exercise lies in the systematic and gradual change in the motion of the lungs. The impact on the autonomic system creates a profound state of rest for the body. As the breathing becomes more shallow, it naturally becomes more rapid. Breathe as quickly as you need to feel comfortable. But you shouldn't have to pant. All breathing should be done effortlessly and without any sense of struggle or panic.

This exercise takes practice. Any disruption of the systematic change in the motion, such as a yawn, makes it less effective. But do not let this discourage you. Even if you do it imperfectly, you're more relaxed than if you do muscle relaxation. Like the muscle relaxation exercise, this exercise is easier to do if you first read through the exercise, and record it on a cassette tape. Then lie in the Relaxation Posture, and listen to the cassette.

### Deep-state Breath Relaxation

Lying in the Relaxation Posture, let your breath become very smooth and even...Let the body do all the breathing for you, you are only the witness to the breathing...Let your breath become very smooth and even... Breathing in relaxation and exhaling all the tension from your body... Breathing in peacefulness and quietness, exhaling all thoughts of the past, and all concerns for the future... Now picture your body like a hollow reed, and you are breathing in from your toes, filling your body with breath to the crown of your head, and exhaling back down and out your toes...Let your conscious mind travel up the body with the inhalation and back down with the exhalation...easily, gently, without any effort and strain, let your body do the breathing for you...Inhale from your toes to the crown of your head and exhale down to and out your ankles, then inhale as if you are breathing in through your ankles back to the crown of your head...easily, gently, letting your conscious awareness travel between the two points with the inhalation and exhalation...Inhale from the ankles to the crown of your head and exhale down and out your knees...Inhale through your knees to the crown of your head and exhale down and out the tip of your spine, and inhale from the tip of your spine to the crown of your head, filling only the trunk, neck and head with breath...

Easily and gently, letting your conscious thought travel up and down with the inhalation and exhalation between the two points...Inhale from the tip of your spine, up the spine to the crown of your head and exhale down and out your navel...Inhale through your navel to the crown of your head, filling only the stomach, chest, neck and head with breath...easily and gently, without any effort or strain...Inhale from the navel to the crown of your head and exhale down and out your heart center, the center of your chest, then inhale from your heart center to the crown of your head, filling only the chest, neck and head with breath...Breathe as quickly as you need to be comfortable, but very easily and gently...Without any strain or effort...Inhale from your heart center to the crown of your head and exhale down and out the base of your throat, then inhale to the crown of your head filling only the neck and head with breath...(Notice that your breath is becoming very shallow, hardly any motion of the lungs at all)...Inhale from the base of your throat to the crown of your head, and exhale down and out the nostrils, then inhale from the opening of the nostrils to the point between the two eyes, and exhale back down and out your nostrils, filling only the nose with breath...Breathe as quickly as you need to feel comfortable, but very gently, very easily, you shouldn't have to pant...(At this point, there is really no breath going at all down into the lungs, just an exchange of air in the nose. Your breath should be extremely shallow and light at this point)...

Now inhale through the tip of the nose to the crown of your head, and exhale from the crown of your head down and out the base of the throat. Then inhale through the base of the throat to the crown of the head, filling the neck and head with breath...Let your conscious thought travel up and down between the two points with the inhalation and exhalation, very easily, very gently...Inhale from the base of the throat to the crown of the head, and exhale down and out the heart center in the center of the chest, then inhale again to the crown of your head filling the chest, neck and head with breath...Remember, there should be no strain or effort, you are only the witness, letting your body do all the work...Inhale from your heart center to the crown of your head and exhale down and out your navel, then inhale from your navel to the crown of your head, filling the stomach, chest, neck and head with breath...easily, gently, without any strain or effort... Inhale from your navel to the crown of your head and exhale down your spine and out the tip of your spine, then inhale from the tip of your spine, up the spine to the crown of your head, filling the entire trunk, neck and head with breath...Letting your conscious thought travel up and down between the two points...Inhale from the tip of your spine, up the spine to the crown of your head and exhale down and out your knees, then inhale through your knees to the crown of your head...Filling your body from the knees to the crown of your head with breath...Easily, gently, let the body do all the work for you... Inhale from your knees to the crown of your head and exhale down and out your ankles, then inhale as if breathing through your ankles, filling the body with breath to the crown of your head...Let your conscious thought travel up the body with the inhalation and back down with the exhalation, easily, gently...Inhale from your ankles to the crown of your head and exhale down and out your toes, completely emptying your body of breath...Then inhale, from the toes, filling the body with breath, peacefulness and quietness to the crown of the head, exhaling from the crown back down and out the toes, completely emptying the body of breath, leaving only the peacefulness and quietness behind...

In your mind you can feel your whole body breathing, as if every pore and cell were breathing in and out...The entire body expands on the inhalation and contracts on the exhalation...very easily, without any effort... For a few moments, concentrate on this feeling of expansion and contraction...

After you become skillful with this exercise while lying in the Relaxation Posture, you can do it sitting. Our minds have difficulty going around corners, so change the base point from the toes to the tip of the spine. You still begin with a deep and complete gentle breath, but then work your way up the spine. The imagery helps make the exercise effortless so you do not become tense from trying to *control* your breath. Once you can change the motion without effort or strain, you no longer need to use imagery. At this point, each breath should be either more shallow or deeper than the one before it, depending on which way you are going.

We can also use the 2:1 pattern of breathing as an effective sleep exercise to minimize and eliminate insomnia, a common and difficult symptom of stress. Whether it is a problem of falling asleep or one of waking up in the middle of the night and not being able to fall back asleep, insomnia is caused by an agitated mind. It is a problem that can easily be remedied with a little training.

Use the following exercise to develop the skill of restful sleep.

### A Sleep Exercise

Practice the following when you go to bed at night.

1. All breathing is 2:1; exhale twice as long as you inhale

2. Use a comfortable count such as 6:3 or 8:4. You are not trying to completely empty or fill the lungs. The 2:1 ratio should be effortless.

3. Pay close attention to your breath. There should be no stops, pauses or shakiness during either the inhalation or the exhalation. Minimize even the pause between inhalation and exhalation.

4. The exercise goes as follows:

    • 8 breaths lying on your back
    • 16 breaths lying on your right side
    • 32 breaths lying on your left side

If you don't fall asleep the first time, repeat the exercise. If you still haven't fallen asleep, then focus on even, diaphragmatic breathing until you do fall asleep. You will eventually train your mind to sleep peacefully throughout the night. This exercise can also help your children overcome the problem of nightmares.

Most insomnia is caused by an overactive mind. By focusing all of our attention on the breath, we minimize distractions in the mind that create tension and sleeplessness.

## Concentration: Achieving the Deepest State of Relaxation

We create the most profound states of relaxation and rest through concentration. The more focused, or concentrated the mind, the deeper the condition of rest and calm in the body. Any concentration exercise calms the body, but the "61 Points" exercise given in Chapter 5 is designed specifically to provide the most profound relaxation in the body. This exercise is particularly helpful in treating and preventing high blood pressure.

When learning deep relaxation, begin with muscle relaxation. As your skill improves, move on to the deep-state breath relaxation. Then polish your skills with concentration exercises. With practice, the fifteen minutes you begin with will change, until you spend only a few moments on relaxation and the rest of the time refining your power of concentration.

## THE OPPORTUNITIES OF IMBALANCE

We can minimize and even eliminate stress by using diaphragmatic breathing and relaxation. We can, and should, become expert at putting out the fires of stress. But if this is all we learn, we end up constantly having to troubleshoot. Why not take the next step? What if you did not create those fires in the first place? If you learn how to *prevent* stress, you do not have to use your valuable time and resources to compensate, or get rid of it. Instead, you can use your time and effort to develop your inner resources and increase your personal effectiveness.

There are many ways to create stress. Let's start with our physical environment. Extremes in the environment, like too much humidity or dryness, crowding, or air and noise pollution create lots of opportunities for stress. Noise pollution is very tiresome for us. For those of us accustomed to a quiet urban or country setting, a trip to New York City means sleepless nights. For the New Yorker who has adapted to the noise level, sleep is generally not a problem. However, take him into the country, and all he wants to do is sleep for the first few days. He doesn't realize just how tired he is, and the price he pays for the constant sensory input until he gets away from it. But after the first few days, the quiet may disturb his sleep.

For most of us, environmental stress is a minor problem. With the exception of noise and air pollution, we seldom place ourselves in extreme environmental conditions. After all, how many of us journey into the Antarctic for vacation?

We can also create stress because we don't exercise enough. Our body's systems are designed to be used, not parked in an easy chair in front of a television, or a desk. The strength and integrity of our body's organ systems require a level of activity that we do not provide when we become too sedentary. Moderate exercise helps us to stay physically and mentally heathy in all aspects of our life. Research reported in *Psychology Today* noted that people in their sixties who exercised had sex as frequently as those in their twenties and thirties. They felt good about themselves and about their bodies, and these were important factors in continued sexual activity and enjoyment.

Not to participate in some kind of moderate exercise is to commit a slow form of suicide. Why hurt yourself this way? It does not matter whether you enjoy sports, ride a stationary bicycle, walk, or swim—only that you exercise. If you are married, a program of exercise or sports with your partner strengthens the relationship as well as your mind and body.

Diet plays a very important role in creating stress. What we eat, when we eat, and how we eat can all contribute to imbalance. Dietary diseases, including cancer of the digestive system, are the second major cause of death in our society. As a nation, we are becoming more sensitive to the effect that food has on the quality of our life. For instance, reducing fat content, eating less red meat, and being aware of cholesterol have led to a decrease in the incidence of coronary and heart disease. But we still have much to learn, particularly about contaminants and alterations introduced into our food chain, such as additives, herbicides, insecticides and, most recently, irradiation. All too often, short-term profits have caused us to overlook the long-term impact on genetic structures, the subtle energy systems of the body, and our health in general.

By far, the most important source of stress is our own sensory mind. You can have the finest food in the world, but if you are emotionally disturbed, that food becomes toxic in your system. The same holds true for exercise. If a coronary-prone Type A, hostile, competitive person becomes a Type-A, hostile competitive jogger, he only increases the pressure on his heart. The value of exercise depends largely on the attitude we have when we exercise.

By taking control of our sensory mind, we gain the power to live without stress, and take another step to mastering our inner resources. This is the next step in developing an Empowered Mind.

## SUMMARY OF PRINCIPLES

1. We create stress when we mismanage our inner resources. Unless we first free ourselves from stress, we can never have an Empowered Mind.

2. There is no such thing as "Good Stress." Whenever we suffer from stress, it destabilizes the body and closes down access to our mental resources. Stress always inhibits performance.

3. Stress is self-created. Through methods of self-management, we can eliminate it and bring balance and harmony to our body and mind.

4. Stress involves the three outer levels of our personality—body, energy and sensory mind. On the physical level, stress is an imbalance within the autonomic nervous system. On an energy level, stress is generated through improper breathing habits. On the psychological level, we create stress by the way we react to events in our life.

5. The necessary first step to managing stress is diaphragmatic breathing. The diaphragm, not the chest, is the body's natural breathing mechanism, and brings balance to the autonomic nervous system.

6. Chest breathing (which is called "normal" breathing) creates problems for our heart in at least four ways:

   - disruptive breathing patterns, such as apnea, can lead to cardiac arrhythmias;

   - by increasing arousal, leading to constriction of the peripheral blood vessels and an increase in blood pressure;

   - by increasing the amount of blood going into the heart, making the heart work harder to pump the blood out, and thus increasing blood pressure;

   - by allowing carbon dioxide to build up in the lower lobes, increasing the level of carbonic acid in the blood, and possibly leading to a deterioration of the linings of the blood vessels.

7. Relaxation skills are the second necessary skill for managing stress. To be relaxed means to have no excess tension. There are three levels of relaxation: structural (muscular), autonomic (accomplished with breathing exercises), and concentration.

# Managing the Reality Generator: Mastery of the Sensory Mind

4

---

*The mind of man is capable of anything—because everything is in it, all the past as well as all the future.*

—*Joseph Conrad*

After all these years, the most important thing to me is a tranquil mind. I feel somewhat that I should be talking about competition, or striving for excellence, or somehow pushing to achieve. In an environment where everyone is caught up with competition, and being driven, I'm not there. I've discovered that in the end, what really pays off is a calm and tranquil mind. It allows me to understand the world around me.

—*Don Miller*
*Exec. Vice President*
*Employee Development*
*Dow Jones Operating Groups*

The power functions of our sensory mind—perception, language, emotion and habit—provide powerful means to understand our environment. But left uncontrolled, they become the source of our stress. You literally worry yourself into ineffectiveness, unhappiness and disease, if not an early grave. To prevent this, you must manage the power functions of the sensory mind, the third crucial skill of stress management.

# THE CHATTERING MIND: INVITATION TO DISASTER

The first thing we notice about our mind is that it is constantly talking. We call it "thinking," but that's a very generous term. When we pay attention to this constant chatter, we find very little real thought behind much of it. Your mind not only talks to itself, it answers itself. You even talk to others in your mind, and they answer you there. This certainly isn't all bad. Your chatter can be creative and productive, and you can use it to solve problems with critical thinking. But left unmanaged, it can be an endless source of stress and suffering.

Time and space do not limit your mind as they do your body and brain. Your sensory mind creates your experience of time and space, but it can also play all sorts of games with time and space. For instance, you can think about your next vacation, dreamily imagining yourself sitting on the beach in Waikiki, sailing around Bermuda, or climbing the Eiffel Tower in Paris. You can just as easily remember what you did last year on vacation. Or you can pay attention to what is happening now in the present. Your mind moves easily in time and space.

But no matter where you go in your mind, your brain never leaves the room. It only operates in the present, or what we call "real time." But that doesn't mean that the brain ignores our mind. The brain is an extremely sophisticated transducer. It translates the subtle energy of the mind into biochemical and neurological energy to carry out the mind's thoughts. Whatever occurs in your mind gets immediately programmed into your body for action. Let's say that you were thinking about picking up a quart of milk on the way home from work. The moment you think about picking up the milk, your brain programs the body to perform that action now. At that moment, your body is ready to literally pick up the quart of milk.

Using sensitive medical instruments to monitor changes, like brain waves, heart rate, skin resistance, and muscle tension, we could actually measure the impact of your thoughts on your body. The moment you thought about picking up a quart of milk, the instruments would show very slight changes going on in your body. The body is prepared for action, but nothing happens to discharge that energy. You and your mind know that this action will take place in the future, not the present. This is not a problem because there is very little emotion connected with the thought of getting a quart of milk. In this case, the level of energy that goes into the body's programming is so slight, you don't even notice its impact.

On the other hand, if you thought about the IRS wanting to review your taxes for the past five years, we could probably measure dramatic changes in your body as you react to the perceived threat of an audit. For most of us, the idea of an IRS audit creates some anxiety, even if we keep our records in good shape. Now we have emotional energy behind the thought, and the changes in our body can become quite dramatic and intense. You might feel your neck muscles tighten, your jaw muscles clench, or your breathing speed up. Or you may begin to feel depressed and helpless.

These are some of the reactions we can have when we allow our chatter to become worrisome. Our mind creates fear when we anticipate something negative or harmful. Fear is our greatest enemy. *Nothing creates more stress, or damages us more, than fear*. It sets off the fight or flight response, and then we suffer from anxiety. On the other hand, when we reach back into our memory and identify with all the hurts, mistakes and disasters of the past, we react with the possum response, and suffer from depression. Many of us do both responses at the same time.

Actually, this mental chatter expresses the creative force of our mind. When we abuse it, this creative power leads to imbalance, disease, and dysfunction. When we manage it, as we will see later in this chapter, this same creative power solves problems, opens new possibilities, and brings balance and harmony to our life. You must take control of the chatter in your mind if you want to use your sensory mind to analyze and solve real problems creatively instead of creating stress and wasting your power.

By taking control of our inner chatter—the language and images we use—we change the way we describe or think about events. This gives us the power to manage our habits and choose our response rather than react. Two basic principles define the power of language in the sensory mind:

- The words we use to interpret our perceptions determine our feelings and reactions. Whether or not we are happy, sad, angry or depressed, challenged or fearful, depends on the language and images we use. For instance, the moment we describe something as *awful* or *terrible,* we key the unconscious emotional habits associated with these words. The more we persist in using them, the worse we feel.

- We can change how we feel and be more effective in what we do by taking control of the language and images we use to interpret our reality.

In *The Quiet Mind*, Dr. John Harvey identifies six different categories of destructive inner chatter: *free and positive*

1. **Demands on others, on ourselves, and on life:** We frequently use terms such as *should, must,* and *have to,* as in the employees *should do* this or that; we *must have* a certain title or position, and you *have to* do this.

2. **Denial:** We use denial words to avoid facing what is happening or to avoid facing the truth of our own actions. This language takes the form of *I can't believe* or *I don't understand* or *How could this happen*? This is the language of someone who plays the role of a victim.

3. **Overreaction:** We often overreact to disappointments and to things that go wrong, using language that adds to the troubles we face. Often referred to as "terriblizing" or "horriblizing" language. It includes words such as *terrible, horrible, awful and miserable,* and such familiar phrases as *I can't stand it, this is awful,* and *it tears me up.*

4. **Always/never:** Many of us project our disappointments onto the future and refuse to believe that things will ever change. Our language takes this prophetic (and pathetic) course: *Things will never change; it will always be like this; I'll never get.........;* and *She always does this.*

5. **All/nothing:** We generalize faults and mistakes into global realities. By not achieving perfection, we become *a complete failure, good-for-nothing, an utter jerk.* Or we wail that we have *totally destroyed our careers.*

6. **Mind reading:** We project our conflicts and negativity onto others and assume we know how they perceive and evaluate us. It includes words and phrases such as *They know I'm a failure;* or *she thinks that I'm unattractive;* or *They know what a fraud I am.*

What can you do about this destructive inner chatter? By consciously choosing to re-interpret, or "reframe" the experiences you have, you end up with different, and better, outcomes: better emotional states, greater clarity of mind, and more effective responses. By using less emotionally loaded words like *interesting* or *problematic* instead of *awful* or *terrible* to describe what's happening, you remain calm and balanced. *In short, you can change how you feel and become more effective and productive in what you do by taking control of the language you use.*

As the wise old umpire knew, our reality becomes what we call it. And our emotions follow the words we use. The more carefully we choose our words, the more control we have over our emotional reactions. For instance, I can describe my children as being *obstinate* , a negative term, or *strong-minded*, a more positive characterization. Each of these characterizations has a certain impact on how I feel about them. By using my language to emphasize their strengths, I create a positive feeling in myself about them, and relate to them in a more productive way. The same can be true for an executive who chooses language that emphasizes the strengths of subordinates. *By taking control of our language and imagery, we gain more response ability and minimize emotional disturbance.*

The best negotiators are very sensitive to the power of language. Often by changing just a few words, contracts can be agreed upon, deals can be made, and law suits can be settled. The arcane language used in the legal system creates more problems than it resolves, particularly for laymen. For example, a real estate broker was unable to close a major deal involving the construction of a large mall because the contractor was upset by some of the legal terms involved. By meeting with the contractor and talking "plain sense," the broker was able to reassure him, and the deal was quickly closed. Not one condition in the contract changed—the language merely was simplified.

By taking control of your language, you can clear your mind of destructive chatter, gain control of your emotional reactions, and become more aware of your inner resources. To do this well, you need three skills:

1. **The skill to manage your emotional reactions.** There are times when our emotions instantaneously flare, and this outburst often leads to even bigger problems. Although you may not be able to prevent an emotional reaction, you can quickly clear it and re-establish calm and clarity.

2. **The skill to take charge of the content of your mind**. You should be able to focus your attention on real problems to solve, and to use your time, energy and effort in productive ways instead of creating fear or indulging in past mistakes.

*- opportunities*
*- optimism*

**3. The skill to make the right choice of language and images.**
You can learn to play with words to re-define your personal
reality, making it more satisfying, and yourself more effective.
You can teach your mind to see "opportunities" rather than
"problems," and generate optimism to help you be more effective and productive.

## BREATH AWARENESS AND TASK ABSORPTION: MANAGING THE MIND

To develop the first two skills, emotional control and content management, you can use a simple but powerful technique called Breath Awareness. This is one of the most useful techniques that you will ever learn.

For fifteen seconds, try not to think. Do not think about anything,
even about not thinking. You will quickly see the difficulty of this. Your
mind is a field of intelligent energy in constant motion. When you are
distracted or disturbed, you try to control your mind with things like
positive thinking, drugs, or even sleep. Unfortunately, most of the techniques you use may not work very well, and they may create even more
serious problems for you. Only one thing works, your ability to focus
attention.

If you think back over your experience, you'll find instances when
you exerted complete control over your chatter. This happened when you
became so focused on your work, or some other activity, that even time
disappeared. Psychologists call this "task absorption." During this time,
your body and mind were completely coordinated. You didn't create fears
by anticipating danger. Nor did you create depression by going over and
over all of your past mistakes and hurts. You simply focused on the task
at hand.

During task absorption, you do your best and most productive work,
solving problems as they arise and working creatively and effectively.
When you finish, you feel wonderfully alive and alert and very relaxed.
Even if the work is physically demanding, you do not feel irritable or
stressed. Instead, the fatigue seems satisfying, the culmination of a difficult job well done.

Keep this in mind: You do not have to wait until task absorption
"just happens" to you. If you take control of your mental chatter, you can
become more adept at creating task absorption. To do this, you should
turn to your breath, the mediating tool between your mind and body. After

diaphragmatic breathing, the single most important stress management tool is Breath Awareness. Breath Awareness gives you direct control over your mind chatter, and it eventually leads to complete control over your emotional reactions. It is also the simplest stress management tool to learn and use.

## Breath Awareness

Be aware of your mind chatter for a few moments. Do not get involved with the thinking; be an observer, a witness. Just watch your mind think. Now, focus your attention on the *feeling* of your breath as it moves in and out of your nostrils. You will feel a slight touch of coolness at the opening of your nostrils when you inhale, and a very subtle touch of warmth when you exhale. Do not think about the breath, focus on feeling the breath as it enters and leaves the opening of your nostrils. Whenever your mind wanders off, simply bring your attention back to feeling the breath. Be aware of how you feel, and what happens in your mind. But keep your attention focused on the coolness of the inhalation and the warmth of the exhalation.

Notice what happens to your thoughts. They disappear! You cannot pay attention to more than one thing at a time. You either pay attention to what you see, or you think about what you see. You may switch back and forth very quickly between these two activities, but you actually only do one thing at a time. When you focus your attention on Breath Awareness:

1. *The chatter in your mind stops, and your mind clears.* The sensory mind cannot think and perceive at the same time. The more you focus on perceiving, the less chatter goes on in the mind.

2. *Your respiratory rate slows down and breathing becomes more stable.* As your mind calms down, your breathing becomes calm and you establish a rhythmic, diaphragmatic breathing pattern, which balances your autonomic nervous system.

3. *You feel a slight release in your body.* Your body relaxes because your brain stops sending demands for action. The body's natural state is one of relaxed alertness, but constant programming from our mind chatter keeps it activated.

## Breath Awareness and Emotional Control

The thoughts and perceptual patterns of your sensory mind trigger your emotional reactions. Most of this happens unconsciously, so people usually do not realize how much control they can exert over their emotional reactions. By the time you become aware of your emotional reactions, you already are caught up in a surge of feelings.

Think of the last time someone came right up to your face and screamed at you. What was your initial reaction? Most of us have a knee jerk reaction, and become angry or overwhelmed and intimidated. But what would happen if you focused your attention on Breath Awareness while such a tirade was going on, and did not allow your mind to chatter about what was happening? By focusing on breath awareness, you could stay calm and collected, and not react emotionally. Rather than repressing an emotional reaction, you would be preventing your mind from creating one. The consequences of your control would either be;

1. The person screaming at you goes completely berserk because you are not reacting to his emotional attack. If this happens, it's a clear sign that he is trying to manipulate you with an emotional outburst, and he is frustrated because his efforts are not working. Don't worry, stay calm. Sooner or later, he will calm down.

2. More than likely, the person calms down because you are not be feeding his emotional outburst with an emotional reaction of your own. In other words, by maintaining control of yourself, you take control of the situation and manage it more effectively. By managing yourself, you can manage others more effectively.

## Breath Awareness and Content Control

When you do not manage what your mind thinks about, your unconscious emotional habits can create some pretty disturbing and unproductive lines of thought. We see this happening almost every day to people we know. Friends or colleagues misread a situation and make assumptions based on their emotional reaction that their boss is out to get them. They act out a scenario that is clearly off base. When they are caught-up in their emotional reaction, their point of view seems obvious, and they don't understand why you cannot see the "truth." Once they calm down and gain some perspective, however, they usually realize their mistake, and feel a little foolish about all the fuss they made.

How is it that your friends' and colleagues' minds can fool them so easily, and so often, while *your* mind *always* tells you the gospel truth?

Your mind can mislead you because you identify yourself with it. You do not see it as a tool, an instrument that presents data or information to you. You see it as "the me" that does the thinking. Consequently, it's difficult to admit mistakes or be objective about your mind. Instead you uncritically accept anything and everything your mind tells you and become thoroughly convinced that you *know* what the truth is.

How can Breath Awareness help you not be misled by your mind? When something pushes our buttons, and we have an emotional reaction, the first thought, image or feeling that pops into our conscious mind grabs our attention. By itself, that one thought, image or feeling seldom has the power to create a strong reaction or a mood. The problem is that we don't stop with just one thought, image or feeling. We allow the first one to start a whole train of other thoughts, images and feelings. Then we build a house with them. Let's say that we think, "*What if I don't get this right?*" This thought alone has little power to disturb us. But then we take this thought and begin to think about how we will look to others if we fail, what they will think about us, what will happen to our prestige, how our boss will be angry, how we might be fired, how we won't have any money to pay for the new car we just got, and how we might have to sell it........... We've built a mansion all from that one thought, "*What if I don't get this right?*"

By the time we finish, we have not only built a village around the mansion, we build an entire city around the village as well. Then we end up paying rent in the form of emotional disturbance, and that becomes very costly. The more we chatter, the more stress we create, the more headaches we have, and the less clearly we think. We spend enormous amounts of time creating fantasy problems, then we spend even more time solving them. The impact on executive productivity can be drastic.

Maybe you cannot control that first thought out of your unconscious mind, but no one says that you have to build houses, villages and cities with it. You have the power to clear your mind. The moment you find yourself in the midst of an emotional reaction, use Breath Awareness to calm and clear your mind. Once you feel centered, and your mind is clear, refocus your attention on the situation. If you do not allow your mind to create a problem, you won't have an emotional reaction. This is not suppression where you consciously avoid thinking about a problem. Nor is it repression where you prevent yourself from being aware of some emotional problem. You simply don't allow your mind to continue a line of thought or imagery that only leads to stress and disturbance.

You do not have to accept everything your mind presents as truth. The sensory mind presents information, based on past experiences and habits all or any of which can be distorted in a thousand and one ways, and which may have very little connection with reality. By using Breath

Awareness, however, you gain some objectivity about what your mind presents to you. With Breath Awareness, you can minimize compulsive emotional reactions, and make better choices about what information to use and what not to use.

Take a few moments to do the following exercise. It will demonstrate how your mind can offer completely arbitrary thoughts, images and sensations that you easily accept.

## The Green Frog Exercise

Sit back, close your eyes and relax. Clear your mind with a few moments of breath awareness, let your face muscles relax, and then scan the rest of your body, relaxing any muscle tension that you find. Then, focus your attention on Breath Awareness for a few moments. Now imagine yourself as a great green bull frog, sitting on a lily pad in the middle of a beautiful, small, clear pool. Over on one side you can see cattails and reeds, and a red-winged blackbird building a nest. Picture a blue sky with puffy white clouds. It's about ten o'clock in the morning of a beautiful August day. The sun is shining, and you feel the heat of the sun on your back. The sunshine feels very warm on your back. Now jump off the pad into the water. Kerploosh! Ahh, the water feels cool and nice on your warm skin. Swim down under the lily pad. You see the stem coming up from the bottom, attached to the bottom of the lily pad. As you look up to the surface of the water, you see the sunshine filtering through the water. Beautiful sight!

Now come to the surface, swim over to the lilypad and climb back on. Now the sun feels really good on your cool, wet skin. Ahhh, life is wonderful!

Now open your eyes. Here you are, back in your own room. Do you really think you are a large, green bullfrog? If you do, this book isn't going to be much help to you. Of course, most of us distinguish easily between our imagination and what is real.....or do we?

Consider this: what makes the thoughts, images and sensations about being a bullfrog any less real than any others that your mind presents? They are all simply mind forms. You alone decide which ones to invest in, and which ones not to invest in. You have the power to determine your emotional states *by consciously choosing what to attend to, and what to dismiss as an unproductive line of thought*. The more you practice Breath Awareness and choosing what to pay attention to, the more skill and power you build.

You can use Breath Awareness virtually anytime, but here are some practical suggestions:

**1. During meetings:** Have you ever attended a meeting that dragged on and on when you had an important appointment to make? Right before it's supposed to end, some fool inevitably stands up and starts to tell everyone about *everything*. As he mercilessly drones on and on, your fingers and toes begin to tap out your frustration, your shoulders and neck muscles tense, your blood pressure starts to rise. Now there are *two* fools in the room. One endlessly talking, the other raising his blood pressure. Do not become the second fool in this situation. As soon as you feel disturbed, clear your mind with Breath Awareness. Then calmly and clearly assess the situation and find a solution. The talking fool won't disappear, but at least you will be free of stress and disturbance.

**2. Clearing your mind between projects.** All too often, the problems and disturbances created in one project carry over into the next. You can prevent this by taking two minutes to practice Breath Awareness. This clears your mind of past mistakes, old ways of thinking and perceiving, and any other negative influences that inhibit clarity of thought and your creative, intuitive resources. By clearing your mind, you prepare it for new work and you reduce stress as well.

**3. Handling the stress of driving in traffic.** Traffic is a daily fact of life for most of us. Along with crowded highways, gridlock in the cities, delays and road repairs, comes traffic stress. Suddenly, it seems as if the world is an unbelievably crude, snarling, choking mass of thoughtless drivers with no concern for anyone else, especially you. The result of all this stress is tightness and pain in your neck and shoulder muscles, jaws clenched in anger, a sense of desperation, even feelings of helplessness. By the time you reach your destination, you are in no shape to really be productive.

You don't have to become a traffic beast yourself. With a little practice in relaxation, and using Breath Awareness during commuting, you can sail through traffic without any stress at all. Below are some common traffic situations where you can use Breath Awareness to bring back balance and clarity of thought:

- when you begin to feel tension and frustration
- whenever another driver cuts in front of you, passes on the shoulder, drops his change in his car instead of the basket at the toll booth, or any number of other "stupid" things

- whenever you start talking to yourself in a negative way, saying to yourself (or others) just how bad the roads are, how terrible the traffic is

- when you begin to worry about being late

- whenever your mind becomes cluttered, and you feel pressured by the traffic

## PLAYING WITH WORDS

Words have power. They have the power to motivate, create emotional states, start wars, bring peace, to create the reality in which we live. Unless we're politicians, diplomats, or negotiators, we do not pay much attention to the words we use. Yet, these words determine how we feel, perform and interact with others. By carefully choosing our words, we have the power to create the reality we want. You can develop that power by playing and experimenting with language.

Take the word "problem." When someone comes up to us with a "problem," it shows in their entire body. Their shoulders slump, their eyes are troubled, and they walk as if they are carrying a large weight around. And they are! Think of a problem that you face, and have not been able to solve—one that really creates difficulties for you. Get as involved in this problem as you can. Feel what it's like to have this problem. Let it really weigh you down. Now, say out loud "I have a problem," and really feel it. Feel just how difficult, how awful, how frustrating this problem really is.

Notice how it feels and sounds when you say "I have a problem." Your intonation, your body language, your facial expression all show that you really have one! Now, change the word "problem" to "opportunity," and try to say "I have an opportunity" with the same intonation, body language and intensity. You will find that it is not possible. Even if the tone is the same, it feels different inside. The word "opportunity" has different connotations in your unconscious mind than the word "problem" does. It is not possible for these two words to express the same inner reality, even though you can use them to describe the same external reality.

Your inner reality determines your ability to perform and produce effectively. If you feel angry, frustrated, depressed—emotionally disturbed in some way—change the words you use to describe the external reality. You will notice a change in your attitudes toward the problems you face, and in your ability to solve them. The following exercises can help you develop your control over language and its power to create inner realities.

## Clarity Exercise

The interpretations and judgments we make often interfere with our ability to understand what's going on. A Chinese proverb warns of the deceptiveness of judgmental words:

> *If you wish to see the truth, then hold no opinions*
> *for or against anything. To set up what you like*
> *against what you dislike is a disease of the mind.*

Shakespeare understood just how arbitrary interpretations and judgments are when he wrote "There is no right or wrong but what thinking makes so." But we are so accustomed to thinking in judgmental and value-laden terms that it seems to us that our judgments reflect the truth. Nothing could be further from the truth.

For one week, strive to not interpret anything that anyone does or says. Do not allow your mind to assign judgmental words to any behavior. For example, if you see someone come into the room, and throw a pencil down on a desk, stick only with words that describe the behavior: "John threw the pencil on the desk." Avoid interpreting the action or using judgmental words such as "John must really be angry," or "John shouldn't do that," or "John is being awful."

This exercise is difficult, particularly for the first few days, because we are so used to interpreting everything in judgmental terms. You may be surprised at how much interpreting your mind does. During this exercise, be sensitive to the effect that *not* using judgmental terms has on your emotions and on your clarity of understanding. After about a week, try to gauge any differences in your understanding of situations and people around you. What do you notice about your own emotional reactions? Does the ancient Chinese proverb have any more meaning for you now than it did before you started this exercise?

## The Equalizer

To help keep your mind free of judgments, use one word to describe everything that happens to you. It doesn't matter which word you use—interesting, extraordinary, fascinating—as long as you use the same word for *every* experience. For example, if you walk into a wall, think *"That's interesting."* If you are offered a wonderful position, think *"That's interesting."* If you are bored, think *"That's interesting."* No matter what happens, use only this one adjective to describe the event to yourself.

For the first few days of the Equalizer exercise, everything will seem to feel the same, and you might feel a little disconnected from the world around you. These feelings will soon pass, and you should experience your world with a greater clarity and intensity. By using one word to define your experience, you can cleanse your perceptions of the unnecessary baggage that words secretly create.

## Word Play

Your mind habitually uses certain words and phrases that lock in limitations. As an experiment, alter the words you use to see what changes that creates. One example of word play is using the word *opportunity* instead of *problem.* You can change *This is awful* to *This is an interesting development*, and you can change *I can't do this* to *Let me see what I can do.* By paying attention to your inner chatter, you can identify certain words and phrases that lead to restrictions, or negative feelings. When you find a consistent pattern of words and phrases like "I should have..." or "I can't....," alter them to more helpful and positive ones.

## Mind—The Sly Fox

Be forewarned. While the words we use are powerful, they are only the front line of deeply ingrained habits in our sensory mind. Our mind will *not* be so easily fooled simply by changing your language. "Thinking positively" alone does not guarantee control of the sensory mind. Often, we will find that a train of thought has already traveled down the track for several minutes before we notice it. And by the time we do notice it, we already have created some disturbance for ourselves.

But we have a far more serious problem to which we are often not sensitive. Most of the time, we think positively to compensate for some unconscious negative thinking. Our sensory mind builds on opposites. If we have cold, we also must have hot. If things are easy, then somewhere things are hard. If we think positively, then somewhere in the mind we have negative thinking. As long as we deal in opposites, we cannot eliminate just one side of them.

As a consequence, our positive statements do not always work as well as we would like. Simply getting up in the morning, looking into the mirror, and saying, "Today is the best day of my life" or "Every day in every way I'm getting better" does *not* bring the instant fulfillment that many writers seem to think. While your conscious mind chirps "Today is a wonderful day," your unconscious mind may very well be muttering "Yesterday sure was lousy!"

Positive thinking, rephrasing our language, or reframing your interpretations, is helpful, particularly if you have been negative about yourself. But you are just compensating, putting out the fires while building new ones. The best action is to *clear the mind completely, so you can stop building the fires in the first place.*

We create the *need* for positive statements because we keep making negative ones in the subconscious and unconscious levels of our mind. Thus, no matter how many positive things we say, as long as we continue our unconscious negative thinking, we continue to create disturbances. The only way to solve the problem is to be sensitive to the deeper habits of our mind and eliminate this negative chatter.

Each of us has some particularly troublesome thought that keeps pressing our button. It may be: *I'm not really smart enough.* Or *I'm not good enough.* Or it may be: *If they really knew how incompetent I am...* Look at how much time, energy and effort you spend in proving that the thought is not true. No matter how many times you prove yourself and overcome this thought, it keeps popping up. Here is what to do: Instead of struggling with the thought, clear your mind with Breath Awareness, and re-focus your attention on more useful activities. The more you clear the negative chatter from your mind, the less time you need to spend on positive chatter. Instead, you will have more time for solving problems, being productive, enjoying your family, or pursuing leisure activities.

## YOUR CHOICE: STRESS OR PERSONAL POWER

You can allow your sensory mind to create stress for you, or you can take command and use this powerful level of your personality to become more productive and effective. Diaphragmatic breathing, deep relaxation skills, and breath awareness are powerful methods to eliminate stress and tension, and help you manage your sensory mind. However, the most effective stress management is to not create stress at all. Keep this in mind: Nearly all stress stems from your reaction to events in your life, so you only need to change your reaction to change the stress.

# THE THREE MISTAKES OF SENSORY MIND

We commit three serious mistakes in our sensory mind—fear, self-rejection (self-hatred) and laziness. These three mistakes are habits that inhibit the use of our inner resources, and lead to stress and emotional disturbances. But when we correct these mistakes, we free ourselves of their burdens, and maximize our inner strengths and skills.

### Fear: Negative Use of Creative Imagination

Our greatest (and some say "only") enemy is fear. Fear can become so powerful and pervasive that it colors our entire sensory mind, distorts our thinking, gives rise to other emotional disturbances, and destroys our bodies. Nothing is more dangerous, more destructive, and more useless, than fear. And yet, when we analyze it, fear is nothing more than a thought or fantasy, a habit of our sensory mind. We do not like to admit our fearfulness to others or even to ourselves. Instead, we talk about worry, anxiety or concern. Yet fear by any other name is still fear. If we realized just how much fear controls our life, we would be staggered.

Another of the great myths of our time says that fear is an innate response that helps people protect themselves. This is not true; no one is born with fear. We are born with a primitive, biological urge for self-preservation. This is more than just physical survival. Self-preservation includes our entire ego-self. In fact, we often place our physical self in danger just to enhance the ego-self. Look at the way we drive, or the way we push ourselves at work. Or look at why many of us begin smoking and drinking.

We mistakenly confuse self-preservation with fear. When we activate self-preservation, we feel an increased, relaxed alertness and a readiness for action. Along with this, we are more concentrated, and more aware of our surroundings. The key is *relaxed alertness*. It allows us to perceive and think more clearly, and to move more quickly and gracefully. This balanced state of readiness allows us to take any necessary action to protect ourselves.

Fear, on the other hand, sets off the alarm response called *fight or flight*, which produces uncoordinated arousal. Body and mind are unbalanced, and out of synchronization. As a result, we experience more stress which leads to more tension and more emotional disturbance. These reduce our awareness of what is going on around us and distort our thinking. Our entire personality becomes more rigid. The more fear we have, the more inflexible we become, and we lose our effectiveness.

Two crucial elements—(1) the way we use time and (2) our ego—determine whether we use self-preservation or suffer from fear. We create fear when we involve ourselves with speculation about the future. We never fear or worry about what is happening—we only fear or worry about what **might** happen. Fear is a projection of "what if." Our mind perceives a threat in the future, our body is acting in the present, and *voila*, we have stress. On the other hand, we utilize self-preservation when we deal with what is happening. Body and mind focus on the same reality—the present. This brings coordination and balance between mind and body.

Once we develop the habit of anticipating threats and creating fear, we set ourselves up for real problems. *By paying attention to imaginary threats, we program these events into our lives.* The more we fear, the more energy and attention we direct toward these possible events—and the more we subtly create the conditions that bring about the very reality we wish to avoid. For example, many of us are intimidated by the thought of addressing a large audience. Our mind begins to worry—What if I forget? What if I stumble when I walk up on the stage? What if they don't like what I say? We can program ourselves so well that by the time we begin our talk, we are so unnerved that we actually commit these very mistakes.

Fear involves our personal sense of I'ness, or ego, and those people and things to which we are emotionally attached: our family, our new car, our position in the corporation. We create fear when we make ourselves part of the problem. Often, however, this happens so subtly that we don't notice that we have just trapped ourselves. Suppose, for example, that the corporation's president assigns you to a major project at work. You are responsible for strategic planning, and you must have a report ready by next week outlining the possible problems and the steps to correct them. You are dealing with the future, but the planning must be done now. To do your best work, you want to be able to think clearly, and use your instincts and intuitive insights. However, you also know that your boss will be evaluating your performance. You want to look good on this one.

If you see this assignment as a challenge and you have confidence in yourself, there is no reason to feel threatened. But if you perceive this assignment as a possible threat, your innate urge for self-preservation is activated. Your mind will begin to play in the future, anticipating what might happen to you, and distorting the natural balance of self-preservation. You are not dealing with a present danger; you are imagining a future danger. The resulting fear and worry in turn create stress, and your mind is then too unbalanced to focus properly. You inhibit your creative and intuitive abilities, and end up with a headache or stomach pain. All of this makes it increasingly difficult to find creative solutions to the problems you face.

We literally train ourselves to fail by the worries and fears we create. Using imagery to bring about results is not a new technique. We have been doing it with fear for years. It is time to put a stop to this. Fear has no value other than to create stress, cloud our mind, inhibit our memory, and close off access to our intuitive and instinctual knowledge.

The next time you begin to worry, examine your imagery and thoughts. Is what you are worrying about *actually* happening to you, or is it something that you *think* is going to happen? Then watch how you deal with an actual situation that is dangerous or harmful. You will find that when you take action, you are not fearful, even though you are intensely alert. This is the essence of martial arts training. In martial arts, you don't anticipate—you remain entirely focused on what is happening in the moment. In this way, you remain free of fear. Your body stays relaxed and balanced, your mind remains responsive to its environment, and your movements are coordinated and graceful. The moment fear intervenes, you become tense, lose your inner balance and become less graceful, and your mind locks into a narrowing range of possibilities.

## Four Steps to Controlling Fear

**1. Deal only with the present.** Focus your attention on what you can do now, not what you might do in the future. Fear can't exist if you focus attention on the present. Solve the problem you face *at this moment*, take the actions available to you now, and let future problems take care of themselves.

**2. Face your fears directly.** When fear, worry or anxiety grips your mind, sit quietly and examine the fear as if you were a court reporter. Examine the assumptions your mind makes. What could be the worst to happen? Keep following the consequences, and don't allow your mind to stop until reaching the very end. Bring everything out in the open for your observation. For example:

> If this happens, my boss will be mad at me. What then?....Well, she will chew me out. What then?....I'll lose her respect, and feel bad and stupid. What then?...I may get fired, not be able to make my

mortgage payments and lose my house. What then?....oh, I probably wouldn't lose my house, I'd just have to find another job.... I'll get over it. What then?.....

As you follow your mind to the end, watch what happens to your fears. Then proceed to step 3.

**3. Use Breath Awareness to clear the mind.** With everyday fears and worries, immediately use Breath Awareness to clear your mind. Whenever your mind chatter brings up a personal threat, depersonalize it so you can maintain mental clarity. Focus on the problem to solve, and avoid becoming part of the problem by imagining all the terrible things that will happen to you. Don't build a village and then pay rent. The greater your skill at managing chatter, the more power you have over fear.

**4. Focus attention on your own power, strengths and resources.** Allowing your mind to chatter about your personal failings, weaknesses and faults only reinforces them, and never solves problems. Instead, focus your attention on what you can do, on your strengths and the resources you can utilize. Now your mind's energy is directed towards your strengths, and will reinforce them. This builds the useful habit of focusing on your strengths rather than your weaknesses.

To sum up, you can free your mind of petty fears, worries and anxieties quickly and easily with Breath Awareness. The stronger and deeper your habits, the more effort and training it takes to free your mind. Fear is only a habit of the sensory mind. But fear can destroy you physically and mentally, interfere with your personal productivity and effectiveness, and inhibit the joy and richness of your life. You can only empower your mind to the degree that you free yourself of fear.

**Self-Rejection: Creating Impotency**

It is not difficult to create a chronic pattern of failure and misery. All you have to do is constantly remind yourself of how awful, weak or incompetent you are, and brood on your past mistakes, hurts and failures. This will set off the possum response, resulting in stress, poor performance, more mistakes and diminishing awareness of our inner power.

Like fear, self-rejection is only a habit of the sensory mind. Rather than imagining a dire future, however, we create a distorted interpretation of our past. We lose touch with the present, and cannot deal effectively and joyfully with it.

There are different patterns and kinds of self-rejection, ranging from self-hatred and suicidal thoughts, to guilt and inferiority complexes—all of which interfere with personal effectiveness and executive productivity. *One of the greatest problems we face is feeling inferior.* Nearly everyone suffers from believing that somewhere they are just not good enough. While this often gives us a strong motivation to succeed, we never seem to have enough success to satisfy our nagging self-doubt. We run into that same old problem of trying to prove something again and again.

When "proving ourself" is our motivation, no amount of achievement brings genuine or lasting satisfaction. We feel compelled to chase after greater wealth, a bigger house, a bigger and better deal. We achieve all the external signs of success, but internally we still feel like a miserable failure, and constantly worry that others will find us out.

Guilt is another way we have of beating up on ourselves. We often use guilt to manipulate—"I've given you so much, and now you....." or "After all that I have done for you....." But even as a manipulative tool, guilt is not very useful, because it reinforces the very behavior about which we feel guilty. When we feel guilty, we become preoccupied with the behavior that makes us feel guilty. The more attention we give the behavior, the greater the probability that it will happen again. Guilt also leads to conflict and resentment, which interfere with our ability to act. The more guilty we make someone feel, the more we interfere with *their* effectiveness.

Guilt has nothing to do with our genuine conscience. Caught in the habit of guilt, we simply repeat the condemnations we learn from others. Our natural, or real conscience, lies in our discriminating mind, a deeper level of our personality. Our real conscience is not punitive, and it does not make judgments. It quietly tells us what is helpful and what isn't. Discrimination provides us with the opportunity to recognize mistakes, learn from them, and make more effective choices.

On the other hand, we build the habit of guilt, called the *superego,* through our interactions with parents, teachers, preachers, and other members of society. Instead of discriminating, our superego calls names, makes value judgments and, most of all, punishes. The conflict it generates damages our ability to function as healthy, joyful, and productive human beings.

## An Exercise for Solving the "Should" Problem

Punitive use of the word "should" is a strong indicator of guilt. We repeat "I should have done...." or "I should not have done....." over and over until we have ingrained the pain of failure in our mind and body. The first time we say "should," it's very helpful—that's when we alert our mind to a mistake and its correction. But we do not stop at just one. We continue to "should" ourselves unmercifully. This habit is damaging, and you can put a stop to it with the following exercise.

## The "Should" Stopper Exercise

When you find your mind repeating that you "should have," or "should not have" walk over to a window. Look up to the sky. If you do *not* see the hand of God writing in indelible gold letters, "John (or whatever your name is), you should not have done that!" then you can figure that what you did or did not do was okay. If God doesn't punish you, why do it to yourself? Accept the mistake and go on.

By taking this action, you weaken the destructive power of the guilt habit. It then becomes much easier to alter or replace the habit with a more functional and productive pattern of behavior, such as paying attention to the task in front of you.

## Laziness: Path to Nowhere

Like any organization, our personality resists change. This resistance comes mostly from our habits. Once we build a habit, it resists change, and can create some formidable obstacles. If we allow this resistance to control our choices and actions, we will have little chance of becoming empowered. Laziness is one way we experience this resistance. Our mind asks us, "Why bother?" It's easier to take an aspirin for a headache, a beta blocker for high blood pressure, or a drink to relax, than spend fifteen minutes a day doing some silly exercise.

It is easier and more familiar to feel a little miserable than create a change. Our fast food mentality constantly hunts for the easiest, quickest way out, whether a lottery, a shorter work week for more pay, or a drink to relax. We do not realize that we are shortchanging ourself. The less effort we invest, the less we gain, and the more damage we do to our personality. Minimum effort creates minimum satisfaction.

To eliminate the habit of laziness, we take action. It is laziness to expect the educational system to prepare us, the company to train us, or our country to feed us. It is laziness to expect someone to make us happy, solve our problems, and make us feel secure. Taking charge of our life is not as difficult as we may believe. It only requires time and effort. We have great capacity to live without emotional disturbance, stress and disease, but we must train ourselves. Our relationships, our institutions and social structures, our culture and society, can only offer us opportunities. What we do with them rests entirely in our hands.

This is not a hard-nosed conservative philosophy, but a recognition that *we alone create the meaning of our world.* Whether you are fearless or fearful, emotionally balanced or disturbed, successful or not, depends on what you do with your own mind. If you want to realize your potential as a human being and create an Empowered Mind, you have no choice but to take full responsibility for yourself.

## BALANCE AND CHOICE: THE DOOR TO SELF-MASTERY

We need inner balance and the freedom to choose our responses. These provide the foundation for developing our inner resources. Without them, we neither understand nor express the creative power, intelligence and wisdom of our inner selves. Each of us is a unique combination of skills, interests, beliefs and experiences. But if we are distracted by negative habits, we cannot express this inner power.

To understand and express the intelligence already within us, we need only to become more of what we already are. Through self-training, we (1) unlearn the habits that restrict our power, and (2) uncover our innate resources. The same tools that bring balance and harmony to our life also allow us choice and control. We can return to a more natural condition of health, awareness and integrity, where mind and body act in harmony. This is *wellness,* a dynamic condition of increase of health, personal effectiveness and self-actualization.

To have wellness means that we feel better physically, we experience more joyfulness in our life, and we are more optimistic and content with ourselves and life. *These inner qualities flow naturally from a balanced mind.* And it doesn't matter how many inspiring speakers we hear, how many pep talks we attend, and how many award dinners are given. If we are not balanced, the very next day it's back to feeling the same old worries and hassles, and acting in the same uncreative and inhibited way.

We experience joy when we face life without expectations, and greet each challenge as a dancing lesson from God. Joy is the natural outcome of undistorted self-expression, free of fear, dejection, and laziness. Whatever limits our self-expression limits our joy. We limit our-selves when we create expectation. The more expectations we have about life, the greater our disappointment. Expectations are different from goals. Goals serve as beacons to our future, lighting the direction in which we must travel. Expectations are the "shoulds" we impose on ourselves, on others, and on life. Instead of accomplishment, expectations bring disap-pointment and cynicism.

When we create an expectation about the way life should be, we operate out of a fantasy. We must have hopes and dreams, create images of the future, plan and set goals, but in the end analysis, however, we can only deal directly with what is, not what should be.

## An Exercise In Letting Go

When you entrap yourself with an expectation that is not met, you can free yourself of disappointment, clear your mind of regret, and move on. First close your eyes for a few moments and focus on Breath Awareness. After you have cleared your mind, allow it to occupy itself with the expectation and the disappointment. Try to see *where* you experience the sense of loss. Are you any different than a few moments before? Are you any less of a person? Has anything essential changed?

If you feel any emotional disturbance, again clear your mind with Breath Awareness, and return to a stable emotional state. Repeat the same self-examination. Once you remain free of disappointment, go on to the next item on your agenda. Do not allow your mind to keep coming back to the same old language about "shoulds" and "should nots."

Optimism emerges from our capacity to face challenges. Optimism plays a significant and often determining role in success. We remain optimistic when we recognize that failure can neither harm nor damage us. Look back at all the mistakes and failures that you have experienced. How did they really damage you? More than likely, the greatest damage comes from carrying that mistake or failure in your mind, holding on to it like a treasure.

> In ancient times, two monks, an old and a young one, were walking together. In this order of monks, any contact with women was strictly forbidden. The two monks came to a stream, swollen by the spring rains. A beautiful young woman stood on the bank crying her heart out. "Why are you crying?" the old monk asked. She replied that she

wanted to go to her father's house to attend her sister's wedding, but that the stream was too high for her to cross.

"No problem at all, " said the old monk, and he picked the young woman up and carried her across the stream. When he sat her down on the other side, she thanked him profusely, and went on her way. The two monks continued their journey. But the older monk could see that his young companion was becoming more and more disturbed. "What's troubling you, brother?" he asked. The younger monk exploded in anger. "You know we're not supposed to have anything to do with women, and you picked that woman up and carried her across the stream!"

"I picked her up and set her down," replied the old, wise monk, "You have been carrying her all this way."

The mistakes and failures that we continue to carry in our mind inhibit the spontaneous expression of joy and optimism that are a natural part of our mind. We are not born with this baggage, but we train our minds to become beasts of burden. It's hard to be optimistic when we constantly feel like a jackass.

Practice letting go of past mistakes. We all have some expectation that we should be perfect, free of any and all error. Once we give ourselves permission to make mistakes, we rid our mind of a great many unnecessary burdens. Then our natural optimism can emerge. One of the best ways to clear our mind is with Breath Awareness.

Developing an Empowered Mind is a process of unfolding potential—physically, emotionally, mentally, and spiritually. To develop our potential, we must build on the firm foundation of inner balance. These past four chapters have shown you how to build this foundation. Once you begin to establish wellness, access to the inner skills of the Empowered Mind becomes a natural second step.

## SUMMARY OF PRINCIPLES

1. The greatest source of stress is the mismanagement of the inner chatter (thoughts and emotions) of our own sensory mind.

2. By taking control of our mental habits, we choose our responses rather than react.

3. Two basic principles define the power of language in the sensory mind:

- How we feel and act is a function of how we interpret and define our reality.
- We can change both our feelings and our actions by taking control of the language, images and sensations that we use to interpret our reality.

4. The most powerful tool for managing mind chatter is Breath Awareness. With it you control emotional reactions, eliminate stress and maintain clarity of mind.

5. By taking control of language, you take control of the power of the sensory mind.

6. We commit three serious errors in our sensory mind: the habits of fear, self-rejection and laziness. Fear generates the alarm reaction of the fight or flight response; self-rejection generates the alarm reaction of the possum response. Because of laziness we fail to correct the habits that destroy our joy, optimism and contentment.

7. We have the power and knowledge within us to free ourselves of stress and continue the journey of self-mastery to the Empowered Mind.

# Concentration:
# 5 The Executive's
# Ultimate Skill

*Depend on it, Sir, when a man knows he is to be hanged in a fortnight, it concentrates his mind wonderfully.*
—*Samuel Johnson*

**Situation:** You are flying into O'Hare Airport, the busiest airport in the world, at five o'clock in the afternoon. As you look at the sky around you, you see at least five other airplanes in the immediate vicinity, all waiting their turn to land. Suddenly, the pilot announces a fifteen-minute holding pattern because of all the traffic in the area. What if you knew that the air controller in the traffic control tower was distracted by worries about his wife, or an argument with his supervisor, or upset about union problems? How comfortable would you be if you knew that this air traffic controller was unable to concentrate on his work?

**Situation:** You have had a very trying day, with a lot of worries about the project that you are working on and several difficult personnel problems to solve. Now the boss asks you to give him a decision about marketing the new product. Several million dollars are at stake, and you cannot clear your mind. No matter how hard you try, you simply cannot focus on the marketing.

**Situation:** You have had another exciting and challenging day. Finally, you get to bed. As you lie there, your mind constantly goes over the new project that you are working on. You are not worried, but really excited about all the opportunities. Instead of getting the rest you need, however, you find yourself going over and over all the possibilities. Just like a little kid looking forward to Christmas Day, you are too excited to sleep, even though you need to.

## FOCUSING THE MIND

In each of the three above situations, the common problem is a distracted or unfocused mind. We usually do not think about concentration until those times when we cannot focus. But concentration affects every aspect of our life. It is the one personal skill we *must* have if we want to be successful. Everything we do, from auditing to zoning, depends on our ability to pay attention. Intense concentration allows a batter to see and hit a 98 mile per hour fast ball, the mountain climber to find footholds and opportunities on a sheer face of rock, the actor to tune in to the audience, and the executive to determine which data he needs to complete a project successfully. Sexual functioning thrives on concentration. Our safety depends on paying attention. Even our sleep is disturbed if we cannot control our agitated mind. While personal styles, job demands and expectations, situations and opportunities all differ, the universal characteristic of successful performance is concentration.

Through concentration, we alter our sense of time and space, become more aware of our environment, think more clearly, and access our instinctual and intuitive knowledge. Concentration coordinates our mind and body, so we remain free of stress no matter how hard we work. Through concentration, we achieve what psychologists call a "peak experience"—a performance that transcends our everyday experience. Because no other personal skill is more crucial to personal empowerment, I call concentration the ultimate skill.

For most of us, concentration is something that just happens. Our ability to concentrate varies from day to day, and we seem to have little control over it. Whatever skill we have is accidental, as very few of us ever deliberately train our power of concentration.

Like breathing, concentration is so central to our life that we pay little attention to it. But we cannot afford to ignore this critical resource if we want empowerment. Without concentration, our mind remains weak and our resources undeveloped.

## CONCENTRATION: THE MIND AS LASER

Our mind is a subtle field of energy. As we interact with our environment, this mental energy creates different mind forms—thought, images, and sensations—which we experience as knowledge. But each pattern stimulates another, and we move from one pattern to another. This makes it difficult to keep our attention focused on one thing for any length of time. Try to hold one thought in your mind. Close your eyes, and focus on the word "blue." Do not think of blue skies, blue shirts, or blue monkeys. Just the word "blue" for thirty seconds. You will find that your mind does not want to stand still. It jumps from one thought or image to the next like a nervous monkey in a tree. This scatters our mental energy, and the more scattered we are, the less we accomplish.

On the other hand, when we pay attention to something, we focus our attention and synchronize our mind's energy into a cohesive flow. The difference between a concentrated mind and a distracted mind is like the difference between the energy of a laser and that of a normal light bulb.

A regular light bulb gives off energy in the form of photons. Each photon, or energy unit, exerts a certain amount of force that we experience as light, not as individual photons. A normal light bulb scatters its photons into the atmosphere in all directions. But the photons lose energy as they run into other sub-atomic units of energy in their path, so they do not travel very far. In a laser, however, the photons, organized and compressed into a cohesive flow, all travel in the same direction. Now the energy of each individual photon is accumulated, and the light becomes a powerful force. Because of this focused and accumulated energy, lasers can penetrate steel plate, or have a touch as delicate as a flower petal, or travel almost infinitely through space with very little loss of energy. The basic energy unit—the photon—is the same. The only difference is that the laser's energy is synchronized.

The energy of the mind is similar to these photons. The individual unit of mental energy—just for fun, let's call them mentons— is too slight to even measure. These individual mentons combine to form thoughts, images or sensations. When our mind is distracted, the mentons go off in all directions. Because they are scattered, their force is weak and can only form superficial knowledge. But when we concentrate, we organize and compress these mentons into a cohesive flow, and our mind becomes powerful in its capacity to enlighten and understand.

### From Homo Haphazardous to Homo Sapiens

Figure 5:1 shows how our mind's energy becomes more synchronized as we become more concentrated.

# CONCENTRATION: THE ENERGY STATES OF MIND

### A

DISTRACTED MIND

Mind energies scat-
tered as mind reacts
to any stimulus; body
in some stress as it
reacts to mind chat-
ter; subtle skills of
the mind remain hid-
den by chatter (noise).

### B

PAYING ATTENTION

Mind energies begin
to be more focused;
less chatter, more
awareness of immediate
environment; body
less distracted;
thoughts more clear.

### C
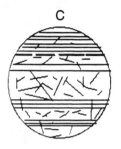

CONCENTRATION

Mind energies more
focused; body becomes
calm; mind skills more
available; thinking
more clear, intuition
more available.
Greater sensitivity/
awareness.

### D
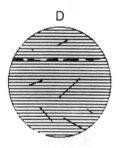

MEDITATION

Mind completely fo-
cused; concentration
effortless and flow-
ing; enhanced aware-
ness of environment
and inner skills;
unconscious mind and
its power available
to conscious control.

### E
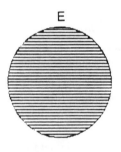

UNITARY CONSCIOUSNESS

Total concentration;
super state of con-
sciousness; mystical
knowledge; complete
mind/body conscious-
ness; all resources
of mind available for
conscious use.

Figure 5:1

Distractions create conscious and unconscious cross-currents which dissipate our mind's energy in a thousand and one different directions (Figure 5:1A). Instead of Homo Sapiens, in this state of mind we should really refer to ourselves as Homo Haphazardous. Sensory stimulation and unconscious emotions and habits dominate our mental chatter, leaving our conscious mind weak and disorganized. The more our body reacts to this unmanaged mind chatter, the more stressed we become.

Then something grabs our attention. We begin to focus our mind, and the energy patterns take a more orderly flow (Figure 5:1B). This conscious act of paying attention alters the condition of our conscious mind. But if we do not intensify our focus, we can still be easily distracted by worries and disturbances that lie dormant in our unconscious mind. For example, if we are speaking on the phone, and our supervisor walks in scowling, we quickly lose our focus and begin worrying about the last mistake we made. His scowl may, in fact, have nothing to do with us. Before he walked into the office, we talked on the phone without any anxiety. His scowl stimulated our unconscious fears, which quickly surfaced, and began to dominate our thoughts. Then we could no longer focus on what we were doing.

## Taking Control: Increasing the Power

By intensifying our focus, we synchronize more of our mind's energy (Figure 5:1C). The stronger our concentration, the weaker the distractions. In this way, concentration purifies and strengthens our mind by minimizing the cross-currents of energy. This gives us three crucial benefits:

- increased awareness of what's really important, and greater clarity of thought.
- greater use of the mind's natural ability to form accurate and penetrating knowledge. This leads to more effective learning.
- enhanced coordination and balance between mind and body, leading to less stress and a healthier mind and body.

We have all felt anger, resentment or regret because we felt forced to do something we did not want to do. In this negative mood, the work seemed dreary, uninteresting and difficult. Then something clicked, spurred our interest, and we began to really focus on what we were doing. The more concentrated we became, the more interesting our work became. We found creative solutions for difficult problems, and we realized that the work we had initially disliked had become very satisfying. Through concentration, we transformed the project into a very positive experience.

You can train your mind to be calm and focused. The following exercise is a concentration exercise that leads to a deeply calm mind. Because of its impact on the mind, and the profound state of relaxation that it brings, we use this exercise in the treatment and prevention of high blood pressure.

## 61 Points

Begin by lying in the Relaxation Posture and concentrating for a few minutes on even, diaphragmatic breathing. Once your breath has become smooth, even and effortless, than practice the Sweeping Breath (page 78) for a few moments. Picture your body like a hollow reed, breathing as if you are breathing through your toes, filling your body with breath to the top of your head. Than exhale back down and out the toes. Continue this breathing imagery until you can feel as if your whole body is expanding when you breathe in and contracting when you breathe out.

After a few moments of the Sweeping Breath, bring your concentration to the mind center, the point between the two eyebrows, and visualize a small blue star or flame. Choose one or the other, but don't switch them around. The star should look like an actual star in the sky, a point of blue light, while the flame should look like the small blue flame that is used in natural gas commercials on television. Picture the star or flame as small, clear and perfect as your mind will allow it to be. Hold this image in your mind for ten to fifteen seconds. Then visualize this star or flame at each of the other sixty points in the body as shown in Figure 5:2. Follow the diagram exactly, as this is a very precise exercise. Focus only on one point at a time. You don't want to light up your body like a Christmas tree.

As you can see in the diagram, you repeat several of the points. The exercise is very systematic and easy to learn. As with any concentration exercise, the more concentrated you become, the more relaxed you feel, so you may feel the urge to fall asleep. Since this exercise leads to the most profound states of relaxation, and you are lying down, the tendency to sleep is even greater. Before doing the exercise, make a strong determination that you will not allow yourself to sleep. Although you may fall asleep the first few times, practice until you are able to maintain alertness throughout the entire exercise.

The color blue is important as it provides a restful focus for the

# 61 POINTS

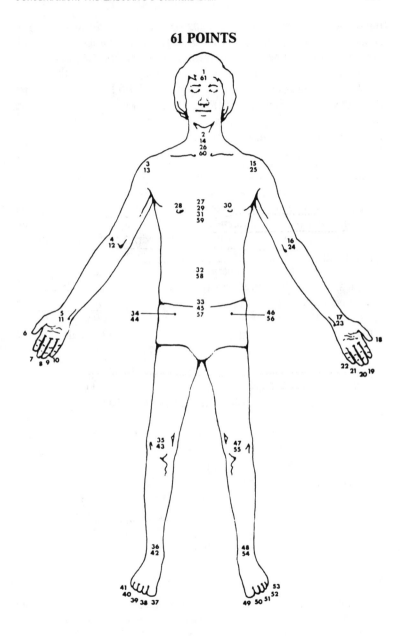

Figure 5:2

mind. Do not substitute colors; doing so will change the effect. If you absolutely cannot visualize a flame or star, substitute a point of warmth or heat, about the same size as the diameter of a pen. End the exercise with a few moments concentration on the Sweeping Breath, and then even, diaphragmatic breathing. As you become more skillful, gradually increase the time you spend at each point to at least twenty seconds. I recommend that you continue this practice on a weekly basis at least. See Appendix B if you wish to tape this exercise.

## A Calm Mind Brings Awareness

All the information in the world doesn't help if we are too distracted to notice it. When we synchronize our mental energies, we create a calming effect that increases our awareness. The less distracted we are, the more we tune into the subtle sensory cues in our environment. As a result, our instincts are sharper, and we make better choices. Let's return to the example of the scowling supervisor. If we are distracted by anxious thoughts, we do not notice the slight swelling in his jaw indicating an abscessed tooth. But if our mind is clear and focused, we will notice the swelling and the pain in his face. With this information, we respond differently. Instead of reacting defensively, we can offer understanding and sympathy which, in turn, enhances our relationship with him.

With a calm mind, we also become more aware of our inner resources. Remember, your mind already has all the knowledge and resources you need. But if you are not aware of this capacity, you cannot use it.

Imagine the unconscious mind as a vast treasure cave. But the cave is so vast and dark that we don't see very much. All we have are hints of the treasures within. When we focus our attention inwardly, it is as if we have taken a very small beam of light and slowly enlarged it to reveal more and more of the hidden treasures of the cave—our innate wisdom, power, and knowledge. The more powerful our light (concentration), the more clearly we see our innate capacities. Consequently, we use them more effectively and make better choices for ourselves.

## Refining Concentration: Making the Mind a Laser

By intensifying our concentration, we create an even more powerful state of mind. As we refine our skill, we synchronize more and more of the mind's energy until we are deeply concentrated (Figure 5:1D). Now our mind becomes like a laser, burning away any remaining distractions. The distractions may not be completely eliminated, but they no longer influence our mind. We become so calm and stable that we can handle anything, no matter what happens around us. Now when a higher-ranking executive walks in with a scowl, we do not have a knee-jerk reaction of worry. We calmly note the fact of his presence, and complete our phone conversation without anxiety.

We make our conscious mind strong through the discipline of deep concentration. Although we are not aware of it, our unconscious emotional patterns constantly influence our thinking. But these have little power against the "laser-strong" power of a trained conscious mind. When we refine our concentration to the degree that it builds this strength in our conscious mind, we call it meditation.

"Meditation" is a technical term indicating an effortless and unbroken stream of concentration, on a single point, over an extended period of time. In this advanced, highly refined state of concentration, the subtle cross-currents in our unconscious are so weak that they can no longer distract or disturb us.

Most people have funny ideas about the term meditation. They consider meditation as closing your eyes and thinking about something. Or they associate the term with a foreign religion, or funny-looking people who have shaved heads and orange-colored clothes, or someone trying to float in the air. None of this, however, has anything to do with meditation.

In meditation, you concentrate the power of your mind on a single point. To do this, you do not have to believe in any particular philosophy, religion or culture. A ruby laser is the same ruby laser whether it's used in Japan, Germany or the United States. Meditation is refined concentration whether it is used by a Buddhist priest or by a New York accountant. The focus point may well be different, but the condition of effortless, unbroken concentration must be the same. If you drive a car built in Japan, you do not become Japanese. Nor do the Japanese become Americans because they like to go to Disneyland. If you practice meditation, you do not become some kind of Eastern hippie. You do, however, open the power of your mind and gain access to your inner resources.

Concentration makes our mind powerful. Focusing our attention is like holding a lens up to sunlight. The lens catches the light waves and concentrates them. Ordinary sunlight has tremendous power when concentrated. We can do a great many things with concentrated sunlight that we can't do with normal sunlight. The energy of the mind is the same. When we concentrate our mind, we achieve things that seem almost miraculous to a scattered and undisciplined mind. When we completely concentrate our mind, there is literally nothing that we can't accomplish in this powerful and potent state.

## Unitary Consciousness: The Crown Jewel of Concentration

When we refine our skill at meditation, and eliminate all cross currents of the mind, we achieve Unitary Consciousness, a very special condition of awareness (Figure 5:1E). Our entire unconscious mind becomes part of our subconscious, and all of the mind's resources and power functions become accessible to our conscious mind. We become completely balanced and we achieve absolute clarity of mind. If we direct our focus outwardly, we gain penetrating insight into the nature of our world. If we direct it inwardly, we gain awareness of our own Center of Consciousness, and experience the power of our human spirit. This profound awareness completely frees us from fear, and we feel an overwhelming sense of love and compassion. This is often referred to as a "mystical experience."

Obviously, this doesn't happen easily, or often. But we do have fleeting experiences of Unitary Consciousness, and we can cultivate it with practice. Unitary Consciousness is the inevitable consequence of total and complete inner concentration. By achieving Unitary Consciousness, we complete our journey, and take full command of all the resources of our mind.

But concentration is a complex skill, and many things affect our ability to concentrate effectively. At least five factors determine our ability to concentrate. By understanding and managing these dimensions, we increase our power of concentration. They are:

1. Making an intentional and conscious choice to focus our attention;

2. The level of positive interest in what we choose to focus on;

3. Whether we focus our attention inwardly or externally;

4. The level of energy we have to bring to our concentration;

5. The degree of skill we develop in concentrating.

## MAKING A CONSCIOUS CHOICE

The first thing to realize is that concentration is a conscious, intentional action. Daydreams, trance states, subliminal learning, and hypnosis may have some value, but they don't strengthen our conscious mind. As mental experiences, they create patterns in our unconscious mind which may or may not be helpful to us. But they don't synchronize our mental energy. *Only by focusing our conscious attention do we achieve this.*

In a trance state, or a state of reverie, such as daydreaming, your unconscious mind controls the flow of your thoughts. Under hypnosis and with subliminal learning, the hypnotic suggestion controls the flow of your thoughts. This actually weakens your will. You have simply built another habit (energy pattern) in your unconscious mind, giving you even more to synchronize. To synchronize the mind's energy patterns, you must consciously and intentionally focus your attention. Without doing this, your conscious mind remains weak, controlled by whatever patterns you have in your unconscious, and you forfeit the benefits of concentration.

Empowerment means choice. It means conscious use of your resources. Building positive habits leads to empowerment. But following another person's suggestion, or allowing another unconscious habit to take control, does not.

## BUILDING THE FORCE: EXPANSION OR CONTRACTION

We pay attention for two basic reasons: interest and fear. Interest takes a variety of forms: income, sexual attraction, self-image, pleasure, personal growth, curiosity, even self-preservation. Fear makes us pay attention whenever we think we might be hurt, or lose something. Both fear and interest grab our attention, but their impact on our mind and our ability to concentrate are quite different.

Concentration and pseudo-concentration are two conditions of our mind that we often confuse. Concentration builds on positive conditions which allow us to fully synchronize the energy of our mind. The more positive interest we have, the more intensely we pay attention, which in turn, expands our awareness. Even though we may focus on a specific object or task, the interest we generate expands our awareness to include everything related to the object or task. This serves to reinforce our interest. We initiate a positive cycle of interest, awareness, focus and more interest, leading to deeper and deeper states of concentration.

The great inventor, Alexander Graham Bell, was not a specialist. He followed whatever stimulated his interest. In fact, his father-in-law once chided him for his aimless scattering of interests, and this happened less than five months before he invented the telephone. Almost everything fascinated Bell. The greatness of his mind wasn't in education or specialization, but in his capacity for total absorption in the concern of the moment. "My mind," he once wrote, "concentrates itself on the subject that happens to occupy it and then all things else in the Universe—including father, mother, wife, children, life itself—become for the time being of secondary importance."

Just the opposite happens when fear motivates us. Fear intensifies whatever emotional cross-currents we have in our unconscious mind, distorting our perceptions and thoughts. Instead of synchronizing the patterns of our unconscious mind, fear disrupts them. Instead of concentration, we have *pseudo-concentration*—our conscious mind is focused, but our unconscious mind is totally disrupted.

Thus, instead of becoming more effective, as we do when motivated by interest, fear makes us *less* effective. When we worry about making mistakes, failing, or being discovered for the nincompoop that we secretly feel we are, we have a greater tendency to make mistakes, fail and act like a nincompoop. The stronger the fear, the more it interferes, and the more it controls our behavior.

### Fear and Awareness: Diminishing Returns

Figure 5:3 shows the difference between fear and interest on our degree of awareness. Interest expands our awareness while fear contracts it. The stronger our fear, the more we focus on "the problem" until we can't see anything else. We become so constricted that we develop tunnel vision. Then all we see is the problem, the thing we fear!

The more disturbed we are, the more rigid our behavior and thoughts become. We even begin to see all kinds of dangers that do not really exist. In pseudo-concentration, our muscles become as rigid as our mind. We behave in compulsive and erratic ways, and even our physical movement is awkward, jerky, and unbalanced. We become a danger to ourselves as well as to others. Pseudo-concentration results in stress, and leads to psychosomatic diseases such as headaches, ulcers and heart disease.

On the other hand, genuine concentration leads to mental and physical harmony. We feel relaxed, attentive and become very aware. When we clearly understand how fear destroys our ability to concentrate, we see with painful clarity the damage done by a manager or boss, who "puts the fear of God" into his charges. He not only creates problems for them, but interferes with their effectiveness, and creates productivity and

# AWARENESS AND MOTIVATION

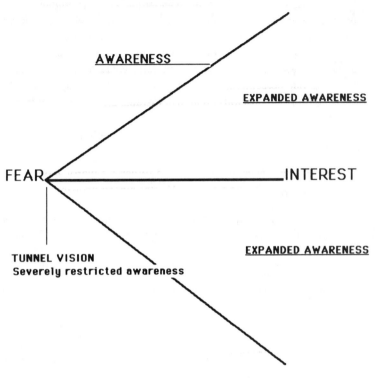

Figure 5:3

morale problems for the corporation. Winning through intimidation is not winning at all—it is losing.

Just examine your own experience. Remember the time when you worried about a meeting with the boss, and all the misery you put yourself through? How well could you work? The more you worried, the more unproductive you became. Contrast this with the times when you were fascinated by what you and the boss were working on together. The more interested you became in the work, the more attuned you became to his thinking and the ways in which he saw the world. During this time, instead of fearing the boss, you became more interested in his ideas and in him as a person. If your boss also concentrated, he experienced the same benefits. The whole experience was a positive one of enhanced learning and performance.

### Steps to Positive Motivation

We can take specific steps to minimize fear and increase our ability to concentrate. The steps to prevent fear (Chapter 4, p. 103) are helpful, along with the following:

1. Follow your interests! Always find something to like and enjoy about whatever it is you are doing. Remember, the more interest you generate for yourself, the better you will do, and the easier the task becomes.

2. Stay present-centered. Focus on what you are doing now. Do not let your mind wander off into fantasies of "what if." Even positive fantasies distract your attention and minimize your concentration.

3. Do not tie your ego to the task. The more ego-involved you are, the greater the possibility of fear and worry.

4. Whenever you find yourself becoming anxious or worried, clear your mind with Breath Awareness, and re-focus your attention on the task at hand.

## THE INS AND OUTS OF CONCENTRATION

We can focus on some inner point, such as a thought or our heart beat. Or we can focus on some external point, such as a person, an event or an object. When we dream, mull over a problem, or practice meditation, we focus inwardly. When we engage in sports, work on a project, or engage in conversation, we orient our attention externally. In less advanced stages of concentration, we can easily shift our orientation back and forth. But as our concentration intensifies, it becomes more difficult to shift, and takes greater skill.

Since we operate in both the internal and external worlds, we must be skilled in both. We spend time and effort in understanding our environment, but we tend to ignore our inner reality. If we remain one-sided, we will find ourselves increasingly handicapped in the age of information technology, dependent on our technology to make decisions. The more dependent we become on our external reality, the more we diminish the power of our own humanity.

## External Concentration: Peak Performance at Work

Our most familiar experience with deep concentration happens when we become so absorbed in some activity that we forget about time. The key is not *what* we are doing, but our ability to *concentrate* on our activity. The deeper our concentration, the more access we have to the treasures in our unconscious mind, and the more we use them in our efforts. During this time, we are more creative, find solutions to difficult problems, and really do our best work. This wonderful experience, called *task absorption*, becomes a peak experience for us because of our concentration.

When we achieve task absorption, we may work for several hours, and not realize it. We may be doing anything—a work project, chopping firewood, playing handball, or even washing dishes. During this peak performance, we go beyond our usual limitations, and expand our capacities. Even if the work is physically demanding, we find the experience extremely satisfying. The idea of success or failure becomes insignificant in the joy of self-expression.

In his autobiography, Bill Russell, one of the greatest and most competitive basketball players of all time, describes such an experience. When he became totally focused on the game, he knew where the ball was and where it would end up, where each player was and where he would be in the next moment. Everything came together in a single effortless flow. In this state of complete concentration, there was no longer any effort or strain, actions flowed into one another, and he experienced a profound satisfaction. At that point, he reports, it did not matter whether he won or lost, the only thing that mattered was participating in the flawless performance. The peak experiences of effortless concentration and complete self-expression made it all worthwhile.

## Inner Concentration: The Realization of Power

Although less familiar to us, inner concentration is even more useful. We need inner concentration to become aware of our inner resources and to develop our capacity for self-management. Through inner concentration and meditation, we gain control of the innate resources that constitute an Empowered Mind, and gain spiritual knowledge and power.

The awareness generated by inner concentration has unlimited value. For example, our ability to use imagery for creative problem solving. One classic and frequently cited example is the dream of Friedrich A. von Kekule:

> I turned my chair to the fire and dozed...Again the atoms were gamboling before my eyes. This time the smaller groups kept modestly in the background. My mental eye, rendered more acute by repeated visions of this kind, could now distinguish larger structures of manifold conformation; long rows, sometimes more closely fitted together; all twining and twisting in snakelike motion. But look! What was that? One of the snakes had seized hold of its own tail, and the form whirled mockingly before my eyes. As if by a flash of lightning, I awoke....Let us learn to dream, gentlemen.

This lucid dream did not just happen. It was the result of von Kekule's intense involvement with his work, and a practiced sensitivity to his inner realities. It allowed him to intuitively discover the unknown structure of certain organic compounds, and fixed his contribution forever in modern chemistry.

## Gazes: From Vision to Skill

We depend heavily on our vision to function in the world. We can use this powerful sense to enhance our power of concentration by practicing gazing. We hold a gaze when the eyes are not allowed to move off the target object, to waver or even blink. We focus all of our attention on the object, ignoring all thoughts and sensations, until our eyes begin to water, or our concentration is involuntarily broken by blinking. At that point, we close our eyes and visualize the object internally. We create an internal gaze and hold it at least as long as we held the external gaze.

Almost everyone has heard of candle gazing. This is not quite as flaky as you might suppose. Light naturally attracts our mind. If someone "flicks their Bic" or strikes a match, we involuntarily glance at the light. We can use this natural attraction to help strengthen our concentration.

Candle gazing can be done in two ways:

1. with direct light, looking directly at the candle flame, which creates a heating sensation in your eyes

2. with indirect light, looking at a reflection of the candle flame in a mirror, which creates a subtle, cooling sensation in the eye

Whether you use reflected or direct light doesn't matter. What does matter is that you train yourself gradually to hold the gaze without blinking or distraction for longer periods of time. To practice any gaze exercise, take your glasses or contacts off. If you wear contacts, you should take them out whenever you close your eyes to do relaxation or concentration exercises. Otherwise, the discomfort of the contacts will eventually distract your mind.

**Gaze Exercise**

Place an even-burning dinner candle approximately an arm's length distance in front of you. The flame should be level with your eyes so you can hold your head steady and gaze straight ahead. If you want to use a reflected light, place the candle behind you so that you see the reflection in a mirror directly in front of you, at the proper height.

In a dark, quiet room, gaze at this steady flame without blinking until your eyes begin to water, or until you feel too much discomfort or strain. Keep the thought of the flame in the mind, ignoring other thoughts, sensations and feelings. When you blink, stop the external gaze. Close your eyes and picture the flame as clearly as you can in the center of your mind. Hold this internal gaze on the image of the flame as long as you comfortably can. The smaller, clearer and more defined the image of the flame, the better the training for concentration. Don't worry if at first the image of the flame is undefined or vague. As you become more skilled with concentration, the image will become more clear and defined.

Don't try to become expert in two days or even two months. Keep a daily practice, and let your capacity slowly expand until you can hold the external gaze for at least twenty minutes. If, at any time, you get a headache, simply reduce the time you spend gazing. Headaches are an indication that you are pushing too hard and going beyond your natural capacity. After reaching this twenty minute capacity, maintain at least a weekly practice of twenty minutes. You might notice an increase in both the intensity of your dreams and in your ability to recall them.

# ENERGY: BALANCE AND CONSERVATION

The fourth dimension—energy—has a complex relationship with concentration. Concentration involves our ability to manage energy. We usually do not experience thoughts as energy, but we do experience their effect on us. Good news, a promotion, or a word of praise may energize us, while criticism may lead to low energy states, such as feeling depressed, worn out, or simply tired. Both kinds of news may interfere with our ability to concentrate effectively. Our level of energy depends on many things; thoughts and emotions, diet, exercise, even the weather. How we manage our energy often determines whether or not we can concentrate.

## Energy Requirements: The Lows and the Highs

If we do not have enough energy, it is difficult to concentrate. When tired, worn out, or depressed, we cannot focus our attention for any length of time. We do not have the strength to bring our mind and its distractions (cross-currents) under control. Have you ever been so tired that all you could do is shuffle papers around, or it seemed as if you had to work harder and harder just to get the same amount of work done? Perhaps you indulged in steak and fries for lunch, and then found yourself sluggish at an important afternoon meeting. Your digestive process diverted your energy for several hours as it digested the red meat and other fats. Regardless of the cause, you cannot do your best thinking in a low energy state because you do not have the energy you need to concentrate.

Having *too much* energy also presents problems. Being overly enthusiastic or too excited likewise can interfere with focusing your attention. In a championship game, a football player can be so "keyed up" that it interferes with his performance. After a few plays, he may settle down to a manageable state of energy. A more common problem for the executive is tension. When we are too wound up, the excess energy creates muscle tension, our mind races, and we find it difficult to concentrate. To concentrate, we must maintain our energy within reasonable bounds. Too much energy, or too little, makes concentration more difficult and less likely to occur.

Thus, the more *balanced* you are, the easier it is to control your mind and its energy fluctuations. Stress management skills and mind-clearing techniques, such as breath awareness, help maintain a calm and accessible energy level. You can use your breath in other ways to manage your energy. The following breathing exercises can help stabilize your energy, and prepare your mind for concentration.

**Energizing Exercises**

When you feel too sleepy or too tired to concentrate effectively, either of these two exercises will increase your energy levels, and return alertness to your mind:

### *Bellows Breath*

In this simple exercise, you create a bellows effect with your lungs. Sit erect in a comfortable position with your head, neck and trunk in proper alignment. The exercise consists of a vigorous, forceful expulsion of your breath by contracting the stomach muscles and pushing the diaphragm upwards. This is followed by relaxing the stomach muscles and allowing a slow, spontaneous inhalation without any effort. This constitutes one cycle. Several cycles are repeated in quick succession. When you first begin this exercise, do only seven to twenty-one repetitions, depending on your capacity. As you practice, your capacity will increase, and you should increase the number of cycles. It's best not to do this exercise after eating. The Bellows Breath exercise has several benefits:

- cleans the sinuses and respiratory passages
- stimulate and strengthens the stomach muscles
- stimulates and increases blood flow to the digestive tract
- increases our level of energy, makes the mind more alert

### *Complete Breath*

In this exercise you use all of your breathing capacity in a very gentle way. Sitting erect, breathe in, using the diaphragm and expanding your belly. Continue breathing in by expanding the chest. Then inhale to the very top of the lungs at which point you will feel a slight upward movement of the clavicles (collarbones). The breathing out is done in reverse. The clavicles drop slightly, then let the chest wall collapse slightly, then let the belly collapse as the diaphragm moves upward, pushing the air out of the lungs. Breathe slowly and smoothly, without any pauses or jerks. Usually after five to ten complete breaths you will feel energized, relaxed and ready to concentrate on what you are doing.

Use the Complete Breath exercise when you are sitting at your desk and feel a lot of tension in your shoulders. A few minutes of working with this exercise will reduce the muscle tension as well as eliminate your mental fatigue and help you restore your level of productivity.

## Calming Breath

The Alternate Nostril exercise can calm an agitated mind and bring your attention into a clear and steady focus.

### *Alternate Nostril Breathing*

This is one of the most important breathing exercises available. This exercise will:

- increase the capacity of your lungs.
- increase your control over the breathing process and the autonomic nervous system.
- calm and focus your mind.
- serve as an effective preliminary exercise for developing your power of concentration, and can evolve into a sophisticated Breath Awareness concentration exercise.

To practice Alternate Nostril Breathing, sit comfortably with your head, neck and trunk in alignment (the back should be straight but allow for the natural S curve of the spine). The exercise consists of exhaling and inhaling through the active nostril and then through the passive nostril. Then you repeat this procedure two more times. The entire exercise consists of only six complete breaths, three on each side.

1. Rest the index and middle fingers of the right hand on the space between the two eyebrows. Determine which nostril is active. (The active nostril is the one through which you breathe out easily, the passive is the nostril that seems to be somewhat or partially blocked. There is a natural cycle that opens and closes the nostrils to shift the air flow from one nostril to another.) If the right nostril is active, press your ring finger against the left nostril, closing it, and gently exhale through the right nostril, counting to six (or about six seconds) mentally as you exhale. Then inhale immediately through the same nostril for a count of six.

2. Now press the thumb gently against the right nostril, closing it off, and at the same time release the pressure on the left nostril. Exhale for a count of six, and then inhale for a count of six through the left nostril.

3. Now press the ring finger gently against the left nostril, closing

off the flow of air, and at the same time release the pressure from the thumb on the right nostril. Exhale for a count of six, and inhale for a count of six through the right nostril.

4. Close the right nostril and open the left. Exhale and inhale for a count of six through the left nostril.

5. Close the left nostril and open the right, Exhale and inhale for a count of six through the right nostril.

6. Close the right nostril and open the left. Exhale and inhale for a count of six through the left nostril.

This completes the exercise. Now bring your hand down and slowly resume your normal breathing. Focus as much attention as possible on the flow of the breath during the exercise. When there are no bumps, jerks or pauses, and when the flow of the breath is evenly distributed throughout the entire cycle, then increase the length of the breath (go from a count of six to a count of eight). Begin with a count which is comfortable and concentrate on making the breath smooth and even at this length. It is the smoothness of the flow which is important here, not how long you can make your breath. The length will increase as your control over the flow increases.

After several months of daily practice, and your capacity has increased, you can shift this exercise into a sophisticated Breath Awareness exercise by doing the exercise without using your fingers. This takes time and practice, but it is powerful technique for enhancing your concentration skills.

## Concentration and Conservation

The more concentrated we become, the more energy we conserve. We use our energy more efficiently and stop wasting it in non-productive ways, such as excess muscle tension. For example, when you change from chest breathing to diaphragmatic breathing, you find that you aren't as tired at the end of the day. Diaphragmatic breathing is more efficient, so your body does not work as hard and uses less energy.

You can also become energized by paying attention, and really getting involved in what you are doing.

The more concentrated you become, the more balanced you become. This results in lower energy demands in your mind and body. Your heart rate, breathing and other systems stabilize and you have less tension. That is why in task absorption you can work very hard, but not have any

# CONCENTRATION AND
# ENERGY CONSERVATION

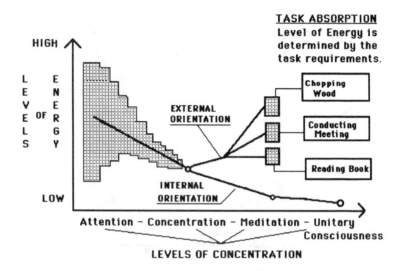

Figure 5:4

stress or excess tension. *The greater the concentration, the greater the coordination and balance, and the more energy you conserve.*

Figure 5:4 shows what happens to our energy as our concentration increases. The energy level first stabilizes, and then begins to decrease, reflecting the increasing balance and coordination of your mind and body. But there is a difference between external and inner concentration.

Both forms of concentration conserve energy. In external concentration, however, different tasks demand different levels of energy. Obviously, you need more energy to play handball than to draw house plans or coordinate a meeting. During intense concentration, we generate only the energy specifically needed by the task. Even with physically demanding work, you can stay balanced, and not get stressed. You may become tired, but it is a satisfying tiredness, free of tension and frustration. The less focused you are, the more difficult it becomes to conserve or balance energy. Your fatigue becomes polluted with excess tension from using your energy inappropriately. This is the fatigue you feel after driving in traffic for an hour, and worrying the whole time about being late for an important meeting.

On the other hand, energy levels in inner concentration can reach minimum levels, particularly when we meditate. The only performance demand on the body is to maintain life-support activities. The pervasive synchronicity of our mind's energy creates a deep harmony, and the body achieves its most profound state of relaxation and rest.

### Pseudo-Concentration: Blowing Our Energy Fuse

In pseudo-concentration, when we pay attention out of fear, we blow our energy fuses. We intensify unbalanced and dysfunctional energy patterns in the unconscious, and end up with acute and chronic stress. The common tension headache is a classic example of misplaced energy. Instead of creating chronic muscle tension which leads to headaches, this misplaced energy could be used for a much better purpose. Unlike concentration, which conserves energy, pseudo-concentration creates excess energy, and uses it inappropriately. The result is stress and ineffectiveness.

## SKILL: THE FIFTH DIMENSION

For most of us, concentration is something that we just do, not something that we systematically develop as a skill. This haphazard approach leaves the power of our mind unused, and our resources undeveloped. This does not have to be the case, however. We can use a number of specific techniques to train our power of concentration. Like any skill we want to learn, we must have:

- a systematic approach.
- the proper techniques.
- a consistent practice.

## Success Insurance: Knowing How to Practice

To develop an Empowered Mind, you must use the proper techniques in a systematic manner. To master your intuitive knowledge, for instance, or use imagery effectively, you must be able to concentrate. To concentrate effectively, you must know how to maintain inner balance. To maintain inner balance, you must know how to breathe properly. Trying to use the mind in a sophisticated way without solving the problem of stress is like trying to play championship tennis without learning how to serve. You build success from preparation. The stronger your foundation, the easier it is to build the inner skills of an Empowered Mind. Consider the following foundation builders:

## Commitment: Dedicating Time to Personal Power

Find and dedicate one fifteen-minute period a day to developing your internal management and personal power skills. This should be at a time—and in a place—when work, family duties, or outside distractions will not disturb you. Early morning is an excellent time to practice. Your mind is still fresh, your body is rested, and it is easier to concentrate. However, any time that is free from distraction and allows you to practice regularly is fine. *Avoid times when you are tired or have just finished eating.* Your energy level will be too low for you to concentrate effectively, and you will not gain much benefit .

## Stress Control

Concentration requires a mind free from worries, anxieties and fears. If you are uptight, or upset about something, it is difficult to clear your mind and focus your attention. Tension interferes with concentration. The more skilled you become at relaxation and maintaining inner balance, the easier it is to increase your power of concentration.

## Posture

To achieve a balanced mind, your posture must allow for balance. If you slump while seated, or walk around with your shoulders hunched, it creates a neurological imbalance and interferes with diaphragmatic breathing. This all interferes with your mind. For practicing concentration, the most helpful posture is an erect, seated one, with the head, neck and trunk in proper alignment. A natural S-curve of the spine keeps the upper half of the body erect without any muscle tension. This upright posture allows you to breathe easily with the diaphragm, properly aligns the neural pathways of the spine, and allows the muscles of the upper body to relax.

Lying down presents another kind of problem. It's helpful for learning relaxation, but *not* concentration. If you lie down for concentration, your mind becomes lethargic and lazy. With a few exceptions, such as the "61 Points Exercise," always practice concentration exercises in the erect, seated position.

### Make Transitions Gently

Whenever you practice relaxation or concentration exercises with your eyes closed, do not abruptly open your eyes after finishing. Doing so creates a very subtle shock to the nervous system, similar to the shock you feel when you wake up to a shrill alarm clock. You feel some momentary confusion as your mind registers the shock of the sudden rush of sensory data. Instead, before opening your eyes, slowly bring your hands up to your face, being aware of every movement you make. Holding your hands about four inches from your face, open your eyes to the palms of your own hands. This eases the transition from one level of consciousness to another. At first, you may not feel any different than if you had just opened your eyes. This changes, however, as you become more sensitive to your inner world. So be gentle with yourself and your nervous system, and gently make the transition between these levels of awareness.

## UNLEARNING THE HABIT OF DISTRACTION

You can help your mind by the practice of doing one thing at a time. Polyphasic thinking—trying to do two or more things at once—leads directly to stress. Actually, the mind only does one thing at a time, but does it so quickly that it appears to be doing two things at once. When you constantly shift your attention, you train your mind to be distracted. You get so much practice at doing this that you become very skilled at being scattered.

It's always a little tough to go against such a long-standing habit, but practice focusing on only one thing at a time. Soon you will find that you are becoming more efficient, and accomplishing things more quickly—being more productive. You will also be more relaxed because you stay more balanced, and have less stress.

You can help your children develop a powerful mind as well, by training them to do one thing at a time. Infants and children have a natural inclination for concentration. But over the years, we train our children, as well as ourselves, to be distracted. For instance, we have our children watch television and play with toys, or study and listen to music, or read while they are eating. As they grow older, they keep reinforcing the practice of doing two or more things at once, until they have built strong, unproductive habits.

## MORE CONCENTRATION TECHNIQUES

There are many different ways to develop your power of concentration. For those who like to work with the body, a number of exercise systems use the body to train the mind. Traditional schools of martial arts, such as Tai Chi Chuan, Karate, and Akaido, use the body to train concentration skills. One of the most sophisticated exercise systems available for training concentration is Hatha Yoga. Hatha Yoga consists of a series of postures designed to bring balance and flexibility to both mind and body by stimulating neural and glandular centers. You can find a variety of classes offered locally in Hatha Yoga and the martial arts.

Another powerful way to train your concentration is to use breathing techniques. You have already learned to use Breath Awareness to manage your sensory mind. Now you will learn how it can be used to improve your concentration.

### Breath Awareness as a Concentration Exercise

To practice, sit in the erect, seated posture. Relax the body and focus the mind by using the Alternate Nostril Exercise. Then focus your attention on the feeling of the breath as it enters and leaves the nostrils. On the inhalation you will feel a slight touch of coolness as the air enters the nostrils. On the exhalation, you can sense a very subtle touch of warmth as the air leaves the nostrils. For the first few moments, just center your attention on this feeling. Then, by paying attention to the feeling of the breath going in and out of the nostrils, determine the dominant, or open, nostril. This is the one through which the air flows most easily. Don't use your fingers; determine this only by your sensitivity to feeling the breath going in and out of the nostrils. After determining the dominant nostril, focus your attention on it for several breaths.

Now switch your attention to the passive, or closed, nostril, the one where the air flow is mostly blocked or diminished. Concentrate on this nostril until you begin to feel the air moving freely through it, and it becomes the dominant nostril. After the air flows freely through this nostril for several breaths, bring your attention back to the first nostril, the one originally open. When you begin to feel the air flow freely through this first nostril, shift your attention to the center between both nostrils. Concentrate on the air flowing freely through both.

Whenever your mind wanders to thoughts or other distractions, bring your attention back to the feeling of the breath. Sit very still, maintaining this focus, for as long as you comfortably can. When you are ready to finish, gently wriggle your toes and fingers. Slowly raise your hands to your face. Holding the hands about four inches from your face, open your eyes to the palms of your hands. Your palms should be the first things you see after opening your eyes.

Air flowing freely through both nostrils indicates complete balance in both the autonomic nervous system and between the hemispheres of the brain. During this time, your concentration can deepen and intensify.

## A Meditation Practice

After learning how to sit quietly and focus your attention inwardly, use these final exercises to refine your power of concentration into a state of meditation and even beyond. Our mind patterns energy into three forms: thought, image and sensation. We know that light (used in candle gaze) naturally attracts the mind, and the color blue (used in "61 Points") has a strong restful effect on the mind. We also know that we can use the sensation created by Breath Awareness as a focus point for concentration.

We can create a deeper state of concentration by using thought as the focus point. But thoughts involve language, and language can be tricky. Words often evoke emotional reactions on an unconscious level that interfere with developing concentration and meditation skills. We must carefully choose the words we use in order to create either a neutral or deeply positive focal point. In Eastern meditative traditions, these special words are called *mantras*. Their effect on the subtle levels of the mind has been researched for thousands of years.

When using thoughts as the concentration point, the key is to learn how to *listen* to the thought, and not "think" it. The thought becomes a sound of the mind. Listening trains your power of observation as well as your power of concentration. When you become skilled at observation, concentration becomes effortless and evolves into meditation.

You can use the sound of your breath to provide a useful, neutral thought. If you listen carefully to your breath, you can hear the sound of "So" on the inhalation and "Hum" on the exhalation. Converting this sound to thought, focus on the thought "So" during the inhalation and "Hum" during the exhalation. These two thought forms, So and Hum, are neutral to the mind, and free of any unconscious associations. They provide a useful focal point for training the mind even at the most subtle levels of the unconscious.

Let us break the meditation exercise into two parts. The first is a Centering Exercise which you will use often in the following chapters. The second consists of a meditation exercise using the words So and Hum.

## Centering Exercise

Begin this exercise by sitting in the erect seated position with your eyes closed. For the first few moments, mentally scan the body, relaxing any tension you may find. Then for a few minutes, practice Breath Awareness until you feel both nostrils open. After a few moments of concentrating on both nostrils flowing freely, follow the next inhalation up as if you are following it into the center of your mind. It is as if you are turning your eyes inward and looking toward the very center of your brain. Then picture yourself sitting in the middle of the mind, watching the body breathe around you. At this point, experience the body like a shell around you. After a few more moments, be aware of the center of the mind, and the inner space around it. Notice that there is an inner space where thoughts, images and sensations seem to be, and an outer space, outside the skin of your body. Your body is like the dividing line between the outer space and this inner space.

Within this inner space, you will find a center of quietness. When you become aware of this center, your body will become effortlessly still, and the mind very calm. You will notice that thoughts, images and sensations seem to revolve around this center, but within this center itself, it is very quiet and peaceful. Enjoy this calm center for a few moments. Learn to watch the thoughts and other activities passing by. You are only the observer, the witness to these activities of your mind. Don't get involved in thinking. Just observe, and enjoy the calmness of this center. Whenever you find yourself being distracted, come back to this calm center.

## Meditation Exercise

Now bring your concentration to the sound of the breath. On the inhalation you will hear the thought (sound) of So, on the exhalation the thought (sound) of Hum. Try to focus on exactly where the thought arises in your mind. Don't try to anticipate or remember, but stay focused on the thought itself as it exists at this moment. All sorts of thoughts will come to your mind. Let them come and go. Whenever you find your thoughts wandering, or off on a tangent, bring your attention back to the So and Hum. Don't struggle or fight with your mind; simply come back to the focus point.

When you are ready to finish, direct your attention to the flow of breath through the inner space of your body. Follow the next exhalation out the nostrils, and focus your attention on the feeling of the breath for a few moments. Now wriggle your toes and fingers gently. Slowly, being aware of every inner movement of the body, bring your hands up to your face. Holding your hands approximately four inches from the face, open your eyes. The first thing you should see are the palms of your hands. Maintain the inner calm and stillness you feel as long as possible throughout the day.

When you first begin, you will be thinking "So" and "Hum." After some months of practicing, learn to *listen* to the mind think instead of doing the thinking yourself. In this way, you train yourself to become the observer of what the mind *does* instead of being the one who thinks. Remember, the thought form is So - Hum, not Ho - Hum, which leads to very different consequences!

## Points to Remember

1. Spend at least ten to fifteen minutes every day practicing this concentration exercise. Consistency is far more important than length of time.

2. Focus your attention on where you first hear the thought or sound arising in the mind.

3. Whenever your mind wanders, don't struggle, simply bring it back to the focus point. At times, concentration seems easy and

satisfying, at other times frustrating and difficult. Don't worry; just let distracting thoughts come and go.

4. Finish the exercise by returning to Breath Awareness for a few moments before opening your eyes to the palms of your hands.

5. Enjoy the stillness. Do not be discouraged, and do not have expectations. It takes time to train your mind to be one-pointed.

You can choose your own thought, but make it very short and simple, such as "peace" or "love." Or you can concentrate on the image of a candle flame, or use Breath Awareness. Remember, the goal is *concentration on a single point*, not day-dreaming or contemplation. And do not use music as your focus point. Music can be comforting, relaxing and enjoyable, but it is not one-pointed concentration practice. Do not allow any external distractions.

# THE EMPOWERED MIND: STEP BY STEP

Achieving an Empowered Mind is not difficult if you systematically build your skills. By building a strong foundation of relaxation, balancing and concentration skills, the rest is easy. It only takes time and practice. Below is a reasonable program of systematic practice to build a powerful foundation. Use it as a guide to tailor your own program to fit your unique needs and situation.

### Fifteen Minutes to Personal Power

Begin gently, and be practical! Do not start off with an hour of practice when you have never taken five minutes for yourself. A fifteen minute period of dedicated time is sufficient if it is consistent. Remember two words: *consistency* and *enjoyment*. Consistency builds habits. And if it isn't fun and interesting, you will not pay much attention, and you will not gain much benefit.

- For the first four to six weeks, practice deep relaxation skills, beginning with Muscle Relaxation (Chapter 3, page 76), then Deep-State Relaxation (Chapter 3, page 79), followed by "61 Points" (Chapter 5, page 116), until you become skilled at deep relaxation.

- For the second four to six weeks, practice Breath Awareness as a concentration exercise. Spend the first few minutes relaxing, then sit in the erect posture and focus on Breath Awareness for ten to fifteen minutes. Develop the art of relaxed stillness.

- For the third four to six week period, work with the candle gaze until you can hold the external gaze for twenty minutes and the internal image for twenty minutes.

- After completing the candle gaze, begin the Centering and Meditation Exercise using "So-Hum," or the image of a candle flame.

## Building Day-to-Day Skills

Experiment, and try different techniques throughout the day. Many of the techniques you have learned so far can be done in a few moments time to clear your mind, become more sensitive to your environment, and create a positive, calm mind. Some of the things you might do:

- Take a two-minute breath break at least twice a day, or as often as you need to re-balance and clear your mind.

- Use memory ticklers (red dots on your phone, a card in your desk) to remind you to practice Breath Awareness as often as you can.

- As you go to sleep, practice even, diaphragmatic or 2:1 diaphragmatic breathing, or work with the sleep exercise.

- Practice doing one thing at a time.

- Be aware of the language you use. Change it around, play with it to see if you can create different realities for yourself.

The possibilities are as unlimited as your own creativity. But there is no substitute for concentration. It is the ultimate skill of an Empowered Mind. It develops your capacity for leadership, vision, productivity and performance. It is the pathway to spiritual knowledge—your capacity to know truth, to be free of fear, and to love. You already have these resources, but you must develop them.

## SUMMARY OF PRINCIPLES

1. Concentration is the primary skill of our conscious mind, and absolutely crucial for personal effectiveness and success.

2. Our mind is a subtle field of energy. Each thought, image and

sensation is a small force of energy. When we concentrate our mind, we concentrate this energy much like a laser concentrates light energy.

3. The more deeply you concentrate, the clearer your mind becomes, and the deeper the balance and rest in the body. The most profound states of relaxation are achieved through concentration.

4. Concentration expands our awareness of both your external world and your internal world.

5. Meditation is a refined state of concentration, an effortless and unbroken concentration, on a single point, over an extended period of time.

6. The most powerful condition of the mind is called Unitary Consciousness. In this state, the entire resources of the mind are available for conscious use.

7. There are five dimensions to concentration: Conscious Choice, Positive Interest, Inward or Outward Focus, Level of Energy, and Skill.

8. Interest expands awareness and leads to genuine concentration which stabilizes the mind and enhances your personal power. Fear constricts awareness and creates pseudo-concentration, which leads to a destabilized mind, stress and personal ineffectiveness.

9. Externally focused concentration leads to task absorption and peak experience while inner concentration leads to meditation, the realization of our inner skills, and spiritual knowledge (mystical experience).

10. Energy levels which are too low or too high interfere with concentration. Concentration conserves energy.

11. The inner skills of the Empowered Mind are built through commitment, a systematic approach, and consistent practice.

# 6 Clear Perception— Optimum Performance: Enhancing Day-to-Day Skills

*I can see clearly now, the rains are gone. I can see all the obstacles in my way.*

*—Johnny Nash*

After a while, I knew when John (my supervisor) was stringing me along. Before I had always sensed that something was not quite right, but I just couldn't pin it down. But now I can recognize the signs. In a way, it's really kind of funny and sad at the same time. I mean, here's a guy who is really a decent sort who knows that he has to do something I won't like, and he tries to make it all right for me. What he doesn't know is that everytime that he tries to convince me of something that he thinks that I am not going to like, he has a little tension line that develops around the corner of his mouth. When I finally realized what the signals were that I was picking up unconsciously, it became real easy for me to read him. Now I just pay attention to him, and the message that he is really giving me, and it makes everything much simpler.

*—Ann K., Manager, MIS*

We rely on our senses to gather information about the world around us. We see, touch, hear, taste and smell our way through life, organizing all this stimulus into meaningful patterns of knowledge. How well we do all this determines how well we get along in the world. This is the work of

143

our Sensory Mind, the most familiar level of our mind. The power functions of our Sensory Mind combine to accomplish two crucial tasks:

- Perceptual sensitivity—The more aware we are of the subtle cues and information in our environment, the better choices we make, and the more effective we become. Perceptual sensitivity allows us to see the whole picture, and not just isolated parts. Remember, Peter Drucker makes the point that success comes to those who have the capacity to walk into a situation and immediately grasp the entire picture.

- Organizational integrity—This is the ability to organize our perceptions in a meaningful and useful way. If we rigidly conform to our habits we lose the flexibility we need to respond effectively to the challenges we face. We use images and thought to direct the power of our mind.

If we empower this function, we empower our ability to creatively solve problems and achieve our goals.

Powered by our concentration, these two actions—perceptual sensitivity and organizational integrity—allow us to engage the world in a safe, creative and imaginative manner. Meanwhile, three important skills determine the *quality* of our everyday performance:

**1. Instinct:** the ability to accurately perceive anything in the immediate environment that affects our well-being. Our instincts depend on perceptual sensitivity. Unfortunately, we often ignore vast amounts of relevant, even critical, information. Our mind chatter distracts us, and we only hear the words, not the real message being communicated. We do not notice the messages given by body language, the changes in the facial muscles, or the subtle changes in the eyes that indicate when an individual is dishonest. We think too much, become too dependent on analysis, and don't trust what our senses are telling us.

By paying close attention to our perceptions, we learn to use our instinct as a conscious tool. We can become so sensitive to others that we can literally "read" their mind. We know who to trust and who not to trust, or who will complete an assignment and who will not complete it. A refined instinct also provides the Empowered Mind with an exquisite sense of timing—the knowledge of when to move forward, when to back-up, or when to hold steady—and a sensitivity to the nuances and rhythms of interpersonal relationships.

**2. Creativity:** The organization of sensory data is the creative force of our mind. Creativity is not something we learn in an art class. It is the natural and constant process of the sensory mind. How successfully we use our creative force depends on our perceptual sensitivity and our ability to consciously direct our perceptual strategies and organization. What we call "a creative response" is actually the product of a matrix of events—our habits, emotions, and beliefs—all of which exert a powerful influence. We are creative to the degree that we free ourselves from the tyranny of our habits and other powerful influences.

Being creative means knowing how to undo the restrictions we consciously and unconsciously impose on our mind. We must be flexible, willing to experiment and change the rules, and attentive to how we create our sets of perception. If we know how to play with our thoughts, we can become deliberately creative instead of waiting until creativity happens to us. Creative flexibility, solving problems in new and more effective ways, is not hard when you can consciously allow your mind to play.

**3. Imagination:** directing the creative force. When we take the personal responsibility to carry out our creative insights, we become innovative. We have a powerful tool called imagination to accomplish this. Our mind expresses energy through thoughts, images and sensations. By consciously directing these mind forms, we can bring about the results we want.

Instinct, creativity, and imagination are the perceptual skills of the mind, and the Empowered Mind maximizes these resources for effective day-to-day performance. Like the other skills of the mind, instinct, creativity and imagination are intimately connected with each other, and it is often difficult to tell when one lets off and the other begins.

## INSTINCT: IN TOUCH WITH THE WORLD

Instinct is a gift from Mother Nature, a built-in mechanism that allows us to know exactly how secure our environment is at any one moment. It is the signaling system of our primitive urge for self-preservation. This self we are preserving includes much more than our physical existence. It includes our entire personality, our ego and everything that we emotionally identify with, such as our family, our income, even our new car.

Instinct allows us to recognize and understand anything that affects our well-being. We can easily know when someone is taking advantage of us, when to buy or not to buy, or when danger threatens us. A good salesperson often knows immediately upon walking into the client's office whether or not the sale will be made. If he uses his instincts properly, and senses that a sale won't be made, he uses the opportunity to prepare the client for his next call. If he uses his instincts improperly, he pushes to make the sale, frustrating himself and irritating his client.

Our instincts provide superb guidance in a wide variety of situations:

**Protection from danger:**  Whether physical danger, such as when the car in front of us suddenly shifts lanes without signaling, or social danger, such as knowing whom to trust, our instincts warn us before we get into trouble. Even when the danger is not apparent, our instincts let us know in plenty of time to prepare ourselves, and take the necessary actions. Using our instincts, we can tell what is actually a danger, and what only appears to be dangerous. This saves us from overreacting, or reacting inappropriately, and creating unnecessary problems.

**Timing:**  A sophisticated and unerring sense of timing is one of the major qualities of an Empowered Mind. We know when to move on a project and when to sit still, when to approach someone, and when not to. The rhythms that regulate life are experienced directly through our instinct. By developing our instinctual ability, we tune in to our environment and the rhythms that regulate the ebb and flow of events.

**Interpersonal understanding:**  Using our instincts we become sensitive to the subtle thoughts and feelings of others. Our instincts allow us to understand each other at a much deeper level, and to communicate more effectively.

To use our instincts, we must develop our perceptual sensitivity. The more sensitive we are, the greater our power of instinct. But we seldom, if ever, train our perceptual sensitivity. Even worse, we learn to distrust our feelings. This diminishes our ability to distinguish fears, desires and other emotional distractions from genuine instinct. To compensate for this self-inflicted weakness, we become dependent on logic and analysis when our instincts would provide more accurate knowledge about the situation. This often leads to failure.

A classic example of this occurred when the American missile frigate, the *USS Vincennes* downed the Iranian passenger jet in the Arabian Sea. Computer data was insufficient to make the correct decision in the short time allowed. There was no genuine threat, only the heightened appearance of danger. Instinctual knowledge would have told the ship's captain that the danger was apparent, and not real. But when we are under intense pressure, such as the captain was, we must rely on our habits. If we are not skilled with our instincts, we must rely on information and analysis. Unfortunately, fear and other emotions invariably color our analyses. We end up with results that are not satisfactory, or just plain wrong.

Another problem is the chatter that goes on in our sensory mind. It does more than create stress for us. It dramatically interferes with our perceptual sensitivity. The more we chatter, the less attention we pay to sensory information. We may get so involved in our thinking that we completely ignore what's going on around us. Can you remember a time you had so much on your mind you drove from one place to another and did not remember the trip? Or perhaps you wanted something to happen so badly that you ignored all the signs and signals telling you that it was not going to happen.

## BREATH AWARENESS: LISTENING WITH THE WHOLE MIND

One of the best ways to train perceptual sensitivity is to use Breath Awareness. By paying attention to the feeling of your breath, you automatically shift attention to your perceptual reality. At first, it will seem like the only thing you are aware of is the breath. But that soon passes. As you grow accustomed to feeling the breath, you will begin to notice all sorts of other information coming through your senses. By using Breath Awareness to stop your mind chatter, you become more sensitive to your perceptions. Suddenly, you are more aware of the world around you.

Perceptual sensitivity is very helpful when you need to listen to someone. Often, the moment we engage in a conversation, we get distracted with mind chatter—preparing a response, solving problems, finding ways to impress, to end the conversation, or to change the topic. We "think" when we should be listening. The more we chatter to ourselves, the more perceptual data we miss—the subtle nuances and shifts in voice quality and tone, the facial changes, the body language. We "think" so much that we end up missing the real message being communicated.

You can use a number of techniques to improve listening skills, but the critical element is *paying attention*. You cannot pay attention when you are busy talking to yourself. Eliminate this distraction with Breath Awareness, and your mind automatically pays attention. With practice, you will become quite skillful. Nothing is more simple or direct. In fact, the only difficulty with this powerful technique is remembering to use it.

When we listen with full attention, we gain insight into the nature of the person to whom we are listening. But we have a strong tendency to get involved in the conversation instead of just listening, and it takes practice to overcome this tendency. It is helpful to first practice during social conversations. You will quickly notice more subtleties in the conversation, and have greater insight into the person to whom you are listening.

## TRUSTING YOUR SENSES

Being aware of the subtle cues in our environment is only half the job. To use your instincts, you must be able to listen to your own self, as well as you listen to others. If you are not sensitive to your own inner messages, such as your feelings, you cannot use the knowledge of your mind.

Our sensory mind and body act like a radio receiver, constantly pulling in and responding to information. As we take in this information, the unconscious part of our sensory mind processes it and immediately communicates any vital data back to our conscious mind. Our instincts originate in our primitive urge for self-preservation. They are closely related to our emotional states, and communicate to our conscious mind through the emotional message path of our feelings. If we aren't sensitive to our feelings and the sensations that accompany them, we do not use our instincts effectively.

It is not hard to develop inner sensitivity. All you have to do is pay attention. The body sensitivity exercises in Chapter 2 are a good start. Exercise systems that focus on internal sensitivity, such as Hatha Yoga and the martial arts, also help develop this sensitivity. The more sensitive we become, the more effectively we read our environment. Even the way we walk with someone gives us insight into their personality and about the nature of our relationship with them. Try the following exercise.

### The Walking Exercise

This exercise can make you more aware of your unconscious reactions to other people. Your reactions partly reflect your own thoughts and emotions, and how you feel about this person. But they also reflect the other person's feelings and personality.

Begin by walking around the room for a few minutes in a way that feels natural and comfortable. Be aware of how this feels. You are establishing a baseline of information about your own inner feelings. After you feel sure of your inner sensations—how it feels to walk by yourself, just being yourself—then stop. Visualize the face of someone you know and have a definite relationship with. It can be a positive or a negative relationship, a family member, friend or colleague. Once you can visualize him or her clearly, then start walking as if you were taking a walk with this person. As you walk be aware of how you walk, how you hold your body, what it feels like to walk with him. How does it differ from when you are walking by yourself? How do your feelings differ? Are you more tense or less tense? Do you have feelings of anticipation or of lowered energy? What are the differences between walking with this person and walking by yourself?

Now stop, clear your mind with Breath Awareness, and visualize the face of someone completely different. Again, it should be someone with whom you have a definite relationship. Then start walking as if you were taking a walk with this person. Again, study how you feel as you walk. How does it differ from the first person, or from when you walk by yourself? What does this tell you about how you feel about each of these individuals, about how they react to you, or about the nature of your relationship with them? Does anything else come to your mind?

You might think you walk differently with them because they have a different stride. But they also walk differently with you than by themselves or with someone else. The next time you walk with someone, be sensitive to what your body is telling you. Later, write down your feelings and any insights you might have had during your walk. Use this record to see which feelings gave you accurate information, and which ones misled you. By doing this, you begin to recognize the difference between your emotional projections and genuine instincts.

When you first pay attention to your body's feelings and sensations, be careful of your emotional states. They can easily pollute your instincts. The next exercise helps sensitize you to another person's thoughts and feelings. It also helps you differentiate between your own emotional reactions and those which come from another person.

## Standing in Another's Shoes

There is a great deal of truth in the saying that if you want to understand someone, walk a mile in his shoes. You don't really have to walk a mile, but by putting yourself in another's position, you can often gain insight into the nature of his personality. By modeling his behavior, putting your body in his posture and making his movements, you gain a high degree of sensory input about his thoughts and feelings. This exercise requires a partner. Have your partner stand in front of you in a comfortable and natural stance. She should then close her eyes, and for a few moments focus on what she feels inside. In the meantime, you should stand in front of her, and as much as possible, assume the same posture that she exhibits. If she unconsciously moves her hands, you should do the same. Whatever else she does, you should also do. Then have your partner describe exactly what it feels like to be her, from the toes all the way up to the top of her head. She should tell you in as great a detail as possible—how her weight is distributed, where there is tension, if her knees are locked—every detail that she can notice. As she describes herself, place your body in exactly the same position. If she has most of her weight on the left foot, place most of your weight on the left. If she feels a slight tension in her left arm, slightly tense your left arm.

As you model the other person's position, be sensitive to any odd thoughts, images or feelings. Do not assume that these thoughts, images and feelings all come from you. Verify with your partner to see if those thoughts, images or sensations have any particular relevance to her.

I demonstrated this technique in one of my MBA classes in preparation for the class to practice it. For my partner, I chose a gentleman about twenty-nine years old. All I knew about him was that he worked for a bank, was completing an MBA in night school, and was married. As he described his posture to me, and I began to model him, a thought flashed through my mind that he was worried about his son. As soon as I had the thought, I also felt strongly that his son would be fine. I immediately checked this out by saying to him, "Look, don't worry, your son is going to be fine."

The fellow literally jumped backwards, exclaiming "How did you know that? My son just broke his arm, and I was worried about it." Needless to say, the class enthusiastically participated in practicing the exercise, and several had rather penetrating insights into their partner's thoughts and life.

This is not magic. It is sensitivity to instinctual knowledge. By becoming another person in even a limited way by placing yourself in the same posture, you gain access to their thoughts and feelings. There really are not any secrets between us. We constantly communicate who we are through our posture, our voices, the way we walk, how we hold our body, even by the way we smell. For those who take the time to train their perceptual sensitivity, the world is an open book, waiting to be read.

You can practice modeling at any time—just don't be obnoxious about it. Practice walking the way you see someone walk, eating the way you see him eat, standing the way he stands. Sensitize yourself to the wide variety of feelings and thoughts that this generates. The more aware you become, the more powerful your instinct.

Being sensitive to our inner thoughts and feelings also leads to the second performance skill, creativity. The more aware we are, the easier it is to consciously play with, and alter, our perceptual organizations, and create new ways of seeing, thinking and feeling. Like instinct, creativity is a power of our sensory mind. We can take command of this power, as we do with instinct, and use it to enhance our day-to-day performance.

## CREATIVITY: PLAYING WITH PERCEPTION

Most of us think of creativity as something that artists and actors have. Only occasionally do we see ourselves as being "creative." By thinking of creativity as a special skill or talent, we unnecessarily and fraudulently limit ourselves. Far from being rare, creativity is a natural, innate action of our mind.

Look at what Webster's Dictionary lists as the definitions for the word "create":

- to bring into existence;
- to invest with a new form;
- to produce or bring about by a course of action or behavior;
- to cause; to produce through imaginative skill; to design.

These describe the operations of our sensory mind as it collects, organizes and interprets sensory data. In other words, *creativity is what our sensory mind does.* What we call creativity involves two clearly separate but related mind skills. The first is the actual creative process where we originate an idea or solution at subtle levels of our mind.

In the second phase—innovation—we transform this creative response into a practical reality. It does little good to have creative idea after creative idea if we cannot bring these ideas into fruition. Implementing an idea not only often requires as much creativity as originating it, but also takes the ability to direct our mind's power to a specific end. This requires imagination, another inner skill. We need both creativity and imagination if we want to achieve the performance levels of an Empowered Mind.

## The Creative Matrix

The power of our Sensory Mind lies in its ability to create meaning from a jumble of sensory data. We call this basic process of organizing and interpreting sensory data the Creative Matrix. The term "matrix" implies an interaction of forces or events that combine and work together to produce an outcome. In our Sensory Mind, these forces operate mostly in our unconscious where we have a vast storehouse of knowledge and experiences. We actually know far more than we can possibly be aware.

The Creative Matrix is dynamic, like a blending of color pigments, with each pigment contributing to the final product. There is a continuous interplay between memory, emotions, habits, beliefs, as well as the sensory data that we collect. The power of habit and our emotions dominate Sensory Mind. Along with our beliefs, these often interfere with the creative function. Since most of this interplay in the Creative Matrix occurs in the unconscious part of our mind, our emotional habits exert enormous influence. In the unconscious, emotional pressure seeks the easiest outlet—our habit patterns, which leave little room for flexibility or spontaneity. The more pressure we feel, the more habitual our responses, until we act in extremely predictable and rigid ways.

For example, the fear of failure inhibits our creativity, and stops a great many projects before they even get started. When we get rid of this fear, we find that we can accomplish anything we decide. The only thing stopping us is our own doubts. By staying emotionally balanced, our Creative Matrix uses emotional energy in creative and spontaneous ways. As a result, our mind creates new forms, new ways to act, novel opportunities for self-expression, and we experience the joy of discovery.

Once our thoughts take shape and move from the unconscious part of mind into the subconscious, other influences come into play, such as our reasoning abilities and our belief systems. We know that our beliefs influence our perceptions. For example, if we believe that our boss is out to get us, we interpret his actions as consistent with that belief. As we become more tense and defensive, reacting to what we believe is his negative attitude toward us, we can actually create a problem where none existed before. We may join the union negotiating team, and under the pretext of fairness, find ways to get even with those in "control." This, in turn, leads to real problems with our boss who resents being made a fall guy for the union. In this case, we used our creative power in a way that

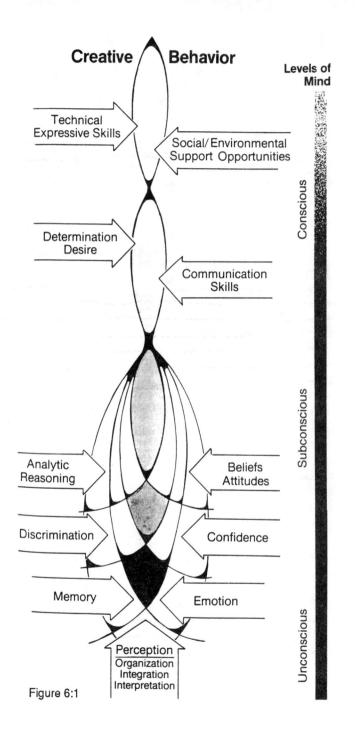

**Creative Behavior**

Levels of Mind

Technical Expressive Skills

Social/Environmental Support Opportunities

Determination Desire

Communication Skills

Analytic Reasoning

Beliefs Attitudes

Discrimination

Confidence

Memory

Emotion

Perception
Organization
Integration
Interpretation

Conscious

Subconscious

Unconscious

Figure 6:1

not only harms us, but leads to a hardening of attitudes that reinforce a negative atmosphere at work. Instead of solving problems, our creativity intensifies our emotional disturbance.

As the creative response emerges into awareness, the more familiar skills—communication, logic and reasoning, our power of persuasion—exert their influence. At this point, our creativity is influenced by our level of skill. For instance, our ability to communicate influences the way in which we think about things. If we lack confidence about our communication skills, we may inhibit the creative process by refusing to try new ways of communicating, or avoiding speaking opportunities. As a result, we limit the quality, as well as quantity, of our thoughts and accomplishments. As skilled and confident communicators, we have more freedom in how we structure our thoughts and ideas.

The end product—the "creative" behavior, idea, or solution—is the culmination of a long chain of events that began in the unconscious, and involves all other aspects of our personality. Our degree of confidence, our intuition, our self-image all influence the Creative Matrix. Even the health and fitness of our body has an impact. *Whatever brings balance and joy, whatever frees us of emotional disturbance, enhances our Creative Matrix.*

If we lack creative ideas and solutions, it is not because we lack creative capacity. It is because we unconsciously limit the inherent and spontaneous creative power of our sensory mind through fears and habits, or because we narrowly restrict the input to our mind. These limits to our creativity are entirely self-imposed. Our environment may reinforce or inhibit our creative expression, but our environment has little power to limit the creative nature of our mind. Only we can do that.

We engage the creative force in every moment as we continue to bring new meanings, interpretations, and reactions into existence. Our personal reality is a product of our fertile and imaginative mind. Our nearly infinite mind creates, sustains and destroys a vast number of interpretations, realities, behaviors, and events. The entire dance of the mind is one continuous creative movement reflecting spontaneity, or restricted by rigid repetitive behaviors.

You can easily see this if you do the following exercise:

## A Brief Exercise in Creative Thought

Sit back in your chair, get very comfortable, and close your eyes. For a few moments, focus your attention on Breath Awareness, clearing your mind of extraneous and unnecessary thoughts......... As you do this, you will feel yourself relax, and your attention will direct itself inward. Next, visualize yourself in your ideal vacation setting............ Imagine as clearly as you can what it feels like to be there...........what you are wearing.......the weather........be as complete as you can......Enjoy this vision for a few moments.......... You have always wanted to live and work in this setting, now is your chance. What must you do to transfer your job and family here.....Mentally go through all the steps it will take to do this........ What does your office or work station look like? Surely, it's quite different than what you have now......... How will you go about conducting your affairs?......... What will you need to do to bring about this ideal setting and work conditions?.... Observe your feelings as you allow your mind to create possibilities for you..........

Now, think of all the reasons why you can't possibly do this, why it wouldn't work........... the company won't move, you can't earn a living, your family doesn't want to move...........Let your mind create all the reasons why it won't work......... This is what interferes with your positive creative force. Be aware of your feelings as you allow your mind to create obstacles for you..........Then open your eyes.

Throughout the exercise, your mind created images, thoughts and feelings. Some could lead to action, some could interfere with action. Your habits structured some of the images, thoughts and feelings that arose, while others were spontaneous, leading to feelings of anticipation and joy. The problem is not whether or not you are creative, but rather *how* you use your creative force. The Empowered Mind consciously takes control of the creative force and uses it to benefit himself and others.

### Taking Control of Creativity

To take deliberate control of your creative force, you must:

- Maintain balance so that you can minimize restrictions to the creative force imposed by habits, beliefs and emotional reactions.

- Become more aware of the workings of your inner creative matrix so that you can more skillfully direct its power.

- Enrich the material available at both the unconscious and conscious levels of your mind.

- Let your mind play by stimulating a free flow of images, sensations and ideas unrestricted by judgmental beliefs or attitudes.

If you learn how to sit back and consciously direct your mind to create scenarios, you can stay more relaxed, feel more in control, and become more sensitive to all the possibilities that your mind will offer. Remember, the tendency of the sensory mind is to follow its habits. If you simply react to a problem, your mind takes the path of least resistance, your established habits, and you will lose touch with the creative process. Automatic reactions diminish your creative capacity and effectiveness in solving problems. By maintaining a calm and reflective attitude, your mind can play, and the Creative Matrix will work for you.

## The Creative Impulse—Stage One: Inner Balance

The various levels, activities and functions must work smoothly together for our Creative Matrix to function at its best. Disturbances anywhere in the matrix inhibit and interfere with the the quality of its output. Psychological research on creativity consistently shows that we are most creative when we have a calm, reflective mind—not a depressed or disturbed mind, but an alert, tranquil, and observant one.

In almost every anecdote of creative insight and discovery, people describe states of mind such as reverie, dreamlike imagery or mental calm. Typically, people report that they go trout fishing, watch a fire, or gaze at the stars in order to let their mind ramble about its internal field in a calm, unhurried fashion. One executive reports that she solves problems by going for a long walk in the park near her home just as the sun begins to brighten the horizon. At this early hour, no one else is in the park, there is no traffic, and the air is calm and still. She relaxes, and allows her mind to create all sorts of scenarios, playful ideas and solutions. By the end of her walk, she has the solutions she needs.

We rarely find creative discovery linked to stress or pressures to perform. The one glaring exception is the unfortunate pairing of creative genius and emotional disturbance. The pairing of art and suffering has long been accepted, but never fully explained. Many great artists are as famous for their idiosyncrasies and erratic behavior as they are for their art. These people, extremely creative in their artistic expression, somehow lacked the balance necessary to channel that creative energy into a healthy life style.

Emotional disturbance, however, is *not* necessary for creative genius. This myth developed because of the strong relationship between the Creative Matrix and our emotions. Great artists are extremely sensitive to, and skillful at, portraying these inner realities. But when they lack the internal discipline necessary to manage their unconscious, their inner sensitivity may lead to emotional disturbance.

We can find similar examples in business where emotionality interferes with obviously creative abilities. Many entrepreneurs are dynamic, creative problem solvers, but do not have the inner stability to manage what they build. In the words of one senior executive, "The country is littered with the bodies of good managers who have tried to work with entrepreneurs." Like so many artists, their potent creative force is undisciplined and narrowly focused. They successfully create in one aspect of their lives, but fail dismally in others.

Then there is the successful corporate leader who is alcoholic, has an unhappy family life, and cannot see beyond his own self-centered view of the world. We have all known those brilliant businessman who are so insecure that they cannot handle criticism. At work, they can compensate by being boss, but their arrogance prevents them from relating to their peers, and they have constant problems with their superiors. At home, they alienate their children and make enemies of their wives. Their rigidly focused emotions provide a driving force for their Creative Matrix but also result in imbalance and personal misery. No matter how "perfectly" they do things, they still feel inadequate and insecure.

Fear (which manifests itself as worry, anxiety, apprehension, and so forth) is the single greatest obstacle to effective creativity. Teaching creative problem solving techniques to people who are anxious, fearful, or under stress, is an exercise in futility. Fear intensifies and distorts our emotional energies, disrupts the balance necessary for effective germination, and inhibits our inner awareness.

## Steps to Managing the Creative Matrix

Like any power, creativity can be harnessed and used efficiently and effectively. You can ensure a stable environment for your Creative Matrix by taking the following measures:

- Maintain a calm, balanced and stress-free mind through the consistent use of relaxation and breathing exercises.
- Become fearless by taking control of our mind with Breath Awareness and other techniques. We create an atmosphere of acceptance and respect to minimize fear within our environment.

- Take time for quiet reflection where we learn to witness the on-going activities in our mind. We gain some perspective, which allows us to examine and evaluate our mind's activities.

## The Creative Impulse—Stage Two: Germination

The heart of the creative process is the *germination* stage, where the raw sensory data is organized into diverse and novel forms. Germination involves all the functions of our sensory mind: memory, habits, emotions, beliefs. For most of us, germination is an unconscious act. We can, however, facilitate and enhance the germination stage by providing a rich mix of information and experience. This is called *diversification*, and provides a broad knowledge base for our mind to play in.

For germination to be rich and diverse, we must have rich and diverse input into the Creative Matrix. We enrich our minds by being very curious about the world and nourishing a wide variety of interests. Those who over-specialize, or who keep their nose to the grindstone literally starve their creativity.

To nourish your creativity, you must nourish a broad interest in life. By taking interest in a wide range of events, becoming informed on diverse topics, and pursuing interests unconnected with your work, you provide a broad base of fertile information for your Creative Matrix. By expanding your experience and knowledge, you enlarge the data bank that your memory draws upon. This increases both the variety and quality of material available to the Creative Matrix.

Richard Ruch, Dean of the Business School at Rider College, exemplifies the creative process. By encouraging innovation within his faculty and developing new programs and classes, he brings a desperately needed creative approach to business education. As a reflection of his own beliefs, Richard engages in a wide variety of activities, including playing in a neighborhood rock and roll band. Recently, he was asked to present the graduation address at Rider College. His talk was devoted to the necessity of expanding interests and exposing oneself to a wide variety of experiences. At the conclusion of his talk, he left the podium, and walked over to a stand where he had placed his guitar. Loosening his tie and donning a pair of sunglasses, he proceeded to play and sing a Beatles' song to the audience. He received a standing ovation from both the grads and their parents.

On the other hand, people who narrowly focus all their energy and learning on their chosen fields may become highly efficient experts, but they rarely come up with creative insights or introduce innovative programs. They become the top-notch technicians who solve problems not in unique, creative ways, but by sheer weight of knowledge. They give speeches that are full of information, but rather boring and quite easily forgotten.

Obviously, specialization isn't all bad, and we solve a great many problems with technical efficiency. But specialists rarely break new ground. They are, for instance, the scientists who fill in the paradigms and theories, the ones for whom science "proceeds step by small step, experiment by experiment." They are also the ones to whom the old saw "science proceeds death by death" applies.

Then there are the Nobel Laureates, the Einsteins, the "mavericks," who make quantum leaps over towering ideologies, dispel whole theoretical paradigms in a single bound, and create revolutions with their creative and unique insights. These are the truly curious ones, willing to explore anything that excites their interest.

Tom Peters knows the importance of diversity. In one of his syndicated columns, he wrote about an advertisement that was intended to sell personal lap-top computers. The ad touted the use of flying time to crunch numbers rather than watch a lousy movie on a tiny screen. Speaking of watching young men and women churning numbers hour after hour on the plane, Peters remarked:

> And I wonder: What do they think? Are they thinking? Is anything even slightly original going on in their head?...One finding pops out above all others. The most successful scientist, inventors and entrepreneurs draw upon wildly disparate sources (art, movies, sailing, flower arranging) to infuse new life into nagging problems, or to create new combinations of familiar things...Never has originality—in strategy or organizational design—been at such a premium. And it is my unshakable belief that originality and breadth of mind are identical twins....

What was the last thing you read or did that was *not* work connected? Does your curiosity feed your Creative Matrix, or do you starve your creative process by a constant diet of sameness? The solutions for increasing the richness of your Matrix are easy, practical and even pleasant. You can find great delight in discovery, even if that discovery has no apparent correlation to our financial "bottom line." The following guidelines can help you get started.

### Guidelines for Diversification:

**1. Read one book or lengthy article a month on a subject** totally irrelevant to your job or profession. Don't read for the sake of reading, but for the sake of curiosity. Diversification does not mean engaging in meaningless activity. It demands your personal interest and involvement.

**2. Use commuter time to "think,"** to let your mind play with ideas, possibilities, scenarios. For example, if I have a consulting job within five driving hours of my home, I never fly. There are two reasons for this. First, this amount of time is close to the breakeven point between driving and flying, and flying is much more of a hassle for me than driving. Secondly, the time I have in my car is quiet time. It is time that I have completely for myself. No one can ask me questions or make demands. Even traffic is outside my immediate environment, and does not disturb me. I use this quiet, solitary time to play with ideas, to think of new ways to communicate, develop new exercises, and to reflect on martial arts philosophy, my studies of Eastern Psychology, or on the latest articles I have read in astronomy. This time is very precious to me. You can make it precious, creative time as well.

**3. Develop real interests outside of your work.** It really doesn't matter what these interests are, only that they appeal to you. In order for diversification to enrich your creativity, the material must be interesting to you. If you have no real interest in what you are doing, you get very little benefit. Volunteer work provides a great many satisfactions. One senior executive brings his expertise in computer skills to teenagers in Harlem. Another dedicates as much time as possible to scouting. Both find that their experiences have contributed to their workplace skills. Hobbies provide many avenues of meaningful experience. Amateur astronomers, for example, have made many contributions to the field. You can find a multitude of ways to provide a rich and diverse data bank for your Creative Matrix.

**4. Explore your artistic sensibilities.** You do not have to have great talent, and your artistic efforts probably will not become a source of income. But they will become a source of creative energy. One of Dean Ruch's many interests, besides rock-'n'-roll, is making furniture. He finds it another creative outlet that (1) relieves the pressure of being Dean of a thriving business school, and (2) opens his mind to new forms and expression. Remember, it does not matter a twit to your Creative Matrix whether or not you make money or become famous from this activity. The only thing that counts is that you create new forms, new expressions, new ways of seeing and being in the world.

**5. People watch.** Few things are as interesting as human behavior. Human nature is a natural and engaging field of study. It has the added value of teaching you about yourself, opening the door to a greater understanding of your own nature and personality habits, as well as providing rich material for the Creative Matrix.

**6. Travel.** When we visit or live in different cultures and express ourselves in other languages, we learn to think in new ways, and see the world from an entirely different perspective. This opens up alternative ways of being, and new ways of perceiving problems and solutions. When we travel and encounter new customs, attitudes, beliefs and language, we must do so with a willingness to learn. If we travel with a closed mind and judgmental attitude, there is little benefit to our creativity.

**7. Maintain an open, experimental attitude about life.** When we become too judgmental, we no longer can learn about the world. Of course we need to discriminate between what is useful or not, what we like or dislike. But pre-judging others, ourselves or our experiences, cuts us off from new and potentially enriching opportunities. By cultivating an open, experimental and non-judgmental attitude toward the world, you open yourself to a wealth of experiences that provide a lasting resource for your creativity.

### The Creative Impulse—Stage Three: Discovery

In the *discovery* stage we step out of our limitations. We consciously stimulate our creative process by trying new ways to think and perceive. Discovery is the focus of seminars in creativity, such as creative problem solving, or creative writing, where we learn techniques to help us go beyond our normal patterns. There are as many techniques to do this as we have the creative genius to devise. But they all have the same goal: to stimulate free association of images, sensations and ideas unrestricted by judgmental beliefs or attitudes. The idea behind all techniques is to allow your thoughts the freedom to speculate, to play with impossibilities, and to allow unrestricted range to your mind's natural curiosity.

The elements that lead to discovery are quite simple.

- *Pay attention, and get absorbed in the process.* Like any mind skill, creativity demands that you focus attention in order to gain insight and knowledge.

- *Creative discovery comes from play, or relaxed effort.* Trying too hard restricts your awareness, and interferes with the creative process.

- *Become a neutral observer, accepting the material from your Creative Matrix without bias or pre-conditions.* You can evaluate the usefulness of your insights later on.

There are a number of different ways to generate creative insights and ideas. As you will see below, we typically use several in combination at any given time.

### Techniques of Discovery: Spontaneous Association

In spontaneous association, we allow our unconscious mind to direct the flow of thoughts and images. We may allow our mind to ricochet from one thought or image to another, creating a spontaneous flow of ideas. This is *free association*, and is used in such techniques as Brain Storming. We can also use day dreaming as well as our dreams to stimulate our creative force to give us answers. The problem solving exercise given in Chapter 7 is one way to use spontaneous association during dreams to find creative solutions.

For your mind to be spontaneous, it's important that you do not judge, or limit the content or expression in any way. The whole point is to allow a "thousand flowers to blossom." Many of the ideas you generate are only useful or helpful because they lead to an even better idea. But without them, it's almost impossible to reach your best solution. Try the following exercise. Commonly called "Brain Storming," and done in groups, it's also an excellent individual exercise to generate ideas.

### Free Association Exercise

When faced with a problem, define it in as broad a way as possible, and in neutral terms. You can start the association process by picking a word at random from the dictionary. Write the word down, and then explore whatever relationship that has to the problem you face. As other thoughts and ideas pop up, write them down, and continue to explore. Do not discard anything as too absurd or foolish. In fact, be as foolish and absurd as you can. Embellish and develop each thought as much as possible. The more playful your mind becomes, the greater the probability that you will find your most creative solution. If you are working in a group, make sure that everything is written down in a way that everyone can see. Remember, no criticisms, no judgments, no evaluations.

## Techniques of Discovery: Directed Association

You can use your reasoning power to focus the direction of your Creative Matrix, and guide its output toward specific ends. Most scientific insights occur because the mind has been directed along specific lines, and then allowed to explore and extend the limits of these categories. The key is to go beyond your normal ways of thinking about a specific topic. You want free association to occur, but from the point of a specific stimulus.

One of the simplest ways to stimulate creative ideas is to reframe the nature of the problem. In Chapter 4, you found that by using different words to describe an event, you create different psychological reactions to the event. You can use this same principle in generating new ideas. By reframing your questions—asking a different set of questions—you can often discover new ways of looking at the situation. This gives you new alternatives to consider.

One of the best statements of a creative approach to problem solving was made by Admiral Kirk in the Star Trek movie *Return Of Kahn*. One of the student commanders was frustrated by a simulation exercise where no matter what decision she made, the end result was disaster. The enemy always won. Learning that the only person ever to "win" at this impossible simulation was Admiral Kirk, she immediately sought him out. She asked "How did you defeat the program, and win the simulation exercise?" He replied " I changed the rules of the game."

One person who loves to change the rules is Clarence (Clem) Cleer, inventor extraordinaire, and President of Highlander Energy Products. Clem and his family design and build high efficiency heating plants for commercial buildings. For Clem, each building presents a unique opportunity to find the most efficient heating designs. His willingness to do things differently has led to a number of patents and heating plants that are now considered to be "state of the art" in hydronic efficiency.

In one installation, the engineers of the boiler manufacturer told him that there was no way that he could vent a large number of boilers without putting an exhaust pipe on each boiler. He installed twenty-four boilers, using an innovative venting system that joined each boiler with a common water-sealed venting pipe. Even after a demonstration, the engineers still would not believe that it would work. One engineer swore up and down that the venting pipe would freeze in the winter. Needless to say, after several years, this system still stands as the most efficient heating plant in the entire city. Not only did it save construction costs, but it spared the side of the building from being riddled by twenty-four exhaust pipes. Clem's patented exhaust muffles the noise of the boilers to a whisper, has increased the efficiency of the boiler by several points, and has eliminated a chronic problem of boiler fan failure.

By changing the rules of the game, we gain an entirely new perspective. We ask different questions, we find different opportunities, and we end up with novel approaches to the same old problem. The next time you need to find a more creative approach to problem-solving, try the following exercise.

### Reframing Exercise: Changing the Rules of the Game

The purpose is to change your frame of reference and develop new and different definitions of the problem. One of the best ways to do this is to ask questions about the problem. Some of the questions you might ask are:

- What is the ideal situation? What would I like to see happen?
- How would someone who is from another country (planet, solar system) look at this problem?
- How broad can I make my frame of reference for this problem?
- What rules govern this problem, and how can I change them?

Another approach is to ask your questions in a "What if" mode, such as: What if we did just the opposite of what we normally do? What if we had a magic genie—what would *he* do? What if we had all the time and resources in the world—what would we do?

Yet another approach is to become the problem itself. Use your imagination to picture yourself as part of the problem, and ask yourself what your next move is. You may become a machine part, or a sum of money that needs to be spent. This lets your mind play from inside the problem, and can create entirely new perspectives.

William Miller, in *The Creative Edge*, calls these kinds of techniques linear because they structure the direction of the inquiry. He provides a number of different techniques that he has found to be very helpful in generating ideas for solving problems.

## MIND TRAPS AND POWER BLOCKERS

Beware of mind traps. Mind traps are ways in which we trap our mind into being mediocre and uncreative. Mind traps are statements such as:

- "But we always do it this way!"

- "That will never work."
- "We have to find the appropriate response."
- "This isn't our responsibility."

or in attitudes such as:

- feeling that you don't have time, and looking for quick answers
- wanting everything done your way
- fear of making mistakes
- fear of being seen as different or strange

When we do not manage our inner resources, we create traps and block the power of our mind. If we try to fight or change our blocks and traps, we end up with conflict, and this only reinforces the blocks and makes the traps even harder to get out of. The key is to focus on what we can do, strengthen our ability to use our inner resources, and transform our present reality into the reality that we choose from our own inner wisdom.

## IMAGINATION—SHAPING MIND POWER

While our creative force provides new alternatives and ways of being in the world, it is our imagination that directs the energy and power of our mind to the goals we choose. The principle is very ancient and very simple: *we achieve whatever we direct our mind's energy toward.* This principle cannot be denied, but our results depend on the quality and quantity of energy that we engage.

Our imagination involves all mind forms—thoughts, images and sensations (feelings). When we use imagination as a power tool, the primary focus is on imagery, while thoughts and sensations play a supporting role. We use imagery in two basic ways:

1. actively, to consciously direct the power and energy of the mind towards a specific goal, such as using imagery to bring about a certain result

2. passively, to reveal unconscious knowledge to the conscious mind, such as our dreams or the imagery exercises that open our intuition

In the following chapter, you will use the passive form of imagery to unlock your intuitive knowledge. For now, we want to explore the active, conscious use of imagery to bring about the future we want.

## EMOTIONAL ENERGY: THE MIND'S POWER SOURCE

The power of your mind lies in emotional energy. You can use this energy to reach your goals and enrich your life, or you can use it to distort your life into emotional disturbances, such as fear and self-rejection. We all use imagination, but we do not all use it effectively. There are a number of ways in which we distort and divert this energy, and interfere with our ability to accomplish our goals.

- We misdirect the energy into worries and fears. The more we focus our attention on worries and fears, the more problems we create. We actually help bring about the things we fear by focusing so much of our mind's energy towards them. For example, when we worry about making mistakes, that's when we are most prone to making them.

- We dissipate our power in conflict and self rejection. We use our imagination in self-defeating ways as we imagine ourselves failing, making mistakes, or being rejected.

- We waste our valuable energy on petty goals and activities. There is an ancient Roman warning: "The gods grant the wishes of those they wish to punish." We spend an enormous amount of energy in attaining goals that are not satisfying, and which only bring more problems. Often, the choices we make are misguided, and we end up with a full bank account but an empty life. Or we waste time in complaining, gossiping, or doing things that have no value for us.

### Engaging the Power

You can take command of the power of your imagination, avoid self-defeating mistakes, and direct this energy towards worthwhile goals through three factors: control, commitment, and concentration.

**Control:** By managing the chatter of your mind with Breath Awareness, making proper use of language, and developing your inner strength, you minimize the amount of emotional energy that you put into unproductive avenues.

**Commitment:** You can direct emotional energy in a positive way by doing what you really believe in. It is common to find that when someone begins their own business, they work harder, longer hours, but find life more satisfying and much more exciting. When you believe in what you do, and wholeheartedly commit yourself to it, you energize your mind.

**Concentration:** All the power of your mind is useless if you do not have the skill to focus it. Much of imagination is little more than daydreaming, and has very little power behind it. We have all imagined ourselves being rich, but where is our wealth? The active use of imagery demands control and involvement. These serve to reinforce your power of concentration. Concentration empowers imagery. When you develop your power of concentration and use it to empower your positive thoughts and imagery, you take control of your destiny.

# THE WIDE WORLD OF IMAGERY WORK

Imagery plays an increasingly important role in six major areas:

1. In *performance*, the learning and refinement of specific skills. In the last fifteen years, since the publication of Steve Galt's *The Inner Game of Tennis*, sports psychology has exploded, both on a professional as well as on an amateur level. Imagery training has become the cutting edge of high-performance training, with most professional sports organizations hiring sports psychologists to work with their athletes. We can enhance any specific skill through visualization. Whatever you want to accomplish will be done better if you practice the situation first in your mind. Just make sure that you visualize yourself doing it perfectly.

2. By using *visualization* to neutralize difficult emotional situations, particularly when they involve feelings of antagonism or anger. If there is a particular situation where you always lose control of your temper, and react in unproductive ways, use imagery to gain a more objective view of the situation and create a positive state from which to proceed. The following exercise can help you build your imagery skills.

**Imagery Exercise for Neutralizing Negative Feelings**

After any situation where your emotional reactions have created hard feelings or interfered with your effectiveness, (such as an argument with a friend, or an unproductive and dissatisfying meeting with a colleague), take a few moments to clear your mind. Sit quietly and calm your mind with a few moments of Breath Awareness. Then use the Centering Exercise in Chapter 5. Once you have centered yourself, allow your mind to replay the encounter, but remain centered. If you find yourself being drawn into the struggle, or becoming tense and upset, again clear your mind with Breath Awareness, and return to your center. Continue this until you can visualize the entire encounter without any feelings of disturbance.

Then picture the person engaged in the situation with you, and visualize them surrounded by a soft blue glow. Allow yourself to feel warmth and good feelings about that person, realizing that they are only acting as they know how to act. Continue this visualization for a few moments until all negative feelings about this person are gone. Then clear your mind with Breath Awareness, open your eyes and continue with your work.

3. In solving *health* problems. While the use of imagery in solving or managing health problems is still in its infancy, it is playing an increasingly important role. Carl Simonton and his wife successfully use imagery in their work with cancer patients. Although the images vary from person to person, a typical image involves picturing the good cells coming along and killing the bad cells. Imagery also plays a major role in clinical biofeedback. While conservative physicians argue the point, the evidence is clear that our mind and emotions play a major role in curing disease states, and in maintaining our health. The Shrinking Headache Exercise in Chapter 9 is an example of using imagery to solve a health problem.

4. In solving *performance* problems. When we visualize a task as already successfully completed, we create subtle conditions in our mind that affect our confidence and our problem-solving abilities. We are telling our conscious mind that we know that the project will be successful, even though we are not yet aware of the steps that will bring about this success. By beginning with

a visualization of the finished work, we can often work backwards to find solutions that we were not conscious of prior to the visualization. By combining both active and passive uses of imagery, we can find answers not available through a rational, analytic approach.

5. In *personal empowerment*, creating effective moods and emotional states. We can use imagery to enhance our interpersonal relationships and our communication skills. Its surprising how much of our performance depends on our mood. When we take on a new project, or even start a new day with an enthusiastic "I can hardly wait to get started" attitude, it creates an extremely positive condition for our mind to function in. By maintaining a positive mood, we not only become more effective, we influence others in a positive way.

## A Positive Start to the Day

Use this simple visualization exercise to create a strong, positive mood state to begin your day. Upon waking up, even before you get out of bed, clear your mind with Breath Awareness and spend a few moments relaxing. (You'll be surprised at how tense you can be when waking up. Dream states will not only affect your mood, but create tension.) Then focus on the things you want to accomplish today. Picture yourself enjoying completing these things. Let yourself feel the satisfaction they will bring, and the happiness you will find in doing what you really like to do. Do not allow your mind to focus on a thought that will bring negative feelings, such as a worry or a bothersome problem. These you will solve as they arise. And do not worry about all the things you have to do that you do not particularly like. By controlling your mood states, you will even enjoy these. Don't spend longer then five minutes on this visualization. Then get up and continue with your normal routine.

Anytime you find yourself worrying, take charge of your mind with this simple exercise and create a positive visualization. If you are going to spend time visualizing, it might as well be positive.

6. In bringing about *future results*. Whatever we can visualize successfully, we can achieve. Creating and maintaining a specific image directs our mind's energy towards our goal by engaging our unconscious power and knowledge. This prepares us to accomplish our goal. When we listen to doubts, fears and

worries, we prepare our unconscios to fail. And we do. By consciously visualizing success, we counter negative patterns in our mind, and prepare our mind for success. The following exercise can help.

## Creating Success

Begin with the Centering Exercise (chap. 5, p. ) making the mind as calm and focused as possible. Now visualize the steps you must take to bring your success about...... See yourself successfully completing each of the different tasks it takes to finish the job.......... Be as specific as you can, visualizing each successive task as your momentum builds towards a successful conclusion................ Then clearly visualize the project as successfully completed......... Be as specific as you can as to exactly what will happen when you are successful............ Enjoy all the feelings of success.......... the satisfaction, the pride of a job well done.............. Listen to the sounds of success—people congratulating you, your boss thanking you for a job well done, whatever indicates that you were success-ful........Then finish the visualization with an affirmation: "I must do it, I can do it, I will do it" and "I am full of confidence, free of worry and doubt."

In the course of the project, when things get tough, repeat the visualization exercise and the affirmations.

There are times when it becomes appropriate to modify, change or even let go of your goals. If you stay balanced, and maintain a calm mind, you will know when change is appropriate and when "hanging tough" is the right choice.

## SUMMARY OF PRINCIPLES

1. The power of our sensory mind evolves from two important functions:

   - perceptual sensitivity—how attuned you are to your percep-tions; and

   - organizational integrity—the ability to organize your per-ceptions.

2. By managing these two functions effectively, you gain three performance skills: Instinct, Creativity and Imagination.

3. Instinct is your mind's ability to know exactly the things in your

environment which affect your well-being. Instinct provides protection, a sense of timing, and interpersonal understanding.

4. Your ability to use your instincts effectively depends on perceptual sensitivity and your abililty to trust your senses.

5. Creativity is the action of your sensory mind. The process of organizing and interpreting sensory data is called the Creative Matrix.

6. The creative impulse has three stages:

   • Stage one: Inner Balance—With inner balance, you create a stable environment for your creative force to minimize fear and other disturbances which interfere with your creativity.

   • Stage two: Germination—You increase the raw material of your Creative Matrix by nourishing a broad interest in life and becoming informed on a diversity of topics.

   • Stage three: Discovery—This arises from the stimulation of a free flow of images, ideas and sensations unrestricted by judgmental beliefs or attitudes. The stimulation of our creative process or trying new ways to think and perceive is the focus of most creativity techniques.

7. Through imagination you can direct the power of your mind towards a specific goal. To empower your imagination, you must direct your emotional energy through control, commitment and concentration.

8. You can use imagery in a number of ways to enhance your performance:

   • to learn specific skills and enhance performance.
   • to neutralize difficult emotional situations.
   • to solve health problems.
   • to solve performance problems.
   • to create effective moods and emotional states.
   • to ensure success.

# The Visionary Mind: Tapping the Inner Wisdom for Executive Decision Making

**7**

*While with an eye made quiet by the power of harmony, and the deep power of joy, we see into the life of things.*
—*William Wordsworth*

I couldn't believe it. I was meeting with this vice-president from Japan, and we were to discuss our developing relationship. The man not only brought out a five and ten year plan, he actually had a 25 and a 50 year plan. Right there on paper, just as complete, useful and important to him as the five and ten year plans. I didn't know what to say. Hell, we don't even have a genuine two year plan. We don't think much about the future, at least not in any significant way. These people not only think and envision the future, they are busy creating it!

—*Larry G.*
*senior executive of a*
*major brokerage firm.*

Now that information moves at light speed, and technology changes almost as quickly, the pace and complexity of our life has increased enormously. Our ability to envision the future accurately, and the skill to bring that vision about, is more critical now than ever. Those with a vision, or sense of the future, move confidently and effectively towards that future. Those without vision, simply react to changing conditions, move from one crisis to the next, and barely survive.

The Empowered Mind is a visionary mind, but what does it mean to be visionary? For many, the term "visionary" evokes pictures of wild-eyed futurists, fortune tellers and crystal balls. The word doesn't seem to fit with our picture of a modern person, with his technological sophistication and scientific knowledge.

But visionaries build the future. They are the Einsteins who blaze new trails in science, the Edisons who create world-changing inventions, the Watsons who build new corporations, the Kennedys who set new political and cultural directions. All visionaries—famous or not—play a crucial role in their corporations, organizations, or communities. They are the builders, the entrepreneurs who struggle against conventional wisdom to bring about the vision they so clearly see. Horst Rechelbacher, owner and President of Aveda Corporation, is one such visionary. His vision of completely natural skin care and beauty products, and his corporate philosophy based on conservation and concern for the ecology, has placed the Aveda Corporation in the leadership position of an entire industry. The driving force behind his success is a vision of beauty based on harmony—harmony within oneself, and harmony with one's environment.

We do not become a visionary by accumulating more information and analyzing it. Our modern technological society is not a world of simple cause/effect relationships. We are part of a global economic community, affected by events that are as diverse and unpredictable as they are uncontrollable. To our dismay, the actions of a petty dictator of a small country, such as Saddam Hussein of Iraq, can lead to severe economic changes that directly affect our economy.

## WHY LINEAR MODELS DO NOT WORK

We often hear the word "chaos" to describe the complex reality in which we live. If we rely only on linear thinking—information collection and analysis—to get answers, we run into some difficult problems:

1. Any one event has multiple causes. Linear thinking oversimplifies complex relationships, and cannot account for the whole picture.

2. The sheer amount of information makes it more and more difficult to sort out critical information from an overload of

irrelevant data. Accumulating more data often only makes the problem worse.

3.  We have less and less time to make decisions, and this prevents in-depth analysis, making it even more difficult to sort out relevant data. We end up with a superficial understanding of both the problem and its consequences.

4.  Purely logical responses ignore long-term effects, particularly those that do not follow a rigid linear sequence. Very few real-life cause/effect relationships follow linear sequences.

Too much information, the need for instant analysis, and sticking rigidly to linear analysis focus our attention on short-term outcomes. We do not recognize the long-term consequences of our decisions, or foresee the problems we create for ourselves in the future. For example, take automated computer trading in the stock market. During the crash of 1988, automated computer trading, reacting strictly to the very latest information, dumped stock and deepened the crisis. This purely logical response ignored non-linear causes, such as psychological events, as well as any consequence of its actions. As we all know, the result was chaos.

**The Sensory Mind as Linear**

We run into the same problems when we rely solely on our sensory mind to solve problems and understand the world around us. Like the computer, our sensory mind ignores information that doesn't fit its pre-existent patterns (habits and beliefs). Our sensory mind relies on partial and sometimes irrelevant information, particularly if it comes from our unconscious emotional needs, wants and fears. Our sensory mind tends to think in the same old grooves, to react without knowing the entire story, and to be biased towards or against certain outcomes. Instead of good, solid critical thinking, our sensory mind runs on automatic, pre-set patterns. It's not surprising that we end up with the same old tired answers.

# DISCRIMINATION: THE NON-LINEAR MIND

One of the most critical steps in achieving an Empowered Mind is developing your power of discrimination, the fourth level of your personality. This powerful capacity forms your visionary skills—intuition, critical thought, and decisiveness. Through discrimination, your mind directly discerns or apprehends cause/effect relationships. The knowledge we gain through discrimination is more accurate than ordinary sensory knowledge. We call this knowledge intuition. Intuitive knowledge is:

- **Flexible:** Habits and emotions are power functions within your sensory mind. They cannot dominate your discriminating mind. Consequently, your discriminating mind remains sensitive to changing conditions.

- **Comprehensive:** Your sensory mind automatically disregards data and information not consistent with its habitual patterns and belief systems, but your discriminating mind remains sensitive to *all* variables, and allows you to understand the complete picture.

- **Accurate:** Your power of discrimination separates critical and decisive causal events from those which have a superficial impact. Through discrimination, you comprehend which events really shape the future, yet you can remain flexible enough to admit critical change elements as they occur.

Intuitive knowledge fits the emerging needs of our society perfectly. Through discrimination, we shake free of both the limitations of time and our past conditioning, and create an accurate vision of the best course of action for us. By refining our capacity for critical thought, we solve the problems we face in bringing about our vision of the future. But this also involves making decisions, the third visionary skill. One of the biggest problems we face is indecision. We are quite capable of making decisions, yet we do not trust our mind. Plagued with doubt and the fear of making mistakes, we hesitate and fail to decide in a timely fashion. We strengthen our decisiveness when we skillfully combine our instincts, creative ability and our intuitive knowledge. These visionary skills—intuition, critical thought and decisiveness—are real strategic skills of an Empowered Mind, and depend heavily on our ability to concentrate.

## INTUITION—THE POWER OF PURE KNOWLEDGE

Intuition has been called a number of things: a subconscious logic, a brain-skill, a subconscious drawing from past experiences, even educated guessing. Most people think of intuition as a sort of emotional or magical thinking, just the opposite of rationality. When we cannot explain the reasoning process behind a correct conclusion, we use the word "intuition." Some people actually even view intuition as "fortune-telling."

Even knowledgeable writers, such as Francis Vaughn, author of *Awakening Intuition*, are vague about how our mind creates intuition. Vaughn defines it as a "way of knowing... recognizing the possibilities in any situation." Philip Goldberg, author of *The Intuitive Edge*, one of the best books written on intuition, defines it by repeating the dictionary definition, "the act or faculty of knowing directly without the use of the rational processes."

Even if we do not know much about intuition, we still rely on it. Studies of how executives think and make decisions show that successful executives rely heavily on their intuition. In fact, they seldom use the linear models of decision making taught in business schools. For example, one survey compared two matched groups of CEOs. The only difference was that one group made successful decisions over 80 percent of the time, while the other group had only a 50 percent success rate. The more successful CEOs used their intuition to guide their decisions, while the less successful group relied only on logic and analysis. The successful CEOs reported that after arriving at a decision intuitively, they used logic to explain and rationalize their decision to others.

**What Is Intuition?**

If we can understand our power of discrimination, we will understand intuition. Discrimination gives us the power to "see into the future," but this is not "fortune telling" as some people think. Both fortune-telling and linear analysis share a common problem: they count on a fixed future. However, the future is not fixed in stone. It evolves, or unfolds. At any time, something can change, a new element emerges, and a new future takes shape.

Through discrimination, we comprehend the vital elements as they now exist, and their outcome. With this knowledge, we know which actions to take, and which to avoid. In fact, our actions may be part of the elements that bring about this vision. As cause/effect relationships change, our intuitive knowledge also changes to reflect the new reality.

We can be misled by the habits, emotions, fears, and desires of our sensory mind. But our discriminating mind never deceives us. Through intuition, we comprehend what is, and what will be, given the existing conditions. Whether or not we like this truth is irrelevant to our power of discrimination. Our judgments, likes and dislikes may interfere with our ability to access intuitive knowledge, or even distract us so we cannot use our discrimination. But judgments, likes and dislikes cannot alter or distort this knowledge itself. At this very subtle level of our mind, we know the truth. Whether or not we accept or face it is, of course, another matter.

You use your intuition more often than you realize. Think of the time when you really wanted something to happen, like the last wrong decision you made. You were all set, had your mind all made up, and were ready to make the decision. But right before you actually made the decision, a very quiet and subtle thought passed through your conscious mind, saying "Better not do that." But it was just a quiet thought, and not very insistent. Besides, you were sure that this was the right decision, and you wanted action. So you went ahead with your plans. Three days later it became painfully obvious that you had made a serious mistake. That's when you said to yourself, "I knew I shouldn't have done it!"

Your discriminating mind tried to tell you the truth, but your desires overrode the subtle, quiet voice of your intuition. Our intuition is our genuine conscience. It lets us know what is really right for us, as opposed to what we desire or fear. It tells us the simple truth unaffected by our emotions, beliefs and past history.

You access your intuitive knowledge through awareness and sensitivity, not through analysis. It is a process of recognition. Because of its purity, intuition can become your most reliable guide. But first, you must use your power of discrimination to create this pure knowledge. Second, you must learn to access it. Both of these skills depend heavily on your ability to focus attention.

## Building the Knowledge Base for Intuition

Let us return to our computer analogy. We know that we can copy a program from one disc to another, using our computer's built-in capacity. How we use that program later on may or may not be appropriate. But in our computer, the program is intact, an exact copy of the original data.

This is analogous to what happens when we want our mind to form intuitive knowledge. As the computer copies an electromagnetic field from one disc onto another, our mind copies the reality around it by modifying its own energy field. Our discriminating mind copies the energy patterns of whatever we focus our attention on. In this way, we acquire pure knowledge, free from the influence and limitations of our sensory mind. Just as a mirror or a clear, calm lake reflect an image, our discriminating mind reflects the reality it finds. We do not inherit a mind prepackaged with pure knowledge, we inherit the power to form knowledge with our mind.

Several factors play an important role in forming intuitive knowledge:

- our ability to pay attention
- inner balance, and freedom from stress
- a flexible, open and playful mind
- an incubation period

**Focused Attention: Loading the Computer**

Your ability to focus attention is the most critical factor for developing your intuition. When we pay attention to something, it is as though we've inserted a program in the computer to be copied. If we are distracted, it is like adding extraneous data, such as a computer virus, to the copying process. This interferes with the program we are trying to copy. The more distractions we have in our conscious and unconscious mind, the less complete our intuitive knowledge.

The more involved in a task we become, the deeper our concentration, and the more intuitive we become. In studies of intuition, the subjects invariably report that their insights came after intense involvement. Take the experience of David K., a project director in the research labs of a Fortune 500 firm. For several months David was intensely involved in trying to solve a difficult technical problem involving the development of an integrated computer robotics program for the analysis of molecular structure. His team had pushed its analytic methods to the limit of available technology, but was unable to achieve the critical values it needed to succeed.

For several months, David and his team spent endless hours, both in the lab and at home, refining the procedures and investigating new technologies. David could hardly think of anything else. He was eating, breathing and sleeping the project. Towards the end of his third month of intense involvement, David began to see new possibilities and explore alternatives. It was as if a dam had broken. His mind started to make all sorts of new connections and saw the problems in entirely different ways. By the end of the fourth month, not only had David and his team solved the problem of reactivity strength, but their novel approach had led to the development of an entirely new product. No one could have foreseen this outcome at the beginning of the project.

Simply collecting information doesn't lead to intuitive insight. We need focused involvement—concentration, which generates relevant information. *The quality of our concentration is far more important than the amount of information we gather.* We use our power of discrimination not to gather facts but to directly comprehend subtle intrinsic connections and cause/effect relationships.

**Increase Attention to Enhance Discrimination**

To enhance your power of discrimination, take the following steps:

- Increase your power of concentration by practicing concentration exercises such as those given in Chapter 5. The stronger your power of concentration, the greater your intuitive knowledge.

- Do whatever you do 110 percent. Those who love their work are often much more intuitive because they are so involved. Whatever you do should fit your sense of purpose and be consistent with your values. The more interest you generate, the stronger your power of concentration, and the greater the intuitive knowledge.

- Do only one thing at a time. Limit your distractions. If it means closing your door, eliminating phone calls, refusing appointments—do so. Every distraction weakens your attention and inhibits concentration. The more absorbed you become, the greater your mind's power of discrimination.

**The Balance Factor**

The relationship between stress and intuitive knowledge is very simple—the more stress, the less intuition. We all face different kinds of pressures in our life. If not managed effectively, they disrupt the subtle faculty of discrimination. The more unbalanced we become, the less clearly our mind represents and understands the reality around it. But if we stay calm and collected, and see demands and pressures as challenges, we become absorbed in our work. This increases our capacity for intuition. To retain our power of discrimination, we must be able to stay relaxed during times of pressure.

# NEEDED: AN OPEN, FLEXIBLE MIND

To be intuitive, our mind needs the flexibility to adapt to the reality it confronts. Fears, desires and beliefs inhibit our mind's flexibility and interfere with our ability to use our intuition. Fear disrupts our mind's energy, preventing the formation of pure knowledge. For example, many of us are limited by the fear of making mistakes. Early in life we learn that mistakes are bad. This becomes an unconscious influence that limits us in adult life. It prevents us from going beyond conventional wisdom, and confines us to the mainstream of thought. Even worse, we forfeit the opportunity to learn from our mistakes.

Strong desires also interfere with our ability to perceive reality clearly. Not only do we bend our perceptions to fit them, they create strong energy patterns which overwhelm our ability to discriminate. Our sensory mind loses touch with reality, and we listen to our desires instead of our conscience. Often this happens at such a subtle level that we are not even aware that our perceptions are skewed, and we are not discriminating effectively.

Sometimes, for example, our desire to be important clouds our judgment about which responsibilities to accept or reject. We may take on extra work, or shoulder responsibilities that rightfully belong to others. Someone flatters us, and we allow him to "put the monkey on our backs." Intuitively, we know that we will regret this extra load, but instead of listening to our intuition, we fall victim to our desire to be important. We let our desire overwhelm our inner wisdom, and then suffer the consequences of taking on extra work. By learning how to listen to our intuition, we can be more objective, and make the right decision.

The belief that things should be a certain way also creates subtle and powerful obstacles to using intuition. A friend of mine was forced to resign from his position in a drug treatment center amidst some very hostile and negative feelings between him and a new supervisor who was very abusive. For good reason, my friend felt mistreated. He and his wife decided to bring suit against the center and his former supervisor. On the way to the lawyer's office, however, his wife had a sense that all of this was a waste of time. But their anger was so strong, that they went ahead and engaged the lawyer. After all, it was a "matter of principle." Actually, there was not much he could really do, and nothing came of the suit. Eventually, he finally dropped the suit, but not until he had spent several hundred dollars in legal fees pursuing his anger.

While our principles and values—such as not lying or stealing—are very important, our beliefs about how things "should be" often dramatically limit our intuition. If we have already decided what should be true, we will not be open to perceiving "what is" true. The more emotionally invested we are in our beliefs, the more rigid and narrow our perceptions. We confuse our beliefs with "truth," and convince ourselves that our way of interpreting reality is not only the best way, but the *only* way.

Such mental inflexibility limits our knowledge and makes it more difficult to be effective in the world. Beliefs are not the truth; they are paradigms that provide a consistent view of the world. We must challenge our own belief systems, refine them in the light of our expanded experience, and allow them to mature. The more flexible our belief systems (paradigms), the more effectively they provide us with practical ways of working in the world. If our belief systems remain flexible and open to change, we respond creatively to the world around us.

A classic example of how beliefs interfere with performance and future success is the development of the quartz watch. When we consider the history of clocks and watch-making, we invariably think of Switzerland. The term "Swiss movement" is synonymous for the highest quality of watch. But when the quartz movement was invented by the Swiss, the Swiss industry failed to grasp the importance of this highly accurate timekeeping. Unwilling to change, they refused to adapt their proven ways to take advantage of this new way of making watches. They did not believe that anything would replace the exquisite mechanical movement at which they excelled. The Japanese, quick to adapt to new strategies and new technologies, developed the quartz watch, and now overwhelmingly dominate the market.

Today we laugh at categorical statements such as "The world is flat," "Man will never learn to fly," or "The horseless carriage will never replace the horse." They are all examples of inflexible belief systems. But what kinds of statements are we making now that future generations will laugh at? Listen to your own categorical statements about what is true and what isn't, how things are one way and will never change. Just like fears and desires, beliefs become limitations, locking us into realities that may be neither useful nor appropriate.

## Maintaining a Flexible and Open Mind

The following techniques can help you maintain a flexible and open mind:

- **Practice Fearlessness**. Work with the exercises given in chapter 4 to minimize fear, and maintain a calm and tranquil mind. Enhance your innate power of self-confidence by establishing a consistent practice of meditation on a daily basis.

- **Use non-judgmental and non-categorical language**. Avoid using language that limits your options, or closes off possibilities. Learn to describe behavior rather than use evaluative language. For example, instead of using "right or wrong," "good or bad," use phrases such as "That's an interesting way to see the world."

- **Develop a sense of playfulness, a willingness to experiment and try new ways of doing things.** Do not condemn your own or someone else's mistakes. Instead, use them as opportunities to learn. Maintain a sense of humor, and do not take yourself so seriously. Learn to respect yourself and others, and be willing to listen and learn from others.

## QUIET TIME: THE NEED FOR INCUBATION

A calm and reflective mind is another critical element in developing intuitive skills. While intuitive insight can happen instantly, it usually takes involvement over a period of time. This is particularly true when you first begin to practice using your intuition. You must allow some time for reflection. When you are constantly on the go, putting out fires, hurrying from one place to the other, your mind remains on the superficial level of sensory knowledge. *The person who must always be in the center of action rarely develops the intuitive insight necessary for effective leadership.*

Commitment and absorption are necessary aspects of building intuitive knowledge, but there must be some period of time when we let go of any conscious effort to find solutions. These incubation periods can be anything from long walks in the country, going trout fishing, watching the logs burn in the fireplace, to even sitting in a sauna. A senior executive of a Fortune 500 firm gains his insight while taking long, leisurely showers. Another colleague reports that he gains his best insights after gardening or chopping firewood.

To develop our intuition, we must allow our minds time to completely relax, and let go of the problems we face. Constant action, though often revered as the sign of success, is, in fact, a block to our inner resources. Give yourself time to reflect, to calm and quiet the mind. *Genuine leisure is an invaluable activity which you cannot afford to miss.* These incubation periods give rise to valuable states of knowledge and awareness that are a necessary part of an Empowered Mind.

A quiet and calm mind is the connecting point between developing intuitive knowledge and becoming aware of that knowledge. Being in nature helps us to quiet our mind. During a leisurely stroll along the beach or through an open field, we become sensitive to the subtle rhythms of life. Since we are also an integral part of nature, we become sensitive to our own rhythms. But the most powerful and effective incubation process is meditation. It deepens our awareness of the subtle knowledge of our mind, and allows us greater access to our intuition.

## THE PATH TO WISDOM: TAPPING YOUR INTUITION

**The key to using our intuition is knowing how and to what to pay attention.** You can use a number of different techniques to tap your intuition, but all involve a simple principle—being aware of what your mind already knows. There are two aspects to this: (1) to become aware of our intuitive knowledge, and (2) to distinguish it from other messages from the unconscious, such as hunches, wishes, desires, and fears.

I remember the story of a good friend who used to love to bet on horses. One day, out of the blue, he felt a strong message to go to the track and bet on a particular horse. At first, he tried to ignore the message as he was busy working on a project. But the thought persisted, and he finally became convinced that he should listen to this strong inner message. He dropped everything and drove to the track in time to bet $200 on the horse. He lost.

Clearly, not all the messages we receive from our unconscious are useful. With practice, we can learn to tell the difference between genuine intuitive knowledge and other messages.

### The Art and Science of Paying Attention

We experience our intuitive insights in three different ways—as thoughts, as images, and as sensations or feelings. But caught up in the everyday demands of life, we get distracted by the chatter of our noisy sensory mind, and we ignore these intuitive insights. Occasionally, our intuition breaks through the noise of our mental chatter, and we have an "Aha" experience. For most of us, however, this is an occasional glimpse, and nothing more. It is *not* that we do not have intuitive insights, we simply are not aware of them.

You can be more intuitive by becoming more aware of the subtle thoughts, images and sensations that pop into your mind. The key, of course, is learning how to *pay attention.*

This is where inner concentration, or meditation, plays a key role. Techniques, such as the ones below, can help us tap our intuitive knowledge. However, if we are not very sensitive to the subtle thoughts and feelings that come from the unconscious levels of our mind, these techniques are not very useful. By practicing meditation, we become more sensitive to our inner reality. Then the specific exercises we use to develop our intuition become far more effective, and we tap our intuition on a day-to-day basis.

## THE BODY KNOWS

We often experience our intuition as feelings or body sensations. It's common to hear statements such as "This doesn't smell right" or "It doesn't feel right to me." Since our body is in constant communication with our unconscious mind, it serves as a conduit for information stored there. Some subtle sense felt in our body lets us know that something is not quite right with our plans, our actions, or our decisions. We sense that something is definitely out of synch.

Once, my daughter came home from school excited about going on a three hour bus trip to New York City to see MaryLou Retton and the American Gymnast team. As soon as she asked my permission to go, I sensed that something was not quite right. I told her that I would think about it, and let her know. Because I felt slightly uneasy, I wanted some time to explore my feelings. After finishing some work, I took a walk by myself to study what my mind and body were telling me. I felt that there would be a problem with the bus trip, but that no one would be harmed, and that everything would be fine. So I gave my permission for her to go. Sure enough, on the way back home, the bus broke down, and they were delayed for three hours. But no one was hurt, and all turned out well.

Our sensitivity is not limited to just anticipating problems. We may also sense that we should do something, such as going ahead with a project that we were not sure of. I wanted my daughter to have this experience. By understanding my feelings, I could separate out my worry for her, and my intuitive awareness of the reality of the situation. I was very comfortable giving her permission to go, even though I knew that there would be some minor problem with the trip.

When we reduce our overall level of tension with relaxation exercises, we become more sensitive to the subtle feelings in our body. The exercises given in Chapter 2 on increasing body sensitivity are also helpful. But one of the best exercises for increasing sensitivity is "61 Points" in Chapter 5. Concentrating on the different points sensitizes us to the energy patterns of our body, making us more aware of changes that reflect unconscious knowledge.

Stretching exercises are another way to become more aware of your body's messages. But the stretching should be done very slowly, and held for several minutes at the peak of the stretch. During this time, focus your attention on both what the body feels and the emotional/mental events that accompany the body sensations. Hatha yoga is the most sophisticated system of exercises for enhancing mental sensitivity and control. Holding the postures creates a stillness which facilitates inner awareness.

## THE QUIET THOUGHTS

Since intuitive knowledge is free from emotional bias, the thoughts which convey the knowledge are not highly energized. Consequently, these subtle and quiet thoughts tend to be easily lost in the noisy chatter of our sensory mind. However, because they are free from emotional distortion, they are very clear. This clarity is one of the confirming signs of intuition. We experience an intuitive thought as a statement of fact, as though we read it from a book. It simply states what is. You may react emotionally after having the intuitive thought, but the thought itself is clear of any emotional coloring.

To use thoughts as a guide to intuition, you must learn how to listen to, or observe your mind as it thinks, rather than do the thinking yourself. This is one of the skills you can gain through meditation. Jeff, a private broker, is known for his intuitive skill at knowing which stocks to buy and sell. A week before the market crash in 1988, Jeff protected himself and his clients by selling nearly every stock that lost heavily. When asked how he knew, he reported that the previous evening, he had sat in meditation. After finishing his meditation, his habit was to spend about thirty minutes allowing his mind to review his work and the market. Suddenly, a clear thought emerged in his mind to sell, and the names of the particular stocks to sell came in alphabetical order. Jeff said that there was no fear or excitement. He had a clear and unworried recognition that these stocks would lose significant value. It was particularly significant to Jeff that he had no prior inclination to buy or sell. The next day, Jeff acted on this intuitive thought. He not only minimized his losses, but was able to use his liquidity to step in and buy when the market was at its lowest point.

To strengthen your ability to use thoughts, learn to observe your mind. To observe means to be non-judgmental, open, and receptive—not distracted by worries, desires or other disturbances. Significantly, Jeff had the insight after his meditation practice, when his mind was focused, calm and undisturbed. By reviewing his work in a relaxed, objective and non-judgmental fashion, Jeff was receptive to the subtle knowledge of his discriminating mind. Through practice, he had gained confidence and skill in using this vital resource. Jeff's payoff both professionally and personally has been significant.

To develop this sensitivity, do what Jeff does. Spend time in concentrating the mind, creating a deep calm and alertness, and then allow your mind to review your work, or any activity for which you need insight. As you become more skillful, you will notice an increased sensitivity to the subtle, quiet thoughts of intuition.

## A PICTURE OF THE FUTURE

Very often, an intuition comes in the form of an image. When this happens, we literally see the future unfold before us. As you saw in Chapter 6, you can create the reality you want by using images to focus our mind's attention. This directs the power of our mind, and we turn our imagination into reality. It is one of the more powerful strategic skills of the mind.

But we can also use imagery in a passive way to create a pathway to intuitive knowledge. Like thoughts, images can "pop into our mind," and give us intuitive insight. As usual, observation and a calm and quiet mind provide the medium to become sensitive to these pictures from our unconscious. By stimulating our unconscious with intentional imagery, we can generate images that reveal intuitive knowledge. Most of the exercises used to develop intuitive skills are based on stimulating images. Regardless of their origin, these exercises generally include most of the following elements:

- **A relaxed and quiet mind**. This is essential to create inner balance and minimize stress, and to allow for depth of inner awareness.

- **A symbolic journey**. This may be a descent, into a cave or basement, or an ascent, to an attic or mountain top. These journeys are used to focus attention and deepen awareness of the unconscious mind.

- **Exploration of the destination**. This creates an openness to experience whatever the unconscious mind presents, and helps minimize pre-judging and habitual patterns of thought and imagery.

- **An interaction with an imaginary person such as a child, an** elderly person, a sage, or even a disembodied point of light. These symbolic figures personify our power of discrimination, and facilitate the communication between conscious and unconscious mind.

- **Questions asked and answered.** This is a direct approach to tapping the wisdom of our discriminating mind.

- **A gift or object brought back from the journey.** This symbolically identifies strengths, indicates direction, or points to either inner or outer resources of which we were not aware.

- **A return journey.** This involves a return to our immediate reality, with the knowledge of how to return to our intuition when necessary, and with the intent to use the knowledge we gained in our journey.

- **A period of musing.** This is important to consider what we have discovered and how to apply this knowledge to the problem(s) we face.

Imagery exercises vary in complexity and sophistication. The more complex, the more information can be gained. However, much of this information is more relevant to self-knowledge than to intuition. Often the more direct and simple the exercise, the more effectively it accesses visionary or intuitive knowledge. However, the more direct and simple it is, the greater the skill required to use it effectively. Below are three different kinds of exercises. The first is very complex, and reveals one's hidden qualities. The second is much less complex and represents more of the classic journey into intuition. The final one is quite direct, and requires a degree of skill in meditation.

## A Journey Into Wisdom

The following exercise provides a sense of direction for our efforts, and evokes a rich field of imagery for insight into our own nature. This is a fairly long and complex exercise. First read through the exercise, and then mentally go through it with your eyes closed. You might wish to first record it onto a cassette tape, and then listen as your own voice takes you through the exercise. When a question is asked during the exercise, simply note the answer in your mind. Be sure to pause at the places indicated by the strings of periods.

Sit in a comfortable and relaxed position, or lie on your back with your feet approximately twelve to eighteen inches apart, your arms slightly away from the body, the palms of your hands facing slightly upward, and a small pillow to support the curve of your neck. Close your eyes, and focus on even, diaphragmatic breathing, allowing your body to become completely relaxed........ Now focus your attention on Breath Awareness, feeling the coolness of the inhalation and the warmth of the exhalation, right at the opening of the nostrils........ Let your mind become very calm and very clear, without any worries about the future or concerns about the past......bring all of your attention to the feeling of your breath as it passes in and out the nostrils.......................

Imagine leaving your home and arriving without difficulty at a very beautiful forested mountain scene. In front of you is a path that leads into the forest and up the mountain. You decide to walk to the top of the mountain, and you feel excited about going there. You know there is nothing to fear, and that you will be comfortable and safe throughout the entire journey.

As you begin your journey along the path, how do you feel about taking this journey?........ What kind of path are you walking on?......... What does it look like?......... As you go forward, and the path climbs up into the forest, how do you like the journey? ........ What does the forest look like to you?.........

Then you come to a fork in the path. You know that both paths will lead you to the top of the mountain, but you must make a choice. Is there a difference between the two paths?........ Which one do you take and why do you choose that one?............. Continue your journey through the forest and up the side of the mountain. As you continue your journey upwards, what is the path like now?............... What does the forest seem to be like now?...............

You have been so interested in your journey that you have forgotten about time. As you climb higher, and the trees begin to thin out, you can look out into the distance. How does it feel to see a great distance?...................

You want to reach the top of the mountain, but it has taken some time, and it's starting to get late. You know that above you there is a large ledge where you can safely and easily spend the night. As you look up towards the ledge, you see some smoke from a campfire. You remember that this is the home of a very special person, a wise person. You realize that your real reason for climbing this mountain has been to visit with this person. So you continue upwards towards the ledge. How do you feel about seeing this person?............................

By the time you reach the ledge, it is dusk. As you approach the ledge, you see a campfire, so you walk towards the fire. As you get closer, you realize that the wise person is sitting back from the fire, watching you. As you see the wise person, how do you feel about this person?........................ What do they look like?........................

**Now switch your identity and become the wise person.** Picture yourself as that wise person. You know that (your name) is coming to visit you. How do you feel about that?.................. As you sit back from the fire, you see this person coming up over the ledge and approaching the campfire. As you see the person, how do you feel towards him?....................... When he sees you, you indicate for him to sit. Knowing that he comes seeking advice and wisdom, what is it that you would like to tell him?...............................

**Again, switch identity and become the traveler.** You are back to yourself again. The wise person sees you and indicates for you to be seated. As you both sit and watch the sunset, how do you feel about being there with this person?.............. You are able to spend the entire night in the company of this wise person, and somehow you are neither tired or cold. You are very comfortable just listening to the sounds of the night and watching the stars.

The wise person indicates that you may ask three questions. Which three questions do you ask and why?........................... What is the answer that you receive?.............. How do you feel about these answers?...............................

**Again, switch identity and become the wise person.** As the wise person, you watch this person in front of you, and you allow him to ask you three questions....................Why did you give him the answers that you did?.................. Is there something that you want to tell him that you feel he should know?.....................As you tell him, what was his response?....................... Throughout the night you observe this person, understanding his innermost thoughts. How do you feel about this person now?........................... As the sun begins to rise, you know that he must return, but you want to give him a special gift to take with him. What gift do you give him and why?..................

**Again, switch identity and become the traveler.** As sunrise begins, you know that it's time to return to your home. But before you leave, the wise person gives you a special gift. How do you feel about this gift?..........How do you feel about leaving the ledge and returning home?...........

The journey home is magically quick, and you find yourself inside your own home. What are your feelings about this journey that you took?............. What do you do with the gift that the wise person gave you?........................... What would you like to ask this wise person that you never asked?...................

Now return to Breath Awareness to clear your mind. After a few moments, gently bring your hands up, holding the palms of your hands about four inches from your face, open your eyes to the palms of your hands. The first thing you should see are the palms of your hands.

Review the journey and the answers in your mind, and record your thoughts and any insights about yourself, your goals, and any directions for further reference.

**The Room**

There are many variations of this common exercise for developing intuitive insight. They share the theme of going down into the mind, accessing our intuitive knowledge and exploring what we find. This exercise is far less complex, and less rich in self-knowledge material, but more direct in developing intuitive insight.

Begin sitting in a comfortable position, or lying in the Relaxation Posture as described in Chapter 3. Focus on your breath and clear your mind with Breath Awareness. Close your eyes and visualize or picture yourself standing in a room. Let the room be any one you wish, but you should feel comfortable in it. Then picture a stairway off to one side. You approach the stairway and slowly descend the steps down into a lower level. What does this level look like?............. The room you are in now is different, but just as comfortable. There is a large question mark on the wall, with a sign that says "Question Room." You realize that this is a room where you can gain clarity about any questions that you need to answer about a personal decision, a problem at work, or a relationship. Allow your mind to formulate a very specific question......... Don't try to answer the question, just state the question clearly and simply in your mind..........

Then you see another stairway that goes down to an even lower level. You are very curious about what may be at the bottom of these stairs. So you slowly descend onto a small landing where you find a door in front of you.

On the door you see a sign that says "Intuition." You are very curious and try to open the door, but it is locked and you do not have a key.

As you turn from the door, someone approaches you with a key. What does that person look like?........... They give you the key, you thank them, and you open the door. As the door opens, you enter the room........ What do you find?............ What does the room look like?............... Feeling comfortable and curious, you begin to explore the room. What do you find in the room?.............How does it feel to be there?.........................

You have just a little time to spend in the room, so how do you spend it?.......... Something in the room catches your eye, something that seems very important to you. What is it?........................ Why does it seem so important?................ Does it relate to the question that you asked?.............

You must leave, so you decide to take something from the room. What do you choose to take with you?...................... As you leave, you don't have to lock the door, and you realize that you can return at any time. As you go back up the first flight of steps and into the question room, what kind of feelings do you have about the intuition room you just left?....... How does it relate to the question you asked when you first entered this room?............... (Does another question come to your mind?......... If another clear question comes to your mind, you can return to the intuition room and search for another answer or object.)

Now you climb the second set of stairs, back into your original room. There, you look at what you have brought back with you. How will you use it?.............. What comes to your mind as you think about the journey you just took?...................Again, focus your breath, clear your mind, and open your eyes to the palms of your hand.

Write down both the question you formulated, and whatever answers you found. Note the feelings you experienced during the journey, and whatever insights you have gained. Later, you can refer back to these notes and indicate how useful or accurate your insights were.

## DIRECT ACCESS

We can use the same process that Jeff used to access his intuitive knowledge. By creating a deeply calm and focused mind through meditation, and then allowing our mind to play with our work, we can often generate a great deal of intuitive insight. Our insights won't always be dramatic, but the time we spend becomes one of our most valued and treasured activities. With practice, we can develop conscious access to intuitive knowledge, and use it effectively to solve problems, set directions and make choices. Developing skill at direct access takes time and practice, but is well worth the effort.

Begin with the Centering and Meditation Exercises in Chapter 5. By now, these should be part of your daily routine. After finishing your meditation practice, sit back, relax and allow your mind to focus on work or whatever problems need insight. Do not judge anything that comes to your mind, allow your mind to ramble. Pay attention to the thoughts, feelings and images that pass through your mind. If you allow your mind to play with possibilities, trying different answers, this can also be a creative problem-solving technique. To develop intuitive insight you must remain a witness, and *not* allow your mind to actively search for problems or try to solve them. Spend a minimum of fifteen minutes—or as much time as you want—observing the contents of your mind. Write down any insights you have for future use, or for a future check of their validity. The more skilled at meditation you become, the more effectively you will be able to access your intuitive knowledge.

## THINGS TO WATCH FOR

While intuitive knowledge in itself is free of error, using intuition can be difficult and problematic. The following factors can mislead us:

- *Not everything that we think, imagine or feel is an intuition.* Are you having a genuine intuition, or are you feeling some desire, need or want? This is particularly difficult to distinguish when you are just beginning to develop your intuitive sense. The mind is quite capable of fooling us, as my friend who bet on the wrong horse found out. To minimize this problem, keep a notebook handy. Every time you think that you have an intuition, write it down. Note everything that you observe about the intuition— how you felt; whether it was an image, thought or feeling; what was your reaction; how strong or clear it seemed. Then, later on, indicate whether or not it was accurate, and note any benefit you gained from the insight. This helps develop your ability to differentiate genuine intuitive insight from the other messages from the unconscious mind, such as hunches, needs, desires, wants or fears.

- *Difficulties may arise in using imagery.* Because of their symbolic nature, images must be interpreted and understood in context. We can check our understanding of the image by cross-checking our body feelings and sensations to see what we feel. Does your understanding of the image feel right? We can often validate whatever thoughts and images our mind generates by consulting our feelings about them.

- *Intuition does not always give a complete answer.* Often, our intuition only points us in the right direction. We will not always know how things will turn out. But by paying attention, we begin to move in the right direction and can better take advantage of the situation. Periodically checking feelings and thoughts about your direction will help keep you on the right track, even when your intuition is incomplete and partial.

## DISCRIMINATION—THE POWER BEHIND REASONING

You can also combine your power of discrimination with your sensory mind. When you apply discrimination to sensory input, you have the power to reason, to think things out. This is when you use your analytic abilities to solve problems and make decisions. The ability to synthesize and analyze data is the most familiar skill of the mind. We call this *critical thinking*. It depends on our capacity to perceive clearly and to discriminate—to understand relationships and discern differences.

When we do not use our discrimination, our mind chatter consists of a series of automatic reactions to whatever stimulus is occurring at the time. The chatter comes right from our perceptual and emotional habits, with little, if any, discrimination. But when we apply our power of discrimination, this chatter becomes a powerful tool for us.

Critical thinking involves more than logic and analysis. Because of the power of discrimination, these elements characterize critical thought:

- the ability to discern critical elements from a mass of data.

- the flexibility to use information that appears inconsistent or irrelevant.

✓ • the ability to perceive the entire picture.

If we become too dependent on logic, our thinking becomes too rigid and narrow. Computers operate on pure logic, and are limited by this. The human mind is far more adaptive and flexible, or, at least, we have the capacity to be. Along with logic, our thinking should reflect our creativity, our commitments, our instincts and intuitive knowledge, and our emotional power. The clarity and perceptual sensitivity produced by discrimination also enhance our memory, giving us a powerful experiential base on which to base our analysis.

If we do not use our discrimination effectively, our habits control our thought patterns. Then emotional reactions, desires and fears color our mind chatter. The judgments we make interfere with our ability to understand patterns. When we are upset, or worried, we do not think clearly, nor do we have the ability for penetrating analysis. The more our sensory mind dominates our chatter, the less ability we have for critical thinking. But when we approach problem solving and analysis with a calm and clear mind, using our power of discrimination, we can think clearly, solve problems effectively, and develop a powerful and penetrating intellect.

### Intuition and Critical Thinking: Dynamic Duo for Problem-Solving

Intuition gives us insight into situations or about the future. But we cannot always generate the insight we need. We may not be able to tap into our intuition, or we only get partial access to it. Time pressures and immediacy demands may interfere; or we may need a rational explanation to convince others. When we cannot use intuition, we can turn to our power of critical thinking to solve problems. By combining both intuition and critical thinking, we can solve virtually any problem.

### Four Critical Steps to Critical Thinking

Education and experience help train our power of critical thinking, but they cannot guarantee that we will utilize this power effectively. We also recognize the need for logic in analytic thought, but logic only helps minimize error. Without discrimination, logic is a mind game that gives us answers, but not necessarily the most useful ones. By strengthening our power of discrimination, both logic and our "common sense" become formidable tools.

To strengthen your power of critical thinking, follow these four steps:

**1. Create a calm and quiet mind.** A number of elements cloud our thinking in such subtle ways that we are not aware that they are even happening. We know that strong emotional reactions interfere with our ability to think clearly. In subtle form, however, fear, self-doubt, and other emotions influence our unconscious in ways we do not recognize. A relaxed and calm mind minimizes these unconscious factors, and facilitates discrimination.

**2. Take time to ponder.** Do not allow yourself to make critical decisions in the midst of emotional reactions. Crisis management is a poor medium for critical thinking. Time pressures exist for all of us, but we can always find a few moments to clear our mind, and allow ourselves the time and space to ponder the question. The more important the decision, the more important to allow your mind the time to reflect.

**3. Absorb yourself in the problem.** The more you concentrate on a problem, the greater your power of discrimination. Absorption allows your unconscious mind to become totally involved in the problem-solving process. Once you have invested your concentration, step back and trust your unconscious mind to solve the problem for you through the power of discrimination. One of the best times to do this is during sleep. The following exercise will teach you how to use sleep as an aid to problem-solving.

### Problem-Solving Through Sleep

Before going to sleep, spend a few minutes with the Centering Exercise and Meditation Exercise in Chapter. Then, prepare your unconscious mind by thoroughly immersing yourself in all the elements of the problem or decision. Do not allow any worry or concern to disturb this preparation, and be as objective and as thorough as possible. As you prepare to go to sleep, instruct your unconscious mind to solve the problem for you. "OK mind, I've given you all the information, I know you can solve this problem for me by tomorrow morning when I awake." Then keep your mind clear of the problem and go to sleep. In the morning, write down any insights or solutions that occur to you on awakening, or anything you remember that was helpful in your dreams. After getting dressed and prepared for work, spend a few moments pondering the decision or the problem. With a little practice, this exercise can prove a very helpful tool.

**4. Be willing to examine any answer your mind gives you.** Beliefs, expectations, desires, needs and wants all combine to create barriers in the knowledge patterns of our mind. When these become habits, they subtly distort our analytic abilities. Be willing to change your beliefs and to try out novel ideas that your mind presents. The moment you believe that you know what can and cannot be, you prevent your mind from utilizing the full power of discrimination. Psychology has long noted that our best performance, our best thinking, is done in a relaxed but alert state, with an open and receptive mind.

## DECISIVENESS: KNOWING WHEN AND HOW TO TAKE ACTION

Elbert Hubbard, an American literary figure of the early 1900s, said: "It does not take much strength to do things, but it requires great strength to decide on what to do." Deciding in time is one of the biggest problems we all face, and indecision one of the major reasons for failure. All our instincts, creative solutions, brilliant problem-solving and intuitive insights have little value unless we bring them into action. A brilliant idea not acted upon is an abortion, and creates weakness in the mind.

An Empowered Mind knows how to decide in time and avoid costly delay. When we are decisive, we take action when the opportunity presents itself. This "seizing the moment" conserves effort and ensures success. On the other hand, it is certainly true that "he who hesitates is lost."

Given the capability of our mind to collect, process and even go beyond available data to understand reality, there is no good reason to be indecisive. The most common excuse is lack of information. But in almost every case, the real reasons for our indecision and inability to act are fear and self-doubt. When we delay out of fear, or out of distrust of our own analysis, or for any other reason, we not only miss the window of opportunity, we also strengthen the fears in our mind.

# Taking Fear Out of the Decision-Making Process

Probably the greatest obstacle to making a decision is the fear of making a mistake. Rather than make a decision, we may argue that we need more time or more information, or that we're waiting for developments to occur. We often use indecision as a way to let someone, or something else, make the decision for us. This way, we can avoid the responsibility if something goes wrong.

There are times when we do not have the information we need, but then we make a decision to get the information as quickly as possible. We commit to an action and keep from paralyzing our mind with worry. But when we use the lack of information as an excuse to avoid making a decision, it makes the problem worse. By delaying, and not facing problems or tasks directly, we damage our will and make ourselves weaker.

With self-training and time, we can free our mind completely of fear. But we cannot hold all our decisions until then. The solution is quite simple. If we acknowledge our fears (to ourselves), and are aware of their influence, we minimize their impact. This truthfulness with ourselves counteracts the limiting effect of our fears and concerns. By facing our fear, we will not necessarily become entirely free of it, but we can prevent it from paralyzing our decision-making power.

In *Dune*, a science fiction novel by Frank Herbert, the hero Paul Atreides uses a short prayer to clear his mind of fear and bring it to a state of calm alertness:

> I must not fear. Fear is the mind-killer. Fear is the little-death that brings total obliteration. I will face my fear. I will permit it to pass over me and through me. And when it has gone past, I will turn the inner eye to see its path. Where the fear has gone there will be nothing. Only I will remain.

Use this prayer as an affirmation to help clear your mind of worries, concerns and fears that interfere with your decision-making. By facing your fear directly, acknowledging your worries and concerns, and then letting them pass, you prevent fear from influencing your decisions. The key is to refocus your attention to your own calm center, and to make your decisions from that center of equanimity.

# Bypassing Self-doubt: Becoming an Experimenter

In the decision-making process, self-doubt is often more subtle than fear. Every time we remind ourselves of all the mistakes we have made, how things never turn out right, or how poorly we always do, we create a problem for ourselves. To avoid feeling bad, we avoid making a decision. If we never test our ideas, we never have to confront failure. We can remain safely in the world of ideas. But the price we pay is more self-doubt and less accomplishment. What we interpret as laziness is often someone whose mind is paralyzed by self-doubt.

As long as we let self-doubt control our decisions and actions, it becomes stronger. Only by making decisions and taking actions do we learn to trust ourselves and our capacities. Even if things do not turn out the way we expected, we always get some result. If the results aren't what we want or need, then all we have to do is refine our actions until we get the results we want. You read this book without knowing the number of revisions and rewrites that have gone into making the final product. With every revision, I used what had been written before as a guide to make the writing more interesting. Without the labor and sweat of the earlier writing, I could not have communicated the skill and knowledge hopefully evident in the final version.

Instead of looking upon each decision or action as *the* event of your life, practice seeing them as one step along the path of creating the results you want. Each decision and each action is an experiment, and each experiment gives you a result. As you continue to experiment, you gradually refine your skills until you achieve the results you want. What you accomplish is rarely ever the consequence of any one decision. Success is the result of a series of decisions and actions, each a refinement and correction of the one before.

## THREE STEPS TO EFFECTIVE DECISION-MAKING

**1. Create a calm and clear mind:** When faced with the opportunity to make a decision, or whenever fear or self-doubt arises in your mind, clear your mind with the Centering Exercise (Chapter 5), and re-direct your attention to solving the problem.

**2. Language:** Avoid emotionally loaded and limiting words like "failure" and "can't." Remember, every effort brings results, though not necessarily the results you expected or wanted. You will have results, however. Using the right language allows you to use any outcome, and reduces the fear of making the decision. If you allow yourself to make mistakes, you learn to discriminate between effective and ineffective actions. If you cannot lose, you minimize fear!

## 3. Check all levels of knowledge:

- **analysis**—logical steps of information collection and analysis, such as listing pros and cons, down-side vs. up-side, risk/rewards.

- **instincts**—Explore your feelings about the decision you need to make, and how you feel after you have made it. Practice develops your ability to distinguish fears and doubts from genuine instincts.

- **intuition**—What insights can you gain about your decision and its consequences? At the most subtle level of your mind, are you comfortable with this decision? Use the appropriate exercises to gain insight.

Our discriminating mind has wonderful visionary power. By taking command of these resources we can create the future that we want and deserve. We are masters of our own destiny, but only if we access and use the subtle resources of our mind.

## SUMMARY OF PRINCIPLES

1. The power of discrimination is the innate power to discern cause/effect relationships without the limitations found in the sensory mind.

2. Discrimination provides a knowledge base that is flexible, comprehensive and accurate.

3. We experience this knowledge as intuition.

4. Concentration provides the key to form and access intuitive knowledge.

5. To develop our intuition, we need a calm and quiet mind that is open, flexible, and free from the problems of stress and worry.

6. We can use our body's feelings and sensations as a resource to intuitive knowledge. We also experience our intuition in subtle thoughts and images.

7. When we combine our power of discrimination with sensory data, we have the ability for critical thinking.

8. Critical thinking requires a calm and quiet mind, time to ponder

information, involvement or absorption in the problem, and the willingness to consider any and all alternatives.

9. Decisiveness is the power to use our resources to come to a decision and take an action.

10. The two factors which lead to indecisiveness are fear and self-doubt.

# Executive Leadership: The Mastery of Inner Strength

**8**

---

*People do not lack strength, they lack will*
—*Victor Hugo*

I decided that I was going to live in Minneapolis and build a world class salon. In the beginning it was tough. I didn't speak the language well, and couldn't read English very well. I started out by going to bars and hustling customers for my salon. I'd meet some young woman, get acquainted, then begin to tell her about how her hair could look so much better. Gradually, the word got around, and we began to grow. I never had any doubts, I was determined to build my career and my company. I'm still that way. Once I decide, I decide completely, and everything that happens only creates either more opportunity or more motivation for me. Whenever I allowed myself to doubt, I didn't have the strength to create and build. I made lots of mistakes, and each one was another opportunity to learn. I still make mistakes, lots of them, because I want to keep learning. But I won't allow any doubts to interfere with me.

—*Horst Rechelbacher*
*President/Owner, AVEDA Corporation*

Powerful minds make things happen. They build companies, win ball games, structure deals—virtually anything. In describing a "powerful mind," we use terms such as *dynamic, probing, creative, visionary,* and *productive.* We look upon such a person with a mixture of awe, respect, admiration, and maybe even a little jealousy and fear.

But a powerful mind is not necessarily more intelligent, creative or visionary. Nor were these people always born with unusual talents. They started with the same innate potentials that all minds share to one degree or the other. Nor can we say that they are the result of education, culture or socio-economic class. Every human mind has great potential strength and enormous power, but unfortunately very few develop this potential or learn how to direct it.

Our mind becomes more powerful through concentration. But power must be applied for it to become useful. The next step in creating an Empowered Mind is to build the dynamic will that ensures success. This demands determination, strength and discipline, all innate qualities of our mind.

Leaders come in all kinds of shapes and styles but the inner qualities which make for a commanding mind—one which inspires others and provides leadership—are part of every mind. The problem is to identify and develop them. Three innate resources form the command and leadership skills of an Empowered Mind:

- *Will*—the ability to consciously marshal our energy and direct it to our chosen goals.

- *Absolute Self-Confidence*—an inner strength unaffected by either success or failure.

- *Self-Discipline*—the ability to follow-through with our choices.

## WILL—DIRECTING MIND POWER

When we pay attention, we focus the energy of our mind on a specific target. The greater our concentration, the more powerful our mind becomes. But once we concentrate our mind, we must know how to direct this power. This is the role of our will. In the exercise of our will, we marshal all of our resources, both internal and external, to achieve our goals. When we think of someone who exercises a strong will, we may think of Lee Iacocca who brought Chrysler back from the brink of bankruptcy; Lech Walesa who led Solidarity into political power in communist Poland; or Jim Abbott, the one-armed pitcher for the California Angels. Heroic in their determination, these people, and others like them, overcame seemingly insurmountable obstacles to reach peak performance and accomplishment.

Some think that achievement comes from luck and circumstance—being in the right place at the right time. This kind of thinking steals our personal power. It leaves us to be the victim of circumstance. We all encounter opportunity and adversity. It is how we react and use them that determines whether we are successful or not. The Empowered Mind, with a fully developed will, translates any crisis into an opportunity for self-expression.

### Three Steps to a Powerful Will

Although central to our personality, our will can be difficult to understand and develop. First of all, the will is complex, and involves other inner resources, such as self-confidence, self-discipline, and concentration. Second, its power comes from emotional springs which lie deep in our unconscious. Third, there is a bit of a "Catch-22" in developing a powerful will: it takes some will in order to do so. There are three different stages in building a powerful and dynamic will. These are:

- **Building a Foundation.** We establish the initial conditions that allow us to unlock our creative force, and free our mental and physical energy from blocks and distortions. We do this in order to concentrate our power and not dissipate it through stress and conflict.

- **Readiness.** Unshakable self-confidence and integrity are essential elements in the execution of a commanding will. Self-doubts breed hesitancy, and inconsistencies between our values, beliefs and behaviors also dissipate our energy.

- **Execution.** We must be balanced and self-disciplined in order to persist and remain flexible. We must also be able to make decisions, establish priorities and accept responsibilty for our decisions. We strengthen our will by taking action to complete our goals. Inaction, half-hearted attempts, and giving up—all weaken our will, making it more difficult to do the next task that comes before us.

## BUILDING THE FOUNDATION

The word "foundation" signifies the strengths on which all else rests. This is certainly true when we speak of will. Each human mind has inordinate power, but often it lies untapped. Occasionally (and particularly in times of strife) the power to command emerges, and a powerful leader is "born" right before our eyes. This power was always there, but it was not used.

You do not have to wait for circumstance to bring out the best in you. You can systematically develop your will into a powerful force. Three steps are needed to build the necessary foundation for a dynamic will:

1. Create a calm and balanced mind and body, free of stress and disturbance so that our physical and mental energy are not dissipated or diminished by tension and disease.

2. Enhance the power of concentration so you can focus your mind's energy on a particular goal.

3. Develop the ability to manage both internal and external conflict so that your mind does not turn on itself or go in opposite directions.

You have already learned many of the skills necessary to build a firm foundation. In Chapters 3 and 4, you learned how to balance the body and calm the mind. In Chapter 5, you learned techniques for increasing your power of concentration. The next crucial step is to learn how to manage conflict. The reason is very simple: *unmanaged conflict divides and dissipates the energy of our mind and weakens our will.* When one part of your mind struggles with another part, you create a house divided. You literally set your mind against itself when:

- You have competing desires.

- You allow your fears to dissipate your determination, such as when you want to take a certain action, but are afraid of what others will think.

- You struggle with self-doubts and guilt, creating depressed energy conditions.

- You create subtle, unconscious conflicts by acting against deeply held beliefs and values.

All of this leads to conflict in the mind. No matter which side wins, your entire mind has become a battlefield. This weakens your will.

The conflicts you have with others are also destructive. They interfere with your relationships, and add to the problems you must solve. But the conflict you create inside your mind is the most damaging. This internal struggle absorbs mental energy that you would otherwise use to accomplish your goals.

## WILL POWER—THE BATTLE ALREADY LOST

A common mistake is to confuse the use of "will" with "will power." When we create internal conflict, we often try to use "will power" to solve the problem. One part of our mind attempts to impose its decisions or desires on another part. To do so, it must overpower any resistance. But what we overpower is just another part of our own mind. For instance, we exercise our "will power" when we make ourselves get up early, when we try to quit smoking, or go on a diet. Instead of solving the problem by focusing on a positive solution, the mind becomes absorbed in the struggle. All day long we tell ourselves that we are not going to smoke that cigarette, or eat that bowl of ice cream while watching TV. The whole day, meanwhile, we have paid attention to smoking or eating ice cream, reinforcing the very habit we are trying to break.

Instead of using our mental and emotional energy to strengthen resolve, find creative solutions, or maintain effort and direction, we waste it in argument and struggle. No matter which side wins, we lose. In essence, our mind becomes a battleground, and the only sure outcome is stress.

Much of our indecisivness is the result of internal conflict. Instead of reaching conclusions and taking actions, we get stuck as one thought struggles with another. Trying to quit smoking, or break a habit of snacking is difficult because part of our mind desperately wants to continue the habit. By forcing our mind, we are practicing conflict, and this leads to even more conflict. The more conflict we generate, the more difficult it is to exercise our will effectively. We spend more time and effort fighting ourselves than in solving the problem.

We use will, however, when our thoughts, emotions and actions are consistent. When this happens, our determination is complete (no internal conflict), and our mind's energy is directed to one point. Now when we decide to quit smoking, or stop snacking, or to complete a project, we make the decision with our entire mind, and there is no struggle.

With "will power," we only have a partial commitment. The use of will demands total commitment. This does not mean that our mind is suddenly and magically clear of any doubts, worries or competing desires. We may still harbor doubts about whether or not we can complete a project, but we use these doubts to motivate us rather than inhibit us. We can learn how to manage incompatible thoughts and feelings so they do not become conflicts.

The same holds true for interpersonal conflict. Two opponents butt heads, as one person tries to dominate another, or one department in an organization imposes demands on another. Whenever we force our way, we create conflict and problems in our relationships. Instead, we must learn to manage any potential conflict and strengthen our relationships.

Ed, a shop foreman, tells of his experience with two different supervisors. When he first became foreman, his supervisor, Dan, had been with the company for some time. Dan knew the men personally, and got involved with them on several company projects outside of work. Using his own warmth and good humor to solve problems, Dan could diffuse any conflict. He was effective because he did not belittle the complaints and problems of those he supervised. When someone was upset, or had a difficulty, he would listen patiently, allowing the person to express himself completely. Even if he was part of the person's complaint, Dan refused to take it personally. By keeping his ego out of the way, Dan facilitated the communication, and eased the way to resolve the difficulty. Morale was high, and Ed's job as shop foreman was challenging, but very satisfying.

Dan was promoted, and another fellow was brought in to take his place. When Ed aproached his new supervisor with a problem, the new supervisor dominated the conversation. He did not listen to the objections that Ed raised, and ruled by fiat. He would quickly become defensive, cut the person off after a few words, and lay down the rules. Within a few months, Ed's job became much more difficult as the employees began to chafe under what they saw as harsh new disciplines. Union grievances tripled within the first six months of the new supervisor's tenure. Inevitably morale fell and productivity slackened. When managers cannot manage conflict, they cannot manage.

## CONFLICT MANAGEMENT: CHANGING 'WILL POWER' TO A POWERFUL WILL

We can easily manage any conflict situation, whether internal or external, if we understand the key role of *opposition*. All conflict involves opposition, some kind of resistance. To manage conflict, we must know how to prevent opposition or resistance from forming. This does *not* mean that we avoid conflict, or that we become passive. It means that we take charge of our mind and the situation, and *not allow the conflict to dominate*.

The critical difference between Dan and the new supervisor was that Dan could handle conflict without being disturbed. He did not resist the complaints and problems of those he supervised. The new supervisor did not want to hear "disturbing" news, or viewpoints that might be different. But by resisting any negative communication, he immediately intensified the conflicts.

You can easily learn to manage conflict. The keys are relaxation and Breath Awareness. Here are four steps that you can use to manage any conflict situation. They also maximize your ability to resolve any difficulties or problems by helping you maintain a calm and clear mind. I call these four steps the RARE model of conflict management:

1. Relax

2. Accept

3. Restrain

4. Explore

## Step 1: Relax

Tension is part of any conflict. The greater the emotional reaction, the greater the tension. Therapists have long recognized systematic relaxation as one of the most effective tools in dealing with inner conflicts. When we stay relaxed, we take a giant step towards maintaining a calm mind and minimizing conflict.

Tension also characterizes interpersonal conflict. If we even anticipate a conflict, we can become tense. Part of our fight or flight alarm response, tension protects us from being hurt when attacked. However, our tension signals to the other person's unconscious that a battle is imminent. In turn, his unconscious mind reacts by increasing tension, and the emotional intensity starts climbing. Instead of protecting us, our tension actually increases conflict and disturbance.

Your first step is to maintain a relaxed state. To do this during conflict takes a great deal of skill, and you cannot wait until you are under attack to practice relaxation. When face to face with someone who is really angry, it is a bit difficult to say "Excuse me. I must go and practice my relaxation tape for fifteen minutes before you continue."

However, if you practice and become skilled at deep relaxation, you can effectively use the technique of *scanning* to stay relaxed during conflict situations. To scan, mentally go quickly from the top of your head to your toes, and then back up, and relax any tension you find. You can scan in a few seconds time. Do it now. Start at your forehead, and then mentally go down through your face, your neck and shoulders, your torso, and then down your legs to your toes. Relax any tension you find. Then come back to the top of your head. You can stay relaxed during any interaction by occasionally making a quick scan for muscle tension. (This is also an excellent technique to use while at the dentist.) Staying relaxed signals to the other person's unconscious that you are *not* trying to give him a hard time or create any resistance to his communication. At the same time, you maintain a calm and clear mind, which is more flexible and creative, and able to find solutions.

## Step 2: Accept

When you reject a part of your personality, or you repress certain feelings or patterns of thought, you create inner conflict. When you struggle with unwanted habits, feelings and thoughts, trying to push them from your mind, the struggle itself is often more destructive than the "unacceptable" thoughts or feelings.

You can eliminate inner conflict by simply accepting negative thoughts or feelings that come to your mind. If your mind says that you are stupid, incompetent, or a failure, you do not have to go to great lengths to disprove it. It is this struggle that creates conflict and weakens your will. Instead, just accept the thought as a thought, and not vest it with any importance. Then you have robbed it of its power to affect you. It can no longer create a conflict for you, or make you feel bad.

These negative habits of thinking and feeling come from our unconscious. We may not be able to stop thinking them, but no one says that we have to believe them. We can let them pass without giving them attention, without reacting either positively or negatively to them. This is self-acceptance in action.

This same principle operates on an interpersonal level. Have you ever had the experience of wanting to communicate something that you felt was important, and halfway through your first sentence, the person you were talking to started shaking his head "No?" How did that make you feel? Most of us get pretty angry. If you want to really anger someone, and create opposition, just refuse to listen. We do not get nearly as angry when someone disagrees with us as we do when we feel we are not listened to.

On the other hand, you facilitate the communication process when you show that you are listening. You do this by simply nodding your head up and down, and saying "yes" or "OK." This does not mean that you agree with the content, only that you are acknowledging the other person's communication.

In Japan, this acceptance characterizes conversations. When one is listening to another, the listener will nod his head affirmatively and say "Hie" which translates as "yes." This only indicates that he is listening to you. When first encountered by American businessmen, this Japanese characteristic was rather disconcerting. The Americans thought that their Japanese counterparts were agreeing with the content of what they were saying. Until they realized that "Hie" or "Yes" only meant that the Japanese were paying attention, they were at a distinct disadvantage in the negotiations.

Nodding your head up and down and saying "uh-huh" is an old counseling technique. It indicates acceptance of the client by the therapist, and encourages the client to talk about himself. When used in conflict management, it signals to the other person that you are listening to him and accepting his communication.

When the other person has finished talking, you can disagree as much as you like. Most importantly, by not creating any resistance to the communication, you diminish any resistance to accepting your communication. Now whatever you want to say back will be heard, whether your listener likes your response or not.

## Step 3: Restrain

This is potentially the most difficult of the four steps because you must be able to control your emotional reactions. If you want to solve problems, you cannot allow your emotional reactions to distort your perceptions and cloud your thinking. Conflict dissipates your mind's energy, leaving you powerless to focus your attention, and dissipates the clarity you need to use your intellect effectively. Your emotions take over and control your reaction.

The key, as we learned in Chapter 4, is Breath Awareness. By controlling your mind chatter, you minimize and even eliminate internal conflict. You can also use Breath Awareness to control external conflict situations.

By focusing on Breath Awareness when the other person is speaking, you perceive more clearly, and you maintain greater control over your emotional reactions. You can easily sidestep another person's emotional reactions. Some people intentionally attack on a personal level as a manipulative technique. They try to control the situation by provoking an emotional reaction. By managing your mental chatter, you can stay calm and clear, however beserk the person attacking may be. By managing yourself, you manage the situation around you.

## Step 4: Explore

There are always more solutions to any problem than what is first apparent. By keeping a calm, clear mind, you become more capable of solving the real problem without getting sidetracked by emotional issues and ego problems. Conflict situations can be productive. They provide a creative opportunity that leads to new ways of perceiving and performing. But you must be able to manage the conflict situation adequately. If you do not, the consequences may damage both your personal abilities for problem solving and your interpersonal relationships.

## READINESS: BUILDING AN INNER CONSENSUS

To exercise a commanding will demands an extraordinary confidence and sense of purpose. The executive with an Empowered Mind does not permit the aimlessness, doubt and uncertainty that plague an untrained mind and interfere with the exercise of will. Unshakable self-confidence and integrity, a consistent expression of values and purpose, characterize an Empowered Mind.

Our values, beliefs and life goals play a subtle, but critical, role in expressing our will. The consistency between our values, beliefs, and our actions determines the strength of our will. If we have faith in ourselves and believe in what we do, we gain enormous strength. But if we are not genuinely self-confident, or we act in ways inconsistent with our inner nature and beliefs, than the strength of our will is shallow, and quickly compromised.

## THE LEVELS OF SELF-CONFIDENCE

We experience self-confidence on three different levels. Typically, we think of self-confidence as something we acquire by being successful in the world. But this is only the first level of confidence and, unfortunately, the most problematic. John C., a senior manager in a large electronics manufacturing firm, typifies this as he speaks about building confidence in his staff. "We try to set goals for our young trainees that make them stretch, but aren't outside their capabilities. We help program success for them so that they become more confident of their skills and abilities."

It's true that we build some degree of self-confidence by being successful in the world. But there are two hidden problems in this method of building confidence. First, by depending on what happens in the world for our confidence, we get stuck with whatever the world presents to us. We cannot control what happens in the world, and we can never be certain that what we will do will succeed. The universal 10-80-10 Rule applies here:

- 10 percent of the time no matter what you do, you are successful.
- 80 percent of the time your ability to influence events varies. You have some input or control over what happens but the outcome is indefinite.
- 10 percent of the time no matter what you do, you fail.

As a consequence:

- 10 percent of the time you are absolutely confident.
- 80 percent of the time you are insecure, with at least some doubt coloring your level of confidence;
- 10 percent of the time you have no confidence at all.

The 10-80-10 Rule leaves us with only 10 percent real confidence and the rest of the time we are in trouble. If we continue to rely only on what happens in the world to build our confidence, we will always be insecure. At the level of our discriminating mind, we recognize that success is fickle, and this knowledge breeds insecurity. Since we do not really have control over what happens in the world, we feel left to the mercy of fate. We become victims to whatever events happen to us. Very little genuine confidence comes from being a victim, waiting and hoping for someone, or the world, to take care of you.

Even more destructive to our confidence are negative self-concepts. We develop the habits of self-rejection early in our childhood. During childhood, the pain associated with "failure"—people laughing at us, being called names or told that you are somehow inadequate, not good enough—has a much stronger impact on our mind than whatever success we achieve. These destructive habits of self-doubt distort and dissipate our energy, and weaken our will. By the time we enter the work force, the self-defeating attitudes learned in early childhood lead to patterns and ways of thinking that interfere with genuine confidence.

You can strengthen your confidence by setting realistic goals, going about your tasks in a systematic way, and being realistic in the challenges you accept. But the real damage is already done when you engage in self-rejection. The inner chatter of your mind is the real culprit. It prevents self-confidence at every turn. No matter how many times you succeed, there is always the little voice that says you are not good enough, not wealthy enough, not intelligent enough, and so forth.

Fortunately, you can solve both problems by working closely with the language you use. By understanding how your mind defines success and failure, you can build a higher level of confidence. This is not any more difficult than changing the language of your inner chatter. Remember, your mind creates meaning through the language you use. By reframing how you interpret events, you can change how you feel about the situation and yourself.

No matter what we do, we always get some result. When it's not the result we, or someone else, expected, we call it a failure. This superficial evaluation keys the negative programs in our mind, and we feel defeated, sometimes humiliated, and doubtful of our skills. We begin to repeat the language of failure in our mind—"I never get things right," "Something always goes wrong," or "It always happens to me." Now we have begun to program failure. How can our will succeed when so much effort and mental energy goes into negative programming?

Instead of allowing yourself to continue along this unproductive track, clear your mind with Breath Awareness, and then consider your results as information. If you let go of your expectations about what was *supposed* to happen, and deal only with what did happen, you discover that you are in the perfect place to take the next step. Erase the word "failure" from your vocabulary. Failure only exists relative to your expectations, or someone else's. Expectations are fantasies, and not the reality in which we live. But when you use the word "failure" in everyday language, you suffer the emotional consequences it brings. As Shakespeare might have said, "Aye, there's the rub. For what emotions we must suffer when we use this foul word must give us pause."

### Steps to Increased Self-Confidence

A few simple steps will not only bring relief from self-rejection, but increase your level of self-confidence as well.

1. When you start thinking (talking to yourself) negatively, immediately clear your mind with Breath Awareness. Do not allow name-calling and disappointment to continue unchallenged in your mind.

2. Re-interpret the situation in terms of cause and effect. You got results. Examine how they came about rather than judging them as adequate or inadequate, good or bad, successful or unsuccessful.

3. Evaluate how you produced these particular results and modify, if necessary, whatever actions you took. Then take the necessary

actions to produce different results, using what you have learned from the last action.

4. Anytime you find yourself focusing on what you can't do, immediately clear your mind with Breath Awareness. Refocus your attention on what you can do. Avoid repeated attention on what you cannot or did not do.

It takes practice to clear your mind of self-rejection and judgmental language, and to train it to stay focused on possibilities. But it gets easier with practice, and your confidence increases.

## Unlimited Self-Confidence: The Gift We Already Have

There is a secret that only a few people learn. Genuine, unshakable self-confidence actually has nothing to do with what happens in the world. Every one of us has it in abundance, but unfortunately, very few know how to access and benefit from it. It is an innate quality of our balanced mind, the most subtle part of our personality. We bury this natural confidence under a constant barrage of negative inner chatter.

We do *not* have to acquire what we already have. We only need to eliminate the destructive negative chatter throughout our mind so we can become aware of our own inner strength.

This has nothing to do with "positive thinking," but rather with not "thinking" at all. We need to reach into our balanced mind, beyond the level of language, thought and knowledge, and tap the power function of inner harmony and balance. This experience of complete calm, contentment and harmony, lasts only a few moments. But during these few moments, we are completely free of self-doubt and worry. We feel refreshed and renewed, and ready to take on the world. This inner balance is the source of our unshakable self-confidence, available whenever we need it. We only need to become skilled at tapping this inner power.

To tap your inner power, you must create a pathway to it, and make it available for your everyday experience. The key is a deeply quiet and calm mind. *The most effective and efficient method of achieving unshakable self-confidence is the consistent practice of meditation.* You can transform partial confidence into genuine confidence, but only if you take control of your mind and focus your attention on this center of calm and harmony.

The more skilled at meditation you become, the more confidence you gain. You experience this as:

- a more calm and stable mind, less distracted by things going on around you
- fewer emotional swings; things don't bother you as much
- clearer thinking; you can perceive cause/effect relationships more clearly
- more effective/efficient work habits because you focus your attention and energy more effectively

Like a ball rolling down a hill, you will pick up momentum as you become more skillful at meditation. The more effective your mind becomes, the less time you spend on negative chatter, and the more confidence you experience. All of this translates into a much more powerful will as your mind's energies become more efficient and coherent.

### A Confidence Exercise

Use the following exercise to train your mind to remain calm and confident when confronted with difficult situations. Use it anytime you feel pressured, or whenever you need to clear your mind and think clearly.

Begin with the Centering Exercise in Chapter 5. Once centered, watch whatever thoughts arise in your mind. Notice how these thoughts appear around the center of your mind, but not from the center. Then direct your thoughts towards the problem you face. As disturbing thoughts or feelings arise, clear your mind with Breath Awareness, and re-center yourself. Keep returning to the problem until you can watch your mind think about the problem without feeling disturbed or worried. As you remain calm, you will notice that you feel more confident about handling the problem you face. At any point, you can open your eyes and take whatever actions you think necessary to solve the problem.

## INTEGRITY: THE VALUE OF KNOWING YOUR VALUES

Those with a strong will are committed to their value system. They have genuine and humane values within a strong personal philosophy. The productive executive with an Empowered Mind will recognize his or her own humanity, and see himself or herself as part of a greater humanity. The resulting confidence will enable the executive to face incredible odds and overcome any obstacle. People with these qualities are the genuine builders of society. Historical figures such as Martin Luther King, Mahatmas Gandhi, and Helen Keller come quickly to mind. But there are many examples of such people today who have overcome incredible odds and even handicaps to build large and successful corporations.

The story of Horst Rechelbacher, President/Owner of the Aveda Corporation, is a classic story of a genuine entrepreneur. Raised in an impoverished family in Austria, Horst gained a reputation as a master hair stylist in Europe by the time he was twenty-three. At that time, he came to the United States, and settled in Minneapolis where he built a successful chain of salons. Through his personal and professional experiences, Horst became dedicated to establishing an approach to health and beauty care in tune with nature and the environment. Using personal and scientific research, he created the *creme de la creme* of beauty and skin care products, completely natural and free of petroleum by-products. More than any one individual, Horst is altering the entire course of the beauty industry.

In the process, he has created a $60 million corporation that promises to be the industry leader within the coming decade. Under Horst's leadership, Aveda has become an environmentally involved corporation, a sponsor of Earth Day, a cosigner of the Valdez Principles, and a leader in providing environmentally sound packaging and products. Throughout, Horst has maintained his vision of effective, healthy and environmentally sound products. The stated principles by which he leads his corporation are founded on compassion, service and harmony.

A strong will can also be used in destructive ways. A "successful" fanatic, sees the world as *me* (or us) against *them*. Ego-centered in his values, the "successful" fanatic is essentially isolated from deeper human qualities. Fear, not self-confidence, drives his will. This warps the power of his will, and ultimately he destroys rather than builds. His emotional distortions and lack of human spirit eventually defeat him. History is also full of these examples. The Ayatollah Khomeini, Nicolae Ceaucescu, Pol Pot of the Khmer Rouge in Cambodia, and Hitler all overcame obstacles through violence, intimidation and the destruction of their "enemies." They left a legacy of death, destruction, fear and hatred.

The executive with an Empowered Mind moves towards fearlessness and genuine confidence so that the will becomes a positive force for the individual and society. Whether we recognize it or not, we all have a personal philosophy—a set of values, beliefs and experiences which guide the choices we make and influence our behavior. As we grow wiser and more knowledgeable about ourselves and the world around us, our personal philosophy evolves to reflect more humane values and beliefs. This evolving personal philosophy benefits us in the following ways:

1. **A guideline for decision-making.** Our philosophy and life purpose provide a framework for our decisions, direction and goals. If we know what we are about, we naturally channel our energies towards our goal(s). Commitment demands purpose. If we have no purpose, no future to work towards, we won't have the strength to overcome the obstacles in our way.

2. **Conflict resolution.** A personal philosophy provides a framework for choices and priorities, which allows us to resolve many potential conflicts before they are even raised.

3. **A yardstick for measuring progress and personal growth.**

4. **A source of strength.** Few things make us feel as good about ourselves as when we act according to our beliefs. The more we do so, the more confidence we experience. On the other hand, when we go against our own values, the resulting inner conflict damages our self-confidence through guilt, suspicion and distrust.

5. **A ballast, providing stability during times of difficulty, change and challenge.**

Most people spend very little time thinking about the purpose of their lives, or seriously examining their beliefs and values. We usually act on what we learned as children, incorporating the values and beliefs of the culture in which we grew up. But what we learn is not always beneficial. Things like people of a certain color are lazy or only those who practice a certain religion are "saved." Often what we learn includes contradictions, fallacies and mistakes that lead to inner conflicts, cynicism and self-doubt. Unknowingly, we incorporate these into our personal system of beliefs and values. As a result, our personal philosophy becomes a source of weakness instead of strength, and prevents the full expression of our will.

We act with integrity when our values and purpose determine our actions instead of emotional reactions such as fear or greed. Unfortunately, our emotional needs and reactions can overwhelm us, and we act in ways inconsistent with our sense of values. Although we may believe in kindness or generosity, fear and greed can lead to very different behavior. There are plenty of examples: the "televangalists" who amass personal fortunes, builders who substitute inferior materials for specified quality materials, the corporation which sells colored sugar water for baby's apple juice, the White House official who sells his influence to obtain Housing and Urban Development (HUD) grants for wealthy friends.

You can always find examples of wrongdoing in the world. Your challenge is not in what others do, but in what *you* do. You must become sensitive to the inconsistencies in your own life. You must discover where you violate your own principles and become aware of the consequences you suffer. You have the capacity to build integrity into your life, and increase both your self-confidence and the strength of your will. You begin by exploring your own values and priorities. What is it that you really believe in? What is it that you really value? The following exercise can help you answer those questions.

## Discovering Priorities: An Exercise in What Is Important to You

To do this exercise, you need to have a pad and pencil available, and about a half-hour of quiet time.

Imagine that you have only ten days left to live. You will not suffer any pain, but at the end of ten days, you are definitely going to pass away. All the doctors agree: no more miracles left, no reprieve. Now consider carefully just how you want to spend these last ten days of your life. You have the freedom, resources, and opportunities to do anything you like, but you only have ten days.

Write down the things that you will do in these last ten days—what you might say to others, what preparations or actions you would take, writing out whatever you think you would do. After you are finished, go back and review what you have written. This list probably reflects your real priorities.

Now, from what you have written down, make a list of the five most important things in your life. They may be spending time with your family, being happy, having time alone, or gaining knowledge. List them in order of priority. Then list the values that you feel are important in your life, the ones that contribute to your happiness and well-being. Finally, write a few sentences of whatever wisdom you would like to pass on to those you care about.

Now ask yourself: how much effort do you direct to these priorities? How much attention do you pay to the people and things that are important to you? Are you doing what you really want to do? Are you the kind of person you want to be? Do you act on the values and wisdom that you would like to give to others? When your actions are consistent with your own values, purpose and wisdom, how does that make you feel? When they are inconsistent, how does that make you feel?

Now comes the critical part of this exercise. Most of us find that we really spend very little time doing what we really want to do, nor do we always focus on what is most important to us. Caught up in the day-to-day demands of making a living and getting along in the world, we lose sight of our real goals. Keep this list handy. For at least a month, take some quiet time everyday to think about and review what is important to you and whether or not you are moving in the direction you want. The list can serve as a focal point for your thoughts. You may want to keep a notebook handy to serve as a journal for your reflections during this quiet time. Do not short-change yourself. This quiet time is critical. It also facilitates the development of your creative force and intuitive skills. At the end of the month, you should have the habit fairly well established so that a time of reflection becomes part of your everyday life.

A useful supplement to this exercise is to spend a day at work and a day at home as if they were the very last day you would spend there. You may be surprised at how much attention you pay to what you do, and the impact this attention has on the quality of your work and interactions with others.

## EXECUTION: THE STAYING POWER FOR SUCCESS

Few things are as powerful as the habit of success. And habits are built with practice, patience and persistence. No one knows that better than Bob "Doc" Fuller, President of Fuller/Jeffrey in Sacramento, California. Bob started out as a radio announcer in Maine, but was determined to own his own radio station. After years of hard work, mistakes and failures, Fuller/Jeffrey now owns twelve radio stations, several of which lead in their market.

Persistence, the willingness to stay the course until he achieved success, is a consistent theme in Bob Fuller's story—and all success stories. Persistence comes from self-discipline, a key factor in the execution of a successful will. Everyone has some capacity for hard work, but not everyone will discipline himself to maintain the dedicated effort necessary for success.

We have a funny relationship to the word "discipline." Too often we think of self-discipline as forcing ourselves to do something difficult or unpleasant that we do because it's "good for us." Nothing could be further from the truth. Self-discipline means practicing doing what we really want to do. Self-discipline is not magic, nor is it a gift from the gods.

To develop self-discipline, you must consciously use the mind's power of habit formation to systematically build the physical and mental habits that you want.

Remember that we express our entire personality through a complex pattern of habits. Most of these were formed unconsciously in our early childhood. We did not sit down with our parents and plan our emotional, mental or behavioral habits. As we grew up, these habits formed the structure of our personality. And every day we practice these habits as we go about our daily life. For instance, we brush our teeth everyday, which reinforces a very helpful habit of good dental care. But for someone who grew up in a family that did not establish this habit in childhood, daily brushing and flossing would require "discipline" until it became a habit. Such a person might even envy those of us who have the "self-discipline" to brush and floss after every meal.

## A PROGRAM FOR TRAINING SELF-DISCIPLINE

To build self-discipline, you only need to practice choosing and working with the habits you want. You can overcome negative habits by replacing them with stronger, more helpful habits. This is not at all difficult if you keep the process simple and direct, and proceed in the following step-by step fashion.

1. Sit down and decide what you would like to accomplish in the next month, six months, one year, five years and even ten years. (You can project as far as you like, but remember that this is only a projection. Allow for change and personal development which will influence your long-term goals.)

2. Write down whatever factors—time, family support, personal qualities—that you think will help you reach your goals. List the specific things you can do to maximize these factors. Then write down whatever might interfere with reaching your goals and list the things you can do to minimize them.

3. Establish priorities. Decide which basic steps must be taken now in order to begin your program and reach your goals. The more specific you can be, the greater the probability of success. Determine what specific behavior or action you must practice, and how much time you are willing to commit on a daily basis to developing this skill.

The crux of the exercise is simplicity, consistency and persistence.

- Keep your self-training program very, very simple. Make only one or two small changes in your daily routine, and practice these changes until they become habits.
- Do not try to change the world or yourself in a day. Make a reasonable time commitment. A fifteen-minute commitment done consistently provides real benefits whereas an hour done haphazardly will lead to little skill development.
- Persist until you have the habit or skill established. If you finish the smallest of tasks, you strengthen your will. If you do not finish a self-assigned task, you subtly weaken your will.

Now apply the following steps to developing your power of concentration. Your goal will be to develop the behavior and habits that will gradually increase your powers of concentration. If you follow the three steps above, we might end up with the following self-training program.

## A Personal Self-training Program in Concentration

**1. My overall goal:** Increase my power of concentration. I need to learn deep relaxation (freedom from stress and emotional distractions), and practice concentration exercises. By the end of:

- *First month*: Establish diaphragmatic breathing as my normal breathing pattern.
- *Second month*: Become skillful at deep relaxation.
- *Third month*: Practice gaze exercise after doing relaxation.
- *Sixth Month*: Sit comfortably and still for fifteen minutes, focusing on Breath Awareness.
- *First Year*: Have the habit of practicing a concentration/meditation exercise on a daily basis for a minimum of fifteen minutes.

**2. What will help me accomplish my goals:** Set up a specific time for practice; be more careful about my diet, not ingest stimulants (coffee) or depressants (alcohol) at a time which may interfere with my practice; be patient with my progress (I am too much in a hurry at times); ask my spouse to reinforce my efforts by complimenting any progress she (or he) sees; read about others who have helped themselves; listen to motivational tapes on the way to work.

**3. What will interfere with the program:** I hate to follow a schedule;

laziness; feeling like I don't have the time, or not taking the time to do the exercises; not seeing any progress; boredom with the exercise routine. Solutions:

- Vary my schedule somewhat, and not make it too restrictive.
- Set up a system of self-rewards for completing a certain series, or reaching a certain level.
- Set a specific time for practice that has minimal chance for interference.
- Focus on long-term rewards.
- Add a new exercise or focus point when I become bored.

**4. How to establish priorities:**

- *First step:* Read *Freedom From Stress;* make or buy a relaxation tape; practice diaphragmatic breathing for fifteen mnutes before going to sleep, and as often as I can during the day. Length of time: one month
- *Second Step:* Practice relaxation exercise at least once a day lying in the Relaxation Posture. Be aware of breathing as often as I can during the day; take breath breaks at work. Length of time: one month
- *Third Step:* Begin practicing candle gaze after relaxation period. Length of time: one month or until I reach fifteen minutes on the gaze.
- *Fourth Step:* Begin practicing concentration on Breath Awareness for at least fifteen minutes. Daily practice, allowing time spent to increase naturally. After three months, review program to add new steps, such as practicing creative problem-solving, intuition exercises, etc.

The example above is a program for self-development. But you can apply the same methods to develop a work project, build a home, establish a relationship, or to do anything else that you want to accomplish.

## DOUBTING DOUBTS

Nothing interferes more with self-discipline, self-confidence and will than self-rejection and self-doubt. These destructive thoughts pop up in your mind right when you least need them, sowing doubt, hesitation, and the seeds of failure. We can always think of good reasons why we cannot do something, why it won't work, why we should stop trying. The more we listen to these reasons, the more our mind persists in the habit of giving us reasons to fail. After all, we are practicing giving ourselves reasons to fail—and practice makes perfect.

We could analyze why we do this—fear of failure, of trying new things, of not making enough—but no matter how well we analyze and "understand," we still do not accomplish anything. Because the moment we focus on the "can't," we are probably correct—we cannot. In Richard Bach's book *Illusions: Confessions of a Reluctant Messiah,* in the Handbook for Messiahs, there is a beautiful and simple statement of truth: "Argue for your limitations, and sure enough, they are yours."

If your mind has the habit of telling you that you will not be successful, that a project is too hard, that your ideas will not work, *you do not have to listen to it.* Once you decide on a project or goal, and your mind begins its negative chatter, do not accept the doubts as real. Clear your mind with Breath Awareness, and focus attention on what *can* be done. Then replace the negative thoughts with positive thoughts.

The power of positive thinking is not often understood properly. Positive thinking is not just thinking of nice things in order to repress or compensate for negative thinking. With positive thinking you argue for your potential and capacity. The power in positive thinking lies in your ability to focus on what you *can do* as opposed to what you cannot do. Do not to worry about the things you cannot do, you will discover those in plenty of time. Positive thinking is powerful because it directs our mind to fulfill our potential, instead of negating it.

About fifteen years ago, my spiritual Master gave me a lesson I have never forgotten. We were in a small back room of a new building, waiting for his lecture to start. I was gazing about the room, and thinking how unattractive it looked. It was a very modern building, and the ceiling was intentionally left to look like unfinished concrete. While some appreciate this style, I felt that it was rather ugly and unattractive.

Suddenly my spiritual Master turned to me and said, "Isn't that a beautiful ceiling?" Taken aback, I hesitated, not wishing to disagree with him, but finally said, "No, sir, quite frankly, I think that it's rather ugly."

He looked at me and said, "Son, if you look at that ceiling and see beauty, now your mind is filled with beauty. If you look at that ceiling and see ugly, now your mind is filled with ugly. Which do you choose?"

That was positive thinking! We have the power of choice, and what we choose determines whether or not we will be successful. How careful are you of the things that you choose to think about? Are you sure you want the consequences of your thoughts?

At times, you will bite off more than you can chew. And there will be times when no matter what you do, your efforts will not succeed as you want. But so what? If you look upon your results as an opportunity to learn and do better next time, you strengthen your resolve rather than destroy it. By learning from your experiences and making adjustments in your efforts, you can always take the next step and move towards success.

## AFFIRMATIONS—USING MIND POWER

You know that your mind can put up some powerful obstacles in the form of self-doubts and self-criticism. Why not use that power to channel your emotional energy and provide powerful motivation and encouragement? This is what happens when you practice the use of affirmations and positive thinking.

An *affirmation* is a mental/emotional confirmation of our own power, or of the reality you want to bring about. You can create an affirmation with thoughts, images or feelings. Even if you do not feel or experience all of your own power, intelligence and value, you can become more aware of them through affirmations. The more powerful you make your affirmations, the more benefit you gain. Your emotional energy is the power that provides the necessary intensity, and your skill at concentration allows you to focus that intensity in a productive way. *Without focused intensity, affirmations only add to the clutter in our mind.*

All too often, we use affirmations and positive thinking in a mindless way. Simply repeating a positive thought or image in the mind does little but add to the already overcrowded condition in the mind. After all, most of us have had fantasies, dreams and wishes about being wealthy, but how many of these images have come true? To be effective, affirmations must be done in the following ways:

- With a strong desire.

- In accordance with what you really believe and value. This ensures that conflict does not distort or dissipate your emotional energy.

- With concentration, to focus emotional intensity and increase the power of our mind.

- With commitment to the goal: if you do not have your heart in what you are doing, it becomes difficult to persist in the face of obstacles.

Affirmation means confirmation. There are no magic affirmations; there are only thoughts or images that our mind empowers. Below is a list of affirmations that I have found particularly helpful:

- I must do it, I can do it, I will do it.
- I am full of confidence, free of worry and doubt.
- I am responsible, able to learn from any situation.
- I am undisturbed by emotional distractions, free of pain and worry.
- Fear is a thought. I will face my fears, let them pass through without resistance, and when they have passed, only I will remain.

Use one of these affirmations, or create one of your own, and practice it for one month. At least once a day, at a time when you will not be bothered, take a few moments to relax, then do the following exercise.

### Using Affirmations Successfully

Begin with the Centering Exercise in Chapter 5. Then focus your attention on the affirmation. Allow your entire mind to be filled with the affirmation until you actually feel the confidence and calm indicated by the words. Once you feel the emotional aspect of the affirmation, clearly picture yourself going through the day, doing your tasks in this calm and focused state. If the affirmation is specific to a particular task, clearly picture yourself completing the task. Spend 5 to 10 minutes every day concentrating on the affirmation and its reality in your daily life.

During the day, any time you begin to have doubts, take a few moments to clear your mind and focus on the affirmation. Do not work with more than one affirmation for any one period of time, whether a week, a month, or longer. Stay with one affirmation until you feel confident of its power in your life.

## WILL—THE UNDENIABLE FORCE

To repeat the quote by Victor Hugo at the beginning of this chapter, "People do not lack strength, they lack will." We have all the resources necessary for a powerful and beneficial will. Through our will we project the incredible power of our inner resources. Without it, we remain impotent and unfulfilled.

You must develop these resources and become skillful with your will. It is not easy - in fact, it's a life-long task. Developing your will requires dedication, effort and skill, the very things that will provides for you. That may seem like a "Catch 22"—you need will in order to develop it! But we all have some degree of will, and we all can start where we are and take the next step.

## SUMMARY OF PRINCIPLES

1. Will is a conscious choice, the ability to marshall all of your resources to achieve your goals.

2. There are three steps to build a strong foundation for will:
   - a calm and balanced body;
   - enchanced power of concentration;
   - increased ability to manage conflict.

3. Unmanaged conflict divides and dissipates the energy of your mind and weakens your will.

4. Will and will power are different. We use will power when we feel like we must force something to happen. Will power implies conflict. We use our will when our thoughts, emotions and actions are consistent. Our energy is directed to a single point.

5. Using the RARE model, you can learn to manage any conflict situation: RARE stands for: Relax, Accept, Restrain, Explore.

6. Self-confidence can be built on three levels. Unshakable self-confidence comes from your inner strength. This is an innate quality of your Balanced Mind, the fifth level of your personality.

7. The most effective and efficient method of achieving unshakable self-confidence is through the consistent practice of meditation.

8. Your will is strengthened when you act with integrity. You act with integrity when your values and purpose, not emotional reactions such as fear or greed, determine your actions.

9. The execution of will depends on self-discipline. Self-discipline simply means practicing doing what you really want to do.

10. You can develop self-discipline by using the mind's power of habit formation in a systematic and conscious way.
11. Your will can be focused through affirmations and imagery. Your ability to use imagery effectively depends on the strength of your desire and the power of your concentration.

# Love, Performance, and Productivity: Bringing Spiritual Skills to Work

## 9

*When love and skill work together expect a masterpiece*
*—John Ruskin*

The inner skills of the mind bring knowledge, power and influence. But in and of themselves they are incomplete, and can even be used destructively. They can be wielded in manipulative, abusive and even tyrannical ways. Power untempered by the human spirit corrupts. If we end our personal journey with only the tools of our mind, we remain tragically incomplete.

There is still one final level to master in the quest for an Empowered Mind: the power of the human spirit. Only the full expression of our human spirit brings genuine success in life, as it is the basis for our happiness and fulfillment.

We can be financially, politically, creatively or socially successful, and still be discontent, unhappy and lonely. In fact, personal misery seems all too often a secret bedfellow to what appears to be a sparkling, successful life. Material success doesn't count for much if we are not successful as human beings. If we are not happy and do not find life joyful, if we do not feel loved and accepted, if we feel insecure and constantly worry, if we do not have the freedom to express ourselves, or if we lose our curiosity and our desire to learn and grow, then we have very little of worth no matter how wealthy we are.

In a recent address to the Congress of the United States, Vaclav Havel, the playwright who rose to become president of a democratized Czechoslovakia, spoke eloquently about the power of the human heart. In speaking of what he has learned from his struggles for freedom, Mr. Havel said that "the salvation of this human world lies nowhere else than in the human heart, in the human power to reflect, in human meekness and in human responsibility."

We have the knowledge and means to fulfill the power of our mind. To be complete, however, we must also fulfill the power of our heart.

We often do not recognize the enormous power and practical application of spiritual qualities in our daily life. As a consequence, we often isolate our finest human qualities from the world of work. A friend of mine, the CEO and president of a large corporation in the communications industry, was talking about his plans for an early retirement. "I want to contribute to making the world a little better place. I want to retire early, go back to school, and become a nurse. In this way, I can be of some genuine service to those around me." Another friend—a senior executive in a Fortune 500 firm—spoke about retiring early to become a priest in order to dedicate part of his life to service. Still another sold a successful garment industry company to become a social worker. All shared the same desire to make the world a better place. What is striking is that *they all felt that they had to leave the world of business in order to make a serious contribution to human welfare.*

Many of us feel strongly that we would like to leave the world better off as a result of our efforts. But there is a pervasive belief that if you want to provide genuine service to humanity, you have to leave business. Both within the business community and outside of it, a strong mind-set exists that business and service to humanity do not mix, and that any commitment to the betterment of the community or the world is much less important than bottom-line profits and the accumulation of power. This narrow and limited mind-set prevents us from bringing the immense power of our humanity into our work.

This mind-set, in turn, plays into an even greater problem. Increasingly, we rely on technology to make decisions that need human compassion and understanding. We create products that increase the bottom line but poison the air we breathe or the ground which grows our food. When we do this, then human beings stand in service to technology and profits rather than technology and profits standing in service to human beings. Instead of using the system to satisfy human needs and solve our problems, we become part of the system and lose our humanity.

Profits and human welfare, technology and human happiness, self-expression and the common good do not have to be in conflict. They are *not* inherently incompatible. But when we focus on profit and power at the expense of human values, we only lose. In the age of information technology, nothing is more critical for success than human qualities, and the ability to work in harmony with ourselves, our society and our world. Look at these important human skills that information technology demands of ourselves and organizations:

- **Flexibility:** Faster response times require mental and emotional flexibility, which in turn requires autonomy, respect for other viewpoints, and a willingness to take chances.

- **Networking:** Cooperation between a service organization, its suppliers and customers means cooperation between different people, points of view, needs and wants, even cultures.

- **Teamwork:** It takes a variety of backgrounds and perspectives to develop the broadest and most creative alternatives to meet challenges and solve problems. This demands openness to, and encouragement of, differences.

- **Service Orientation:** Service requires attention to customer needs instead of corporate needs. Service also means service to others within an organization. Employees must know that leadership values them as an integral part of the organization.

- **Values-driven:** Compassion, integrity and cooperation result in personal and professional excellence because they increase personal effectiveness and better relationships with co-workers and customers. Leaders and executives must demonstrate strong ethical and moral leadership as well as effective problem-solving abilities.

- **Smaller Work Force:** Competition for a qualified workforce will be fierce. While some third world countries have an excess of people, the countries of the developed world face a shortage of skilled workers. This makes for an employee's market. Thus, the work conditions and attitudes at a company either attract competent workers, or make them look elsewhere.

Our human, or spiritual qualities, allow us to work with others effectively and efficiently. These qualities form the foundation for excellence. Teamwork, morale, even individual personal effectiveness, all depend heavily on the skillful application of our spiritual qualities. Above all, the Empowered Mind personifies this human spirit, the qualities of cooperation, compassion, and concern, that represent the finest aspects of our humanity. These qualities emerge from our innate capacities for experiencing wholeness and community, humility, and love.

## COOPERATION: THE EXPERIENCE OF WHOLENESS/COMMUNITY

The most sophisticated organization in the world is our personality, where body and mind work together. No other organization—whether a family, a corporation, an agency, or a government—functions as efficiently or as effectively as our own personality. All the levels, functions, and systems of our personality work together, doing whatever is necessary to maintain the personality and its needs and wants. Each part, organ and function serves the whole organism, and is served by the whole organism. The personality is a model of interdependency and cooperation.

But what would it be like if our body functioned on a competitive basis—our liver fighting our stomach; our heart trying to limit the influence of our lungs; our brain intimidating the spine; or our limbs going on strike? Can you imagine the struggle and difficulties? How much could we accomplish then?

Our very first lesson is cooperation—working together to create a wholeness much greater than the sum of our individual parts. We begin our life through the cooperative effort of a male and female, and on a more basic level, through the egg and sperm. This initial cooperative effort gives birth to a complete person, an integrated unit, not a bunch of individual pieces that can be added or subtracted.

This principle of cooperation operates throughout nature as a fundamental law of life and organization. One species depends on another, all species depend on the eco-system, and all eco-systems are interrelated. In a family, we depend on each other to make the family a place of joy and peace. In a corporation, sales depends on marketing, marketing depends on product development, product development depends on manufacturing, manufacturing depends on sales. The more complex the system, the greater the interdependency and the more cooperation needed to make it all work together effectively.

In infancy, in play, in creating a family, in building a business, in maintaining a healthy environment—all aspects of our life are involved somehow in a cooperative effort. We have a natural capacity for cooperation, and for experiencing the powerful feelings of wholeness and satisfaction that cooperation brings. Belonging to something greater than ourself is very powerful and motivating. We find strength when we are united. The thrill of victory is sweeter when shared, and the disappointment of losing is more bearable.

For example, loyalty is a strength for any business, whether it's a loyal and dedicated work force or a loyal customer base. But loyalty cannot be forced, nor can it be bought. Contrary to popular belief, money plays little part in creating loyalty. One entrepreneur paid the highest salaries in the business. He was convinced that high salaries would create dedicated and hard working employees. Instead, his business suffered from low morale and a high turn over. The office was riddled with politics. Decisions were made in secret, and he constantly played one employee against the other. This created an atmosphere of rampant blame, frequent arguments, and distrust between individuals and between departments.

As a result, few friendships were formed within the corporation and there was no sense of community. Despite the high salaries, it was no wonder that talented people could hardly wait to leave.

In modern corporations, loyalty is in very short supply. Internal competition, conflict between management and labor, superiors who are "out for themselves," and corporate policy that does not respect individual needs and concerns, all breed disloyalty. The cynicism found in American companies is a clear sign of this. Phil Mirvus, author of *The Cynical Americans*, found that fully 80 percent of the work force doubts the truth of what management tells them. Disloyalty, apathy, and self-serving occur because we do not experience ourselves as part of a larger whole. In other words, we have no sense of community in the workplace.

Cooperation and the experience of community go hand in hand. We develop loyalty when we feel that we belong, that we play an integral role within the group or organization. Where cooperation is limited, loyalty is in very short supply as the Communist leadership in Eastern Europe discovered to their dismay. The power of togetherness is dramatically demonstrated by freedom movements that occur in all cultures—with Gandhi in India, in Czechoslovakia with Havel, with Solidarity in Poland, and in the United States with Martin Luther King.

Isolation, fear, mistrust, and loneliness destroy our sense of community and capacity for wholeness. We cannot genuinely share and cooperate with others when we don't experience our own wholeness and inner strength. The more we "look out for number one," or become preoccupied with our own personal issues, the less capacity we have to share. We grow even more isolated and alone.

## BUILDING COOPERATION

The greater our inner strength, the greater our capacity to cooperate and share. The first step is to minimize whatever interferes with this natural capacity. The following factors create divisive emotions and isolate us from each other:

**Fear:** The more fearful we are, the more difficult it is to reach out to other people. The very walls we build to protect ourselves also isolate us, and prevent us from experiencing any sense of belonging or community. When we regard others with suspicion and distrust, it's difficult to share and cooperate. We see this in corporations where people are afraid to tell their boss the truth, or where a manager is afraid of hiring someone better than himself.

**Self-rejection and lack of self-respect:** When we judge ourselves harshly, we judge others harshly. If we do not respect ourselves, we will not respect others. The more critical we are, the less comfortable others feel around us. In any setting, criticism and personal invective antagonizes and creates barriers. If we do not respect others, we can never gain respect.

**Stress:** Under pressure, we revert to more rigid and defensive behaviors, lose our flexibility to respond, and our behavior becomes more disruptive. Executives who manage through stress, fear and intimidation dramatically reduce the effectiveness of their employees. The employees become less creative, less willing to excel, and suffer lower morale and greater absenteeism.

**Dependency:** Dependency actually interferes with cooperation and a genuine sense of community. When we feel incomplete and insecure, and depend on others to make us whole, we set up expectations and demands that lead to disappointment and resentment. Creative problem solving requires independence of thought, and the freedom to take responsible actions. When the parent, or the boss, makes all decisions, growth is limited, and individual performance becomes stunted.

**Beliefs and values:** The more rigid and narrow our belief system, the less flexible, creative, open-minded and tolerant we become. The fears generated by issues of "us" vs. "them"—whether between different factions in a department, divisions of a company, members of a family, or between cultures and countries—lead to distrust and hostility. Extremism, founded on prejudice and fanaticism, destroys cooperation. The greater our capacity to accept alternative viewpoints, the greater our capacity for progress and creative problem solving.

## Personal Empowerment

The productive executive with an Empowered Mind can build inner strength and unlimited confidence through a consistent practice of meditation. As our confidence grows, so does our recognition of the fundamental unity of the human family. We experience this as a sense of wholeness and community, a recognition that we all belong to the same family of life. This is the experience that allows us to "love our neighbor as ourselves."

Through meditation, we experience a profound sense of peace and tranquility, and become aware of our inner strength. From this vantage point, we can take command of our personality and its resources. In more practical terms, we can become so strong that we can allow others around us to be strong. And since the source of our power comes from within, we do not have to control our external environment in order to feel secure or in control of our life. We have the flexibility to explore alternative solutions, discover new ways of doing things, and allow others the freedom to express themselves.

## Empowering Others: Building Community

Out of our personal empowerment, we empower others. Kim Breese, the Chief Administrative Officer for Dow Jones, exemplifies this kind of strength in his management approach. When a subordinate approaches him with a problem, Kim engages him, or her, in a discussion about the problem and possible alternatives. They discuss the problem thoroughly, and Kim brings out points and counterpoints that occur to him. Then he asks his subordinate what he or she thinks should be done. After listening to the employee articulate a solution, Kim simply says "Why don't you go and do that?" By allowing the direction to come from his subordinates, Kim empowers them, and provides them the opportunity to make their own decisions and grow from the experience.

Many of us have experienced the opposite approach—a parent who dominates the life of a child, the teacher who stifles originality of thought, the boss who can't allow his management team to make their own decisions. Fearful that they might lose control, these frightened individuals insist that their way is the only way. In one company where I briefly served as a consultant, the boss would rant and rave how no one took responsibility; but then would dictate to his management team exactly what it was supposed to do. If someone took an independent action, he or she was subject to verbal abuse in front of peers, and in a few cases, fired on the spot. Ultimately, the management team became afraid to question or contradict any proposed course of action, and difficult problems were swept under the rug because no one would take the risk of bringing bad news to the boss.

If parents do not empower their children, the children learn dependency and grow up not trusting themselves. If a teacher does not empower his students, they never learn to think independently or creatively. If the boss or manager does not empower others, problems remain unsolved, and cooperation withers. Consensus-building depends on the inner strength of the manager: his ability to listen to divergent points of view, to allow others to discover their most effective solutions, and to provide an atmosphere where mistakes are utilized as opportunities, not as focal points for punishment and negative examples. Then leadership becomes an orchestration of a variety of talents and ideas, providing the widest possible base for problem-solving, and ensuring a high level of morale and loyalty.

Ben and Jerry's Homemade Inc., a Vermont premium ice cream company, represents one such business. The owners, Ben Cohen and Jerry Greenfield, have built a successful company on the principles of cooperation, sharing and product excellence. Recognizing the importance of supporting the wider community of which they are a part, 7.5 percent of their pre-tax profits go to an employee-chosen worthy social cause. Within the corporation, no one, including the CEO, can earn more than five times the lowest salaried employee. This is quite radical given that the average CEO salary is a bloated ninety-three times larger than the average U.S. factory worker's. At Ben and Jerry's this approach is not to minimize earnings for executives, but rather to create an equitable sharing of profits throughout the company. Any executive is free to earn as much as they can from increasing profits, but only as long as he or she brings along all the people in the company who help make those earnings possible. Needless to say, both morale and productivity are high.

## An Exercise in Empowerment

The increasing emphasis on team building in corporations reflects the need for cooperation in the age of information technology. In any effective team, the critical elements are communication and cooperation. Team building does not deny the importance of leadership. Rather, it allows leadership to function most effectively. As William Torbert points out in *Executive Mind, Timely Action,* an important sign of executive greatness is the "capacity to generate more than one great team during the executive's career." Leadership does not mean doing the work yourself, it means developing and leading a cooperative effort. This demands the personal strength to empower others.

Creating an atmosphere that encourages and empowers others is much easier than creating an atmosphere of distrust and hostility. We only need to create a an environment that allows our natural cooperative nature to express itself. As shown below, the process can be broken down into four elements.

## Four Critical Elements to Creating Positive Relationships

**1. Sincerity:** A genuine acceptance of, and caring for, yourself and others. This also means the ability to control your expectations, and be realistic about the strengths and weaknesses of your colleagues.

**2. Integrity:** Saying what you mean and meaning what you say. People trust consistency. A dedication to honesty and candor builds solid relationships. We do not have to agree with one another, but we do have to trust that we both mean what we say.

**3. Attention:** One of the most powerful ways to create a positive relationship is also the most simple: *pay attention.* No one likes to feel ignored, taken for granted, or dismissed as unimportant. This is particularly true during any communication. Using the RARE model in Chapter 8 and Breath Awareness, train yourself to give complete attention to the person before you. Skilled attentive listening generates significant dividends in both information and good will.

**4. Positive Reinforcement:** "You catch more flies with honey than with vinegar." The value of reinforcing strengths is as well known as the destructiveness of constant criticism. We all respond to recognition and encouragement. By building on strengths, we also create a reservoir of good will to draw upon when criticism is necessary.

Here is a simple technique that has a strong, positive effect on your own mind as well as the people around you.

## Reinforcing Strengths

At least once a day, find some action to compliment in those who work for you and with you. The compliment must be genuine, and must reflect a real appreciation for the action. Be direct, to the point, and brief. Do not miss a single day. If you cannot find a praiseworthy action one

day, then choose a quality, such as persistence, thoughtfulness, cheerfulness, and so forth. But avoid repeating the same compliment day after day. Repetition can lead to insincerity, or may at least make you *seem* insincere.

This exercise will reinforce the qualities that you praise, and create a positive exchange between you and your staff, or whoever you compliment. While this will have a positive impact on how they feel about you, it will have an even stronger impact on your own mind. It will:

- Create an appreciation of this person in your mind;
- Develop your sensitivity to the strengths of those around you, allowing you to utilize them more effectively;
- Create a positive state of mind for yourself.

HUMILITY: THE POWER OF A HEALTHY EGO

It is not easy to speak of humility to people who are constantly told that they must be the best! When we hear or see the word "humble," we think of meekness, of a lack of drive, even of someone who plays doormat to the rest of the world. After all, life can be tough, and it's a competitive world out there. The idea that humility might have something to do with personal power and effectiveness seems more than a little soft-headed.

Genuine humility has little relationship to meekness, or passivity, however. Probably the rarest of all inner skills, humility is one of our most powerful qualities. Like the other mind skills, humility arises naturally from inner strength and health. It has its origin in the sense of awe that we experience when we participate in the birth of a child, gaze at the stars, experience the power of a thunderstorm, or stand on a high ridge and look at the mountains. Humility is the recognition that we are one small but integral part of a reality that is far larger, more profound and mysterious than our ego.

Think about the time when you were in an audience listening to musicians who really "put it all together" and gave the performance of their lives. The audience was part of this experience, and felt the same thrill and wonder that the musicians themselves felt. How did that make you feel? Was it a remarkable experience? You were actually a part of something transcendent. As you left the hall, you felt a kinship with everyone there. There was no longer any need to feel more important than the next person. Everyone was part of the marvelous experience.

If we ignore or limit this inner sense of awe, we limit ourselves to a very narrow view of the world, and cut ourselves off from new and rewarding

experiences. We build barriers through defensiveness about our ignorance, and through fear of being found out. The more fearful we are, the
weaker our ego, and the more effort it takes to prop it up. Nothing is more
pathetic than the person who already knows it all, and cannot say "I don't
know." When we cannot admit to our limitations, they enslave us.

## Humility and Curiosity: The Desire to Know

Our natural sense of awe stimulates our curiosity and allows us to
learn, to appreciate other ways of living, and to be tuned to the rhythms
of life around us. Despite all our sophistication and accomplishments, we
still command vast areas of ignorance. By recognizing this, we open
ourselves to the desire to learn, to explore, to grow. This desire for
knowledge is in every human child. We call it "curiosity." When we allow
our curiosity to grow and flourish, we learn, grow and flourish. But once
we believe that we already know it all, we stop growing and stagnate.

Curiosity leads directly to enhanced personal power and understanding, and greater wisdom. Without humility, we are not curious, and
we do not learn.

## I Am, Therefore I Think: The Ego Faculty

Humility has to do with our ego, and we all have one. Most of us
are all too familiar with the ego, particularly when the one in question is
someone else's. The term "big ego" makes us immediately think of people
who reek of self-importance, and who need to always have the biggest
and best. We speak of inflating and deflating egos, building egos, leaving
egos behind, even destroying someone's ego. At times we are egotistical
or egocentric, and some of us become egomaniacs. Most of the time when
we speak of ego, we speak negatively.

Yet the ego performs a critical boundary function. It defines what
does and does not belong to the bundle of habits we call a personality. Our
ego provides our sense of "I-ness." It defines one's self as distinct and
unique from the rest of the world. This is "my" book, "I" wrote it, not you,
not the editor, not anyone else. So "I" am responsible for what's in the
book. If my ego is threatened, I will not listen to your comments. After
all, if you know so much, write your own book. However, if my ego is
strong, I can listen to your comments and see if I cannot use them to make
this an even better book. But my ego still "owns" the book. The writing
belongs to this individual called "Phil," not Tom, Dick, or Harry.

The ego also functions as a manager, supervising the operations of
the mind in order to sustain and enhance the total organization. It directs

the sensory mind's organization of sensory data, deciding what is important and what isn't, and it decides when to use instinctual and intuitive knowledge. The ego's job is to oversee operations and make sure that the activities of the mind and body are properly integrated.

But do we use our ego, or does our ego use us? Its important managerial function becomes destructive when the ego comes to believe that it is the owner, and not the manager. It then directs all efforts towards its own gratification, and begins to act as if it is the only important thing in the world. When this happens, a manager mistreats his subordinates, a politician maneuvers for greater power, an actor becomes childish and self-centered, and a parent thinks only of how his child's behavior or accomplishments reflect on him. When our ego considers itself the owner, we have real problems.

The world is full of individuals caught in a spiraling need to have more and more. Their inflated egos eventually lead to their destruction. J. Paul Getty's disintegration is a classic tale of misguided fears and needs. John Belushi and Janis Joplin, both with great creative talent, were destroyed by drugs and their inability to handle fame and fortune. Ivan Boesky is a financial wizard whose name has become synonymous with greed and excess, and who has ended what appeared to be a brilliant career with a jail sentence.

As adults, we operate with habit patterns established in early childhood. These habit patterns inevitably include some negative self-concepts that interfere with our success and happiness, and we may struggle with these glitches in our personality for years. They may be ego-deflating thoughts, such as "If they really knew how little I really know" or "I'll never be successful (enough)" or "If only I were better looking (smarter, thinner, richer, etc., etc)." Or these habits may be feelings, such as anxiety, worry, or depression. Sometimes they appear as images, and we picture ourselves as failing, being ridiculed, put down, or hurt. These patterns carry powerful negative emotional charges. To compensate, we turn to ego-gratification, which only creates more problems.

This is what neurosis is all about. We must remember that our ego also includes the bad habits of our mind as well as the good ones. When we feel bad about ourselves, we do something to try and create some good feelings. Often we use pleasure as a way to feel good about ourselves. We might eat when we feel lonely, or go on a shopping spree when our spouse rejects us, or find a new lover when we have problems in our relationship.

Unfortunately, while these distractions give us some pleasure, they do not really solve the problems we face.

Our ego may also inflate itself with thoughts such as "No one can do this as well as me, so I'll have to do it myself," or feelings of snobbishness, superiority and "holier than thou." We seldom realize that an inflated ego is really an over-reaction to a weak ego. There is no such thing as a superiority complex. It is an inferiority complex in disguise, trying desperately to compensate. Weak egos also compensate through excessive control and manipulation: an endless need to make bigger and better deals; an endless search for ever more power, money and prestige. Unfortunately, inflating our ego never really resolves the feelings of inferiority; it only makes them stronger and even more difficult to overcome.

## Ego: The Biggest Problem in Life

Problems are puzzles to solve, and we have all the resources necessary to do so. Problems require our intelligence and skill, but by paying attention we can always find solutions. The really difficult problems in life are ego problems. Building fiefdoms, carving out empires, protecting one's tail-end, personality conflicts—all are ego expressions that create conflict, even wars, inhibit personal effectiveness, and make problems very difficult to solve.

For example, a manager secure in her own skills and knowledge encourages her staff to bring in new ideas and new ways of doing things. An insecure manager protects her position by consciously or unconsciously discouraging innovation and risk-taking by her staff. When confronted with this behavior, the insecure manager indignantly denies this, swearing that she fully encourages people to try new things and takes risks. Her ego needs prevent her from even recognizing the problem, let alone resolving it.

A strong ego will seek out role models in order to enhance its skills and performance. A person with a weak ego has difficulty learning from others, and thus expanding his knowledge base. An inflated ego creates problems that interfere with genuine learning, thereby dismissing the opportunity to learn from a role model since it already knows more than that person, anyhow. Someone with a deflated ego will put the role model on a pedestal, and will either spend the rest of the time in a dependency role, or in taking pot-shots at the person on the pedestal to try and knock him off.

## The Qualities of a Strong Ego

Having a strong ego does not mean that we will not have weaknesses or problems. No one is perfect! But a genuinely strong ego has the capacity to (1) integrate weaknesses and (2) focus effort on building strengths. A STRONG EGO is:

- **Strong:** free of fear and self-rejecting patterns of thought.
- **Truthful:** unafraid to see and deal with reality as it is.
- **Relates to others:** compassionate, concerned, able to form deep and satisfying relationships.
- **Open:** innovative, willing to explore new experiences, different ways of seeing the world, willing to learn new ways;
- **Non-manipulative:** lets others take the lead when appropriate, able to give genuine friendship—does not demand that others behave or believe in a certain way;
- **Giving:** able to give of himself; unselfish; generous mind.
- **Experimental:** A risk taker; free to meet challenges head-on, and free to walk away when necessary;
- **Goal oriented:** Expresses skills and abilities coherently, persists until the goal is achieved, and still maintains the necessary flexibility to change.
- **Observant:** sensitive to others and to the currents and rhythms of life.

## Five Steps to a Strong Ego

We build a strong ego through self-discipline and training. The key, as always, is to discover our own inner strength and confidence. We must strengthen the role of ego as a manager, not as an owner. To do this, we can place the ego in a position of service, where it shares with others the decision-making power. The following five steps can start the building process:

**1. Undertake a course of study under a master—** in art, martial arts, astronomy, mathematics, language—whatever interests you. Recognition of superior knowledge and skills, and willingness to place yourself in a position of respectful learning, provide excellent training for the ego. For example, martial arts training incorporates specific forms and expressions of respect for the teacher and other students as part of the discipline.

**2. Practice letting others find the "right" solution**—You do not always have to have things go your way. There are a thousand and one ways to solve any problem. By allowing others to be in control, make decisions, determine direction, you not only train the ego, but benefit from gaining new perspectives and alternative ways of solving problems. This also contributes to the development of an effective executive team, one in which all members feel and take responsibility for the welfare of the entire organization, enterprise or community.

**3. Spend time with the vastness of nature**—in the mountains, on the sea, looking at the night sky. Cultivate the sense of awe and wonder. Outward Bound activities, for instance, offer transforming experiences because of nature's power to bring inner harmony and balance. Participants report that their sense of teamwork, of community, and of personal satisfaction are enhanced by participating in shared activities so close to nature.

**4. Practice genuine charity**—Give anonymously of resources, time and effort. Many of us are generous as long as it benefits someone we know, such as family, or an organization to which we belong, such as our church. Or we give because we can get a tax break, or gain some recognition for our good deeds. While all charity benefits someone or something, only when we are free enough to give without benefit to ourselves do we loosen the hold of our ego. Genuine charity is a gift to ourselves. It loosens the limits imposed by the need for ego gratification.

**5. Practice saying no**—All too often we go along with someone only because we have a need to be liked, and want this person to think well of us, or at least, not be angry with us. When we do this, we not only reinforce this weakness in our ego, we also create an inner state of resentment and anger. This resentment can poison any relationship. There is a very simple rule: **Do only what you really feel like doing; give only what you can freely give.** Gradually, you will realize that you are genuinely free to do what you choose. This will end resentment and minimize fear in your life. The other side of this rule is: **Whatever you do, do freely and completely.** If you decide to do something, free yourself of any doubts, and do not keep wishing that you did not have to do it. Practice being 100 percent in everything you do.

The most powerful and direct way to gain humility and to experience wholeness and a sense of community is to learn the art of loving. Love is the most powerful of all human qualities, and of all the innate skills of the mind, the most talked about, and the least understood.

# LOVE: THE FINAL POWER

Love plays a powerful role in our life, but most of us have an extremely limited view of love. We must expand our understanding and experience of love. **In its most powerful form, love is the expression of selflessness, the ability to give to another.** That giving may be to children, to our partner, to colleagues, to customers, even to strangers. Love is a force that we *express,* not something that we try to take for ourselves.

The enormous power of love to transform an individual, a situation, or an organization stems from the expression of selflessness. Occasionally, we experience this power, but do not clearly recognize what is happening. Our needs, problems and wants distract us, and we do not understand the role that selflessness plays. So we miss out on the power we have to build satisfying personal and professional relationships.

Selfless love releases us from limitations of our ego. The more loving we become, the less limited we are. We can understand this if we analyze the nature of pain. Whenever we experience pain, whether physical or psychological, we also experience a boundary or limit. Ask someone who has physical pain where it hurts, and they will always point to a specific area. Those who suffer from chronic pain, which medication or surgery can no longer help, learn to eliminate the pain by visualizing and then eliminating the boundary lines around the pain. Once you eliminate the boundary around the pain, the pain no longer exists.

This is done in a number of different ways, but usually involves relaxation, concentration and imagery. By mentally restructuring how we experience the pain, we alter our experience of it. With practice and skill, we can resolve any pain problem. I often use the following exercise to talk people out of headache pain. Usually the headache is gone within a few minutes.

## Pain Release Exercises

These exercises can minimize and even eliminate headache or any other kind of pain. The more complex or involved the pain, the more skill is required. It will help if you have another person take you through the exercise, or record the exercise on a tape, and listen to the tape.

## Shrinking Headache Exercise

Sit quietly, let your breath become very smooth and even........Picture your forehead becoming very smooth and even, all the lines and bumps becoming as smooth as a piece of glass.........Bring your attention to your breath at the opening of your nostrils.......Clear you mind by focusing on Breath Awareness, concentrating on the feeling of coolness of the inhalation and the feeling of warmth of the exhalation at the opening of your nostrils......Now tell me how long is your headache (indicate by using your hands or by telling me in inches)......How wide is your headache?...............How deep is your headache?........... What shape is your headache (round, square, triangle, oblong, etc.)?.......What color is your headache?.................Now clear your mind with Breath Awareness.

After a few moments, again repeat the questions. Continue alternating the questions with Breath Awareness until the headache or other pain is gone.

By forcing the mind to step back and describe the headache in measurement terms, you are breaking your identification with the pain and forcing the boundaries of the pain to change. When the limitations that define the pain change, the pain must also change. In the next exercise, we systematically alter the images of the boundaries that come to our mind. By changing these images, we can often eliminate the pain.

## Imagery Release Exercise

Sit quietly, and relax your body as much as possible..... Picture your forehead as smooth as a piece of silk...........Bring your attention to Breath Awareness for a few moments and clear your mind of all thoughts and concerns............Now direct your attention to the pain that you feel..........What kind of image comes to your mind?..........Is it a knotted rope, or a dark hole?..........Let your mind give you a picture of the pain............As soon as you have a clear picture of the pain, try changing the picture to allow yourself more flexibility, or space, or size........If you picture a knot, then loosen the knot.....If an image of a tight fist came to your mind, slowly open the fist in your mind..........If there was a black hole, slowly introduce light into the hole......... If there was a fence around the pain, begin to take down the fence...........do whatever you can to alter the image, making it more open, more accessible, lighter................after a few moments of working with the image, clear your mind with Breath Awareness...........After a few moments of Breath Awareness, repeat the process, and continue working with the images and clearing your mind until the pain is minimized or eliminated.

## Love: Letting Go of Self-imposed Limitations

There is no difference between physical pain and psychological pain. Just as physical pain is characterized by limitations, we create psychological pain by imposing limitations on ourself. We believe that we cannot be successful, or that awful things will happen to us, or that we will always be lonely. Or we accept negative judgements about ourself, and we worry about what others think of us. These limiting thoughts create pain for us. When we allow them to define our self-image and our value as a human being, we stop accepting and loving ourself. This is the source of psychological pain.

The first step to eliminate this self-created misery is to refuse to accept the limitations presented to us by our mind or by others. When we clear our mind with Breath Awareness, or work with the exercises to eliminate fear and self-rejection, we eliminate pain. This frees us to focus our attention on developing and using our inner resources.

Just as we use imagery to free ourselves of physical pain, we can use it to free ourselves of psychological pain. After all, it is the negative images that we have in our mind that create our unhappiness. Why not take charge and create positive images that lead to love towards ourself and those who are disappointing or frustrating us. Use the Imagery Exercise for Neutralizing Negative Feelings in Chapter 6 to clear your mind of hostility and resentment. Do not carry these burdens around like priceless treasures. By using imagery to restructure your emotional energy, you operate from your strength rather than from weaknesses. What you experience is an increased capacity to love the very person who was the source of your disturbance, and a greater ability to solve the problems they present.

Our greatest limitation is our own ego. The world of a single, isolated ego is very small indeed. We can easily gauge the degree of neuroticism and unhappiness a person feels by counting the number of times he uses the words "I," "me," or "mine" in a conversation. The more self-centered you are, the more pain you create for yourself. The more limited the ego, the more the ego must focus on its own problems. On the other hand, the more concerned you become about solving another's problems, the less time you spend worrying about your own.

This does not mean that you can safely ignore your limitations, nor can you ignore your own emotional issues. Neither do they require constant focus. This only makes them greater. By accepting your limitations, then concentrating your attention on your strengths and on helping others, you build your strengths. You also weaken your limitations in the process.

Service to others doesn't mean that you become a martyr, however. In one of his novels, Graham Greene described a martyr in the following way: "Alice lived her whole life for others. You could tell 'the others' by the haunted look in their faces." We all know or have met, somone who lives only to help you, and you better damn well be grateful. This is not loving, it is manipulation. Doing favors to gain favor, using guilt to insure payback, or creating dependencies have little to do with genuine love.

When our ego is small and isolated, our limitations and emotional issues seem large and forbidding. As we expand our ego to include others, our limitations seem smaller and smaller. We become less and less disturbed, and function more effectively. To put it simply, the more we love, the better we function.

## SELFLESS LOVE—THE END OF FEAR

The greater our fear, the less we can love. Love is a spontaneous experience when we eliminate fear, negative judgments, and self-rejection. These are all limitations. By freeing ourselves from them, we can express ourselves in unlimited ways. When we love others, we allow them to express themselves. Through love, we provide a supportive atmosphere of respect and caring where we and others around us feel free to explore, to develop and to create.

## LOVE AND THE BUSINESS WORLD

Love is not the usual topic of discussion in the corporate board room. To most people, love is associated with romance and sex, and has little to do with a corporate mission. Given the volatility of emotional involvements, and the growing sensitivity to sexual harassment, most people rightly feel that this kind of love is best excluded from the office.

But if we understand selfless love as freedom from limitations, it is not hard to see its value to the corporate environment. Think, for instance, of the mentor relationship. A senior, more experienced individual takes someone young and capable under his wing, and provides him with all the benefit of his experience and knowledge in order to help the novice become even better than the mentor. This is an act of love in which both grow and benefit. The corporation also benefits from the improved effectiveness of both people. However, if the senior person is insecure, afraid of being shown up or supplanted, then he cannot function as a mentor. He will be too busy protecting his turf, subtly reinforcing his fear and insecurity to the detriment of himself and his corporation.

### Love As Service

An even more powerful application of love in the corporation is service. To the degree that we are self-centered, we are incapable of giving genuine service. To the degree that a corporation is self-serving, focused solely on bottom line profit, it will be unable to provide genuine service. But when the bottom line includes service to the customer as well as profits, the business becomes successful. Rick Goldberg has built an extremely successful distribution company in Minnesota called Beauty Enterprises Progressive. His entire philosophy involves a single concept—legendary service. He will bear any expense to provide service to his customers. One of his customers in North Dakota once called him on a Sunday morning. They were involved in a show and expected a representative from his firm to be there to provide a seminar for their customers. The problem was that the company's sales representative had not shown up.

Within fifteen minutes, Rick was in his office, checking the schedule. A mistake had been made and the wrong date had been scheduled. Within a half-hour, Rick charted a private plane, and flew to North Dakota, where he rented a car and then drove for ninety minutes to his customer's program. He gave a two hour presentation and returned home. The cost was far greater than the immediate sales generated by this odyssey. But the good will he engendered by this one action gained his company a life-long loyal customer.

This "legendary service" that Rick has used to build his company is an act of love, a dedication to servicing the customer. But we make a mistake if we limit this concept of service to the "customer." To be effective, it must permeate the corporation. Most people never see the end user of their organization. Their "customer" may very well be the sales department, the design team, or the MIS function.

Often, managers and supervisors have the attitude that those who report to them are there to serve them when, in fact, it's the other way around. The more authority you have, the more responsibility you have for serving those below you. Providing service, in this context, refers directly to your ability to help your subordinates do a better job. Leadership based on coercion fails in the long run.

## QUALITY LEADERSHIP BASED ON THE PRINCIPLES OF SERVICE

The Tao Teh Ching speaks simply and eloquently about this principle of service and leadership:

> If the sage would guide the people, he must serve with humility.
> If he would lead them, he must follow behind.
> In this way when the sage rules, the people will not feel oppressed;
> When he stands before them, they will not be harmed.
> The whole world will support him and will not tire of him.

The complexities of modern life demand quality leadership—leadership with the courage, compassion, vision and skill to create genuine value, not just increased cash flow. It must build teams based on individual responsibility and empowerment instead of forced compliance; it must be dedicated to service instead of to building fiefdoms. Without quality leadership, individual knowledge and skills are lost, and corporations, institutions and even countries cannot compete successfully.

Quality leadership is a life-time journey of self-discovery, a chipping away at self-imposed limits. Leadership effectiveness builds on inner strength. It is truly "personal power," emerging from the knowledge and mastery of all our resources.

Quality leadership is potent because it is sensitive to nuance, and acts with a conscious, spontaneous responsiveness to the immediate needs. It strives for harmony without any fear of conflict. Flexibility, sensitivity and compassion allow all the elements of the group to emerge. For the empowered leader, leadership is not winning, but a dedication to service and the empowerment of others. Through genuine humility, the empowered leader makes the group the superstar and gains superstar work from the group.

## LOVE AND STRENGTH

Most people, unfortunately, think that love and compassion in business means weakness and softheartedness. Just the opposite is true. The more fearful we are, the weaker we feel, and, like the classroom bully, the "harder" or "tougher" we must act in order to protect ourselfves. But it's all a front to keep people from seeing how scared we really feel. Fear leads to extremes, overreactions and violence.

Strength, however, does not lie in rigidity and egocentrism, nor in victimizing others. There are times when really difficult and tough decisions must be made—people must be fired, plants must close down, projects must be halted. This is reality. If we are free of fear, and direct our efforts for the benefit of others, we stay free of inner conflicts, and remain strong regardless of the circumstances. If tough actions are called for, we execute them without overreacting. Knowing that we are not acting in self-interest allows us to make these decisions with a clear conscience. We maintain clarity of thought that allows us to function at optimum levels. Most importantly, we can sleep easily at night and face ourselves in the mirror in the morning.

## NON-ATTACHMENT: FOUNDATION FOR SELFLESS LOVE

The key to loving is non-attachment. Non-attachment does not mean withdrawing from life, commitments, action or feeling. Nor does it mean becoming a martyr, doing things that you do not want to do. On the contrary, you can find more joy and greater effectiveness through non-attachment. Non-attachment means non-ownership—freedom from the compulsive need to own things, people or ideas, or to have everything done in a certain way.

The more we need, the less we can love. The greater our wants and desires, the more self-centered we become. This is not to say we should ignore our needs or become a monk. But let us realize that we can satisfy our needs in an infinite number of ways. We do not have to become obsessed by the "perfect" deal, job or person. If we need things to be a certain way in order for us to be happy, than we're bound to be disappointed. Through non-attachment, we gain freedom from our expectations, and from the disappointment they bring. The more skilled we become at non-attachment, the less driven and needy we are, and the greater our capacity for compassion and love.

Non-attachment has other far-reaching practical implications—such as the freedom to explore and find alternatives, the capacity to develop an objectivity about the world around us. Through non-attachment:

1. **We minimize the fear of losing.** If we are not wedded to a particular outcome, we have the freedom to develop alternatives. This flexibility allows us to move forward, to gain even when our plans do not materialize in the way we had anticipated. We can adjust, create, move forward or backward, as the reality demands, and still achieve our objectives. When we are skilled in non-attachment, we can go into negotiations knowing that at any time we can walk away from the deal. We have the confidence that if one deal does not work out, another will.

Ron Oehl, President of Stonehenge Capital Corporation, has become a skilled negotiator in his business of buying and selling commercial real estate. Ron goes into negotiations confident that he can find some way to make the deal work. He maintains a calm and clear mind, free from the fear of loss or desire for gain. By keeping his focus on the details of the negotiations, he finds creative solutions to seemingly insurmountable differences.

**2. We develop greater emotional stability.** Inner conflicts weaken our will and inhibit our actions. Emotional stability allows us to remain calm and steady in the face of adversity. In so doing we gain self-respect and the respect of others. Then we can direct our emotional energy to motivate and inspire others. Like a good coach who inspires his team to out-perform the other team, we direct emotional energy towards a positive outcome. A great leader knows just what to say to build emotional intensity and then direct it to the chosen goal.

**3. We gain clarity of mind.** Emotional needs distort our perceptions and our ability to think clearly. The more we emotionally invest in an outcome, the less clearly we see alternatives. A scientist uses formal protocols to insure that his research is as objective as possible. He knows that objectivity is necessary if he wants to discover the truth. Our need to understand our reality is no less compelling. Through non-attachment, we gain objectivity to perceive and think clearly and without bias.

We practice non-attachment in three ways:

- By gaining sensitivity to our internal compulsions and drives, and by taking steps to reduce the emotional pressures they cause. With the centering exercise in Chapter 5, we can free ourselves from emotional compulsion and gain an objective view of our actions. Our inner sense will tell us when to persist and when to explore alternatives.

- By accepting both success and failure with equanimity. The language we use can either help us or create obstacles. Use the consequences of your actions to refine your skills and knowledge, not to berate yourself or pat yourself on the back. Instead of value terms. use language that is non-judgemental, free from emotionalism, and descriptive of outcomes.

- By doing selfless service. Spend one day a month working in a soup kitchen; teach adults how to read; become a Big Brother or Big Sister to a child who needs guidance; volunteer time in a charitable institution or to your favorite cause—the list is as endless as the need is great. We all feel satisfaction when we provide a genuine service and help others. And as we spend less time creating problems for ourself, we gain an even greater benefit. Our mind becomes more and more calm. We begin to realize that genuine satisfaction doesn't come from accumulating things or gaining power, but from expressing ourselves freely.

## THE POWER OF A REFLECTIVE MIND

Thoughtful reflection is fast becoming an outdated luxury. We are so busy making decisions, handling crises, faxing the latest figures, taking phone calls at any time in any place, and carrying our portable computers everywhere so we can crunch data at every spare second, that we hardly take the time to really think. It is a tragic mistake for us to become so action-oriented that we lose our power of reflective thought.

Reflection and stillness are critical to the development and expression of an Empowered Mind. They provide:

1. **A doorway to the mind skills:** A common theme runs throughout the various exercises we use to develop an Empowered Mind—the ability to maintain a calm and quiet mind. Only through quietness and reflection can we access the inner skills of the mind. If we remain in the field of action, we neither develop nor exercise an Empowered Mind. With a calm and reflective mind, we:

- Minimize distractions, gain clarity of thought and intensify our concentration.
- Facilitate access to our intuitive knowledge.
- Develop sensitivity to the subtle sensory cues and feelings of instinctual knowledge.
- Develop the patience necessary for proper timing and the exercise of will.
- See things in perspective which expands our depth of understanding and wisdom.
- Can be playful, stimulating our creativity and imagination.

2. **An experience of time as a restraint, and as timelessness.** Unless

we can play with our time frames, we cannot transform our dreams into actions and realities. In order to see where we are heading, we must remove ourself from the demands of action and take a larger look. If we are always busy, we can't step outside of the action to gain a greater perspective. To step outside of time constraints takes time.

Time rules us when we do not stand back to evaluate where we are going and to determine what we really want—to listen to our own inner wisdom. **Involved with time, we cannot sense the rhythms of time.**

To control what we do, and understand where we are going, we need the detachment that comes from reflection. We must step outside of time pressures and take a clear, unpressured look at who we are, the actions we take, and what we have accomplished. As Jean-Louis Servan-Schreiber says in his insightful book *The Art of Time,* "Achieving detachment *(non-attachment)* is prerequisite to any mastery: to make progress, we must observe and judge what we are doing while we are doing it." This can only be achieved through reflection.

One of the most dramatic ways to understand the need for reflection is to take Servan-Schreiber's advice and substitute the word "life" for the word "time" in those common phrases where we impose limits on our time, such as:

- I don't have the *time* (life)
- Using my *time* (life) well
- Losing *time* (life)
- I'm going to spend *time* (life) on it

It only takes a few times to realize that when we take charge of our time, we take charge of our life.

**3. An inevitably pathway to our spiritual center and skills.** Our spiritual skills are not part of our mind. They originate in our Center of Consciousness, the well-spring of our strength. When compulsive busyness dominates us, and we ignore our inner realities, we deprive ourself of our most essential resource.

## COMING HOME TO THE CENTER

Let's go back to our computer analogy. The computer has many abilities and potentials, but it is the owner of the computer who decides how these will be used. This is analogous to our personality, which has almost unlimited power and potential, but the final control is the owner, the Center of Consciousness. By refining the skill of inner concentration, we achieve a state of meditation. By refining our skill of meditation, we achieve unitary consciousness. Through unitary consciousness, we realize completely our inner strength and potential, and achieve fulfillment.

Experiencing our Center has profoundly practical ramifications. It is the necessary final step in freeing ourselves from fear and self-rejection. More importantly, the more freedom we gain from these two errors of the mind, the greater our capacity to love.

We gain knowledge from experience. Reflection allows us to use this knowledge in our day to day life. But few take the time reflect deeply enough to gain the wisdom that their experiences generate. The greater our depth of concentrated inner stillness, the greater our power of reflection, and the greater the potential for wisdom. Our most profound experience is that of our own Center, and our most profound wisdom comes when we understand its relationship to our life.

In the tape series *The Power of Myth*, Joseph Campbell points out that actions, if they are to be transforming, must originate from the center of our being. He goes on to talk about how top athletes, dancers, and performers center themselves in order to achieve peak performance and the experience of absorption that Bill Russell talked about so movingly. But the realization of our spiritual Center leads to much more than peak performance and achievement. The culmination of the Empowered Mind is the fulfillment of the human spirit, the realization of the very best of who we are as human beings.

## SUMMARY OF PRINCIPLES

1. Spiritual skills are the qualities which characterize the human spirit. They are the most essential part of our personality.

2. The fulfillment of the human spirit makes work and life worthwhile.

3. Our spiritual qualities allow us to work with people effectively to achieve excellence.

4. Cooperation is a fundamental law of life and organization. Without cooperation, we cannot even exist as an individual, let alone achieve success.

5. Cooperation is the basis for community, and provides the foundation for loyalty.

6. We can empower others to the extent that we ourselves are empowered.

7. Humility is the expression of genuine inner strength and health. It stems from the recognition that we are one small but integral part of a greater reality.

8. Most problems in business, as in life in general, are ego problems.

9. The ego serves a critical management function, but it should not be confused with the Self, and allowed to function as the "owner" of the personality.

10. A genuinely strong ego has the capacity to integrate all aspects of the personality, minimize weakness and focus effort on building strengths.

11. In its most powerful form, love is the expression of selflessness, the ability to give to another.

12. Selfless love releases us from all limitations, and allows the mind to be creative. It provides the strength necessary for the difficulties and hardship of effective leadership.

13. Love has an important and immediate application to the world of business. Two examples are service and the mentor relationship.

14. We achieve the ability to love selflessly to the degree that we practice non-attachment. Non-attachment means non-ownership or non-possessiveness.

15. When we experience the Center of Consciousness, we free ourselves of all fear and self-negation. This is achieved through refined skill in meditation.

# Appendix A
## Summary of Exercises

## Chapter 1

| *Exercise* | *Page* | *Purpose and Value* |
|---|---|---|
| Expanding Awareness | 7 | Increases awareness of musclar tension and the impact of your mind in creating tense or relaxed states. Gives you the opportunity to choose whether or not you keep tension in your body. |
| Taking Responsibility | 13 | Increases awareness of the emotional power of taking responsibility for your thoughts and feelings, and what happens when you become a victim by not taking responsibility. |

## Chapter 2

| *Exercise* | *Page* | *Purpose* |
|---|---|---|
| Traveling Exercise | 26 | Gain awareness of the different levels of our personality and the power functions operating at each level. |
| Body Check | 32 | Become sensitive to the information and knowledge states that our body provides. |
| Sensitivity | 33 | Develop sensitivity to body language, others' thoughts and feelings. |
| Body-Energy-Mind | 37 | Enhance awareness of how body affects our energy levels and our moods. |
| Habit check | 45 | Experience how habits unconsciously regulate our behavior. |

# Chapter 3

| *Exercise* | *Page* | *Purpose* |
|---|---|---|
| Relaxation Posture | 72 | Allows all the muscles of the body to achieve a state of relaxation; helpful in learning deep relaxation. |
| Diaphragmatic Breathing | 72 | The natural moment-to-moment breathing pattern; absolutely necessary to achieve balance in the body. |
| 2:1 Diaphrag. Breathing | 73 | Creates a deeper state of balanced rest in the body. |
| Two-Minute Breath Break | 73 | Simple relaxation/mind-clearing exercise to use at any time during the day. |
| Muscle Relaxation | 76 | Systematic exercise to learn deep relaxation on the structural level. |
| Sweeping Breath | 78 | Often used as a preliminary relaxation exercise for concentration exercises or for other relaxation techniques. |
| Deep-State Breath Relaxation | 79 | Sophisticated breathing exercise that creates a deep state of relaxation by manipulating the autonomic nervous system. |
| Sleep Exercise | 82 | An effective sleep exercise that minimizes and even eliminates insomnia. |

# Chapter 4

| *Exercise* | *Page* | *Purpose* |
|---|---|---|
| Breath Awareness | 92 | Provides direct control of mind chatter. The single most important tool for stress management and mental clarity available. |

## Chapter 4 (Con't)

| *Exercise* | *Page* | *Purpose* |
|---|---|---|
| Green Frog | 95 | Develops awareness of how language can provide invalid information; helps gain objectivity toward own thoughts and images. |
| Language Games<br>Clarity Exercise<br>Equalizer<br>Word Play | 98 | Increases conscious control over the way we use language. Helps develop the skill to use language rather than be used by our habitual language patterns. |
| Four Steps to Control Fear | 103 | Enhances the power to manage and eliminate worry and fear. |
| "Should" Stopper | 106 | Disrupts the habitual pattern of the mind to rely on "should" and "should not" as a method of self-punishment. |
| Letting Go | 108 | Clears the mind of disappointments and regrets. |

## Chapter 5

| *Exercise* | *Page* | *Purpose* |
|---|---|---|
| 61 Points | 116 | Sophisticated concentration/relaxation exercise which provides a profound state of relaxation, useful in preventing hypertension. |
| Candle Gaze | 127 | An efficient concentration exercise combining an external and internal focus point. |
| Bellows Breathing | 129 | Increases our level of energy, makes the mind more alert; increases lung capacity. |
| Complete Breath | 129 | Increases level of energy, reduces fatigue and reduces muscle tension. |

# Chapter 5 (Con't)

| *Exercise* | *Page* | *Purpose* |
|---|---|---|
| Alternate Nostril | 130 | Calms and focuses the mind; increases lung capacity and control over the autonomic nervous system; can be extended into a sophisticated concentration exercise. |
| Breath Awareness | 136 | Can be used as an excellent concentration exercise, particularly when combined with the Alternate Nostril Exercise. |
| Centering Exercise | 138 | A basic exercise to establish a steady point of internal awareness. It can be used at the beginning of any meditation exercise, and for exercises involving other inner skills, such as intuition, imagery work, and conflict management. |
| Meditation Exercise | 139 | Used with the Centering exercise, it uses thought as the focal point; trains the mind for one-pointed inner concentration. |

# Chapter 6

| *Exercise* | *Page* | *Purpose* |
|---|---|---|
| Walking Exercise | 148 | Develops sensitivity to the subtle feelings in your body as you react to other people. Gives insight into the nature of your mental and emotional states, the other person's personality and your relationship with him. |
| Standing in Another's Shoes | 149 | A mind-reading exercise. Develops sensitivity to another person's thoughts and feelings. |

# Chapter 6 (Con't)

| *Exercise* | *Page* | *Purpose* |
|---|---|---|
| An Exercise in Creative Thought | 154 | Demonstrates the creative force of our mind to either help us or create problems for us. |
| Managing Creative Matrix | 157 | Three steps to provide a stable environment for our Creative Matrix. |
| Guidelines for Diversification | 160 | Seven steps to increase the variety and quality of the raw material for our creative force. |
| Free Association Exercise | 162 | An exercise in creative problem-solving, often referred to as brainstorming. |
| Reframing: Changing the Rules | 164 | A directed association exercise in creative problem-solving designed to create new perspectives. |
| Neutralizing Negative Emotions and Feelings | 168 | An imagery exercise to clear the mind of unproductive negative feelings toward another person, and to clarify and resolve conflict situations. |
| A Positive Start | 169 | Imagery technique to create a strong, positive mood as you start the day. |
| Creating a Successful Future | 170 | Imagery exercise to facilitate success in completing a project. |

# Chapter 7

| *Exercise* | *Page* | *Purpose* |
|---|---|---|
| A Journey into Wisdom | 187 | A complex exercise to develop self-knowledge and intuitive insight about personal direction. |
| The Room | 190 | A technique to develop access to our intuitive knowledge through imagery. |

## Chapter 7 (Con't)

| *Exercise* | *Page* | *Purpose* |
|---|---|---|
| Direct Access | 191 | A methodical approach for direct access to intuitive knowledge. |
| Sleep Problem-Solving | 195 | A technique for using the unconscious mind to solve problems during sleep. |
| Three Steps to Effective Decision-Making | 198 | Three steps to enhance decision-making abilities by taking control of our mind, and using all three knowledge states. |

## Chapter 8

| *Exercise* | *Page* | *Purpose* |
|---|---|---|
| RARE Model | 207 | Four steps to effectively manage both internal and external conflict. |
| Steps to Increased Confidence | 212 | Four steps to using inner language to minimize self-negation and increasing your level of confidence. |
| Confidence Exercise | 214 | Establishes a pathway to the Balanced State, the fifth level of our personality, and the source of our inner strength. Useful technique to enhance problem-solving abilities. |
| Discovering Priorities | 217 | An exercise to help you determine your real values and priorities. Facilitates development of a reflective mind which is necessary in creativity and developing intuitive skills. |
| Self-Discipline Exercise | 219 | Step-by-step program for building self-discipline through self-training. Followed by an example of a self-training program in developing the power of concentration. |

# Chapter 8 (Con't)

| *Exercise* | *Page* | *Purpose* |
|---|---|---|
| Affirmations Exercise | 224 | Used to focus the power of the mind on a particular goal or task you wish to complete successfully, or a particular quality that you wish to develop. |

# Chapter 9

| *Exercise* | *Page* | *Purpose* |
|---|---|---|
| Four Steps to Creating a Positive Relationship | 235 | Creates an environment that builds cooperation and empowerment. |
| Reinforcing Strengths | 235 | Creates a positive relationship, reinforces desirable qualities, creates a positive state of mind for the user, developes sensitivity to strengths. |
| Five Steps to a Strong Ego | 240 | Strengthens the ego in the role of manager; builds self-discipline and inner strength. |
| Shrinking Headache Exercise | 242 | Minimizes and eliminates head pain; an example of the power of removing limits. |
| Imagery Release Exercise | 243 | Minimizes pain through systematically altering the characteristically limiting images that come to the mind; teaches how to use imagery to dissolve boundaries. |

# Appendix B
## Detail of 61 Points Exercise

"61 Points" is a concentration exercise, and leads to the most profound level of relaxation. To do this exercise, lie in the Relaxation Posture. During this exercise, concentrate on either a blue flame or a blue star (as you would see a star in the night sky) at 61 different points in or on the body (see page 117). At each point, let the star or flame be as clear, as small, and as perfect as your mind will allow it to be. If you are unable to picture the star or flame, simply concentrate your attention on a point of warmth about the diameter of a pencil. Concentrate only on one point at a time for approximately twelve seconds. When first beginning to work with this exercise, you may fall asleep. Don't get discouraged, just keep practicing the exercise. Each time you begin the exercise, make a clear determination that you will stay awake throughout the entire exercise.

Lying in the relaxation posture, close your eyes and concentrate on making your breath very even, very steady, and very smooth...you are not trying to fill your lungs completely, or trying to empty them. Breathe easily and gently, letting your body do all the work for you. Your breath should be smooth and even, letting your inhalation and exhalation be smooth and even... The pressure of the flow of the breath should be even, maintaining the same flow or pressure at the end of the exhalation as you do at the beginning and in the middle. Don't allow any pauses, jerks, and shakiness in your breath. Even minimize the pause between the inhalation and the exhalation.

Now mentally scan down the body, checking for any excess muscle tension...wherever you find tension, simply release the tension in the muscles... Now using your imagination, picture your body as being a hollow reed. Breathe as if you are breathing through your toes, filling your body with breath to the crown of your head, and exhaling back down and out your toes again. Breathe easily and gently, no strain and no effort... Again, you aren't trying to fill your lungs, or empty them completely, just an easy deep, slow and gentle breath, breathing in through the toes to the crown of your head and exhaling back down and out the toes.

In your mind you can feel your whole body expanding when you inhale and contracting when you exhale, as if every cell in your body were breathing in and breathing out... easily, gently, no strain, no effort...

And now bring your attention to your mind center, the space between your two eyebrows. Picture as clearly as you can a small blue star or flame inside the space between the two eyebrows. Let the star or flame be as perfect, as small, and as clear as your mind will allow...and now at the base of the throat, the throat center, picture a small blue star or flame...in the center of the right shoulder joint...in the center of the right elbow joint...in the center of the right wrist joint, a small blue star or flame, as clear and as perfect as your mind will allow...on the tip of the thumb of the right hand...on the tip of the forefinger of the right hand...on the tip of the middle finger...on the tip of the ring finger on the right hand...on the tip of the small finger, a small blue star or flame, as clear or as perfect as your mind will allow...again in the center of the right wrist joint...in the center of the right elbow joint...in the center of the right shoulder joint, a small blue star or flame...again, at the base of the throat, the throat center, visualize a small blue star or flame...

Now in the center of the left shoulder joint, let the star or flame illuminate the entire center of the joint...in the center of the left elbow joint...in the center of the left wrist joint...now on the tip of the thumb of the left hand...on the tip of the forefinger of the left hand...on the tip of the middle finger of the left hand...on the tip of the ring finger...and on the tip of the small finger of the left hand, a small blue star or flame, as perfect and as small as your mind will allow it to be...Again visualize the star or flame in the center of the left wrist joint...in the center of the left elbow joint...in the center of the left shoulder joint...again at the base of the throat, the throat center, a small blue star or flame...

Now visualize the star or flame in the center of the chest, between the two breasts, the heart center...on the nipple of the right breast, visualize a small blue star or flame...back again to the heart center...now on the nipple of the left breast...back again to the heart center... Now visualize the star or flame at the navel center, just behind the navel...

Now visualize a small blue star or flame at the genital center, just slightly up and behind the genital area...in the center of the right hip joint, let the star or flame illuminate the entire center of the joint...in the center of the right knee joint...in the center of the right ankle joint...at the tip of the large toe of the right foot, a small blue star or flame...on the tip of the second toe...on the tip of the third or middle toe of the right foot...on the tip of the fourth toe...and on the tip of the small toe of the right foot, a small blue star or flame as clear and as perfect as your mind will allow it to be... Again, in the center of the right ankle joint...in the center of the right knee joint...in the center of the right hip joint...

Now visualize a small blue star or flame at the genital center...in the center of the left hip joint...in the center of the left knee joint, let the star or flame illuminate the entire joint area...in the center of the left ankle joint...At the tip of the large toe of the left foot...on the tip of the second toe...on the tip of the third toe of the left foot...on the tip of the fourth toe...and on the tip of the small toe, a small blue star or flame, as perfect and as clear as your mind will allow it to be... Again, in the center of the left ankle joint...in the center of the left knee joint...in the center of the left hip joint...and again at the genital center, a small blue star or flame...

At the navel center...at the heart center in the middle of the chest...at the throat center at the base of the throat...and in the mind center, the space between the two eyebrows, let the star or flame be as clear, as perfect, and as small as your mind will allow it to be...

Now using your imagination, picture your body as being a hollow reed. Breathe as if you are breathing through your toes, filling your body with breath to the crown of the head, and exhaling back down and out your toes again. Breathe easily and gently, no strain and no effort...Again, you aren't trying to fill your lungs, or empty them completely, just an easy deep, slow and gentle breath, breathing in through the toes to the crown of your head and exhaling back down and out the toes.

In your mind, you can feel your whole body expanding when you inhale and contracting when you exhale, as if every cell in your body was breathing in and breathing out... Easily, gently, no strain, no effort...

Gently wiggle your fingers and toes. Being aware of every movement—open your eyes to the palms of your hands, then gently lower your hands. Remain aware of the inner calmness and energy that flows within you, and remain calm and aware throughout the rest of the day.

# INDEX

## A

Abbott, Jim, 202
Acceptance, conflict management, 208-209
Action, versus fear, 103
Activation stage, possum response, 63
Affirmations, 223-224
    keys to effectiveness, 223-224
    nature of, 223
    technique for, 224
Alarm stage
    fight or flight response, 62
    possum response, 63
Alternate nostril breathing, 130-131
Apnea, 71
Arousal, versus stress, 59-60
Artistic efforts, for diversification, 160-161
Art of Time, The (Servan-Schreiber), 251
Association
    directed association, 163-164
    free association, 162
Atrophication stage, possum
    response, 64
Attention, and relationships, 235
Autonomic nervous system
    balance/harmony and, 66
    and breathing, 69, 71
    functions of, 61
    and pulse, 67
    regulation of, 67
Autonomic relaxation, 78-79
    sweeping breath exercise, 78-79
Awakening Intuition (Vaughn), 175-176
Awareness
    and concentration, 10, 118, 126
    direct experience as, 7

Awareness (cont.)
    exercise in, 7-8
    and power, 6
    versus fear, 122-124

## B

Bach, Richard, 222
Balance
    and creativity, 156-157
    and diaphragmatic breathing, 69, 71
    dynamic form of, 66
    and energy, 128-129
    harmonious form of, 66
    imbalance and stress, 66
    and inner harmony, 50
    maintaining balance, 66
Balch, Dewey, 30
Beliefs, as limiting factors, 180-181,
    232-233
Bell, Alexander Graham, 121-122
Bellows breath, 129
Biofeedback
    control of physical, 7, 13-14
    early research, 30
Blaming, negative aspects of, 12-13
Brain, versus mind, 38
Brain storming, 162
Breath, and energy, 35
Breathing
    apnea, 71
    and autonomic nervous system, 67,
        69, 71
    and depression, 73
    diaphragmatic breathing, 68-74
    emergency breathing, 69

Breathing (cont.)
    and emotional state, 71
    neural systems affected by, 69
    test of normal breathing, 68
Breathing exercises
    alternate nostril exercise, 130-131
    for autonomic relaxation, 78-79
    bellows breath, 129
    breath awareness exercise, 92-97, 136-
        137, 147-148
    calming breath, 130-131
    complete breath, 129-130
    deep-state breath relaxation, 79-82
    energizing exercises, 129-131
    for muscle relaxation, 75-78
    progression to deep relaxation, 82
    sleep exercise, 82
Breese, Kim, 233
Burn-out, 62

## C

Calming breath, 130-131
Calming stage, fight or flight response, 62
Campbell, Joseph, 252
Candle gazing, 126-127
Capabilities
    capacity inventory, 2
    improvement of, 3
Carbon dioxide, and breathing, 71
Center, experience of Center of
Consciousness, 251-252
Charity, 241
Children
    development of concentration, 136
    empowerment by parents, 234
Cleer, Clarence, 163
Commitment
    to engage power of energy, 167
    to personal development, 134
Community
    and cooperation, 230-236
    creation of positive relationships, 235
    destroyers of, 231-232
    empowerment of others, 233-234
    and humility, 236-241
    and love, 242-245

Community (cont.)
    sense of community, 19
Complete breath exercise, 129-130
Compliments, effects of, 235-236
Concentration
    and awareness, 10, 118, 126
    benefits of, 111, 115-116
    breath awareness exercise, 136-137
    centering exercise, 138-139
    comparison to laser, 112-113, 118-119
    as conscious action, 120-121
    developing in children, 136
    and discrimination, 179
    distraction, nature of, 115
    and energy of mind, 113-115, 119-120,
        121-122
    and energy state, 128, 131
    to engage power of energy, 167
    examples of unfocused mind, 111
    factors affecting ability to con-
        centrate, 120
    and fear, 122
    focus point exercise, 137-138
    gaze exercise, 126-127
    importance of, 9-10
    increasing
    intensification of con-
        centration, 118-119
    61 points exercise, 116-118, 261-263
    steps in, 124
    unitary consciousness, 120
    inner concentration, 126
    and intuition, 178-179, 184
    and meditation, 119, 137-138
    as mind's executive skill, 10
    and peak experience, 111, 125
    and peak performance, 125
    posture for practicing concentration,
        135
    power of focused attention, 6-7
    psuedo-concentration, 122
    and relaxation, 82-83
    self-training program, time
        frame, 220-221
    shifting concentration, 124-125
    and task absorption, 92, 125

Conditioning, of habits, 44
Confidence
    and leadership, 17-18
    and will, 17-18
See also Self-confidence
Conflict, causes of, 204
Conflict management, 206-210
    acceptance, 208-209
    exploration, 209-210
    and personal philosophy, 216
    relaxation, 207-208
    restraint, 209
Conscious mind, 5
    focused attention of, 6-7
Control, to engage power of
    energy, 166-167
Cooperation, 230-236
    builders of, 233-236
    destroyers of, 231-232
    and loyalty, 231
    as natural law, 230-231
Creativity, 151-164
    changing frame of reference, 164
    creative matrix, 152-154
    management of, 157-158
    and diversification, 158-161
    and emotional disturbance, 156-157
    exercise in creative thought, 154-155
    and fear, 157
    and imagery, 15-16
    and imagination, 15-16, 165-166
    and interests, 158-161
    limitations to, 152, 154
    meaning of being creative, 145
    and mind traps, 164-165
    nature of, 15, 145, 151
    and perception, 42
    phases of, 151
    discovery stage, 161-164
    germination stage, 158-161
    inner balance stage, 156-157
    problem solving
    reframing exercise, 164
    reframing problem, 163-164
    taking control of, steps in, 155-156
    as tool, 145

    unlocking, 15
    use and abuse of creative power, 88
Critical thinking, 193-196
    characteristics of, 194
    and intuition, 194
    nature of, 193-194
    strengthening of, 195
Curiosity, and humility, 237
Cynical Americans, The (Mirvus), 231

D

Danger, intuitive sense for, 34
Daydreams, 120-121
Decision making, 196-199
    and fear, 196-197
    importance of, 196
    and personal philosophy, 216
    and self-doubt, 198
    steps in effective decision making, 198-
        199
Decisiveness
    skills related to, 17
    as visionary skill, 17
Demands, language of, 89
Denial, language of, 89
Dependency, negative aspects of, 232
Depression
    and breathing, 73
    and parasympathetic nervous system, 73
Diaphragmatic breathing, 68-74
    advantages of
    autonomic balance, 69, 71
    better coronary function, 71-72
    carbon dioxide cleansing, 71-72
    efficiency, 68-69
    steps in
    balanced 2:1 breathing, 73
    diaphragmatic breathing, 72-73
    relaxation posture, 72
    two-minute breath break, 73-74
Diet, and stress, 84
Discovery phase
    creativity, 161-164
    directed association, 163-164
    free association exercise, 162

Discvery phase (cont.)
spontaneous association, 162
Discrimination
and concentration, 179
developing discrimination, 46, 48
enhancing power of, 179
and intuition, 174-175, 176-177
nature of, 46, 174-175
and non-linear thinking, 174-175
power functions
analysis and thinking, 46
intuition, 48
Disease
and biofeedback, 7, 13-14
and imagery, 168
psychoneuro-immunology, 14
stress-related disease, 28, 30, 58
Distraction
chattering mind, 88-89, 147
nature of, 115
prophyasic thinking, 135
unlearning habit of, 135-136
Diversification
and creativity, 158-161
guidelines for, 160-161
importance of, 158-159
Doubts, 221-223, 221-224
and affirmations, 223-224
See also Self-doubt
Driving, using driving time, 160
Drucker, Peter, 14-15

**E**

Ego, 237-241
functions of, 237-238
and humility, 237
inflated ego, 239
and neurosis, 238-239
and problems of life, 239
strong ego
development of, 240-241
qualities of, 240
Emotional attack, staying calm during, 93
Emotional energy, 166-167
distortion of, 166

Emotional energy (cont.)
engaging power of, 166-167
and habits, 45
Emotional power
creating positive state for, 43
and success, 43-44
Emotional problems
effects of, 43
out of control habits as, 8-9
Emotions
control of
breath awareness, 92-97
task absorption, 91-92
through language, 90-91
effect of out of control habits, 8-9
Empowerment
of children, 234
daily exercises, 141-142
and ethics, 20
exercise in, 234-235
and imagery, 169
from inner resources, 3-4
meaning of, 121
methods toward, 134-135
personal power as, 20-21
techniques for building skills, 141
Energy
and ability to concentrate, 128, 131
and balance, 128-129
as basis of life, 37
body/energy/mind exercise, 37
and breath, 35
emotional energy, 166-167
excess energy, 128
and exercise, 37
exercises for
bellows breath, 129
calming breath, 130-131
complete breath, 129-130
and habits, 45-46
and health, 37
as life force, 35
mind's sensitivity to energy fields, 40
wasting power, forms of, 166
Entrepreneurs, lack of balance and, 157

Environmental stress, 83
Ethics, and empowerment, 20
Eustress, 62-63
Executive Mind, Timely Action
    (Torbert), 234
Exercise
    and energy, 37
    lack of, and stress, 83-84
    and sexual activity, 83
Expectations
    letting go exercise, 108-109
    negative effects of, 108
    versus goals, 108
Exploration, conflict management, 209-210

**F**

Fanaticism, 215
Fatigue stage, fight or flight response, 62
    Fear, 101-104
    and breath awareness, 104
    and concentration, 122
    controlling fear, steps in, 103-104, 124
    and creativity, 157
    dangers of, 88, 101, 102, 103
    and decision making, 196-197
    facing fears, 103-104
    fear of failure, 152
    and fight or flight, 101-102
    and isolation, 232
    and love, 245
    mechanisms in creation of, 102-103
    as negative use of creativity, 101-103
    versus action, 103
    versus awareness, 122-124
    versus self-preservation, 101, 102
Fight or flight response, 61-63
    alarm stage, 62
    calming stage, 62
    fatigue stage, 62
    and fear, 101-102
    goodbye stage, 62-63
Flexibility
    and intuition, 179-181
    maintaining open mind, 181-182
Focus point exercise, 137-138

Free association
    free association exercise, 162
    nature of, 162
Fuller, Bob, 218
Future, and language, 89

**G**

Galt, Steve, 167
Gazing exercise, 126-127
    candle gazing, 126-127
Generalization, language of, 89
Germination stage, creativity, 158-161
Goals
    nature of, 108
    versus expectations, 108
Goldberg, Philip, 176
Goldberg, Rick, 246
Goodbye stage
    fight or flight response, 62-63
    possum response, 64
Gorbachev, Mikhail, 10
Green, Elmer, 30
Green frog exercise, 95
Guilt
    effects of, 105
    as manipulative tool, 105
    and superego, 105

**H**

Habits
    conditioning of, 44
    definition of, 44
    effects of bad habits, 45
    and emotional energy, 45
    and empowerment, 121
    and energy, 45-46
    exercise in habit sensitivity, 44-45
    habits of power, 45
    and inflexible mind, 45
    pervasiveness of, 45
Harmony, and balanced mind, 50
Harvey, John, 89
Havel, Vaclav, 227-228
Headaches
    and gaze, 127
    shrinking headache exercise, 242-243

Headaches (cont.)
    tension headaches, 31-32
Health
    body as information resource, 31-32
    body check exercise, 32
    and energy, 37
    and imagery, 168
    importance of wellness, 11
    wholistic medicine, 14
Heart
    and breathing patterns, 71-72
    preload and afterload, 71
Hobbies, for diversification, 160
Hubbard, Elbert, 196
Humility, 236-241
    and curiosity, 237
    and ego, 237-241
    and ego strength, 19
    nature of, 236-236
    power of, 19
Hymes, Alan, 72
Hypertension, 82
    and breathing, 72
Hypnosis, 120-121

I

Iacocca, Lee, 202
Illusions: Confessions of a Reluctant
    Messiah (Bach), 222
Imagery
    active imagery, 165
    creating success exercise, 170
    and creativity, 15-16
    and empowerment, 169
    and health, 168
    passive imagery, 165
    and performance, 167, 168-169
    positive start for day, 169-170
    and visualization, 167-168
    Imagination, 165-166
    and creativity, 15-16
    nature of, 15-16, 145
    as tool, 145
Immune system, psychoneuro-
    immunology, 14
Information technology, demands of, 229
Inner Game of Tennis, The (Galt), 167

Insight, and intuition, 16
Instinct
    emotional basis of, 41
    functions of
    interpersonal understanding, 146-147
    protection from danger, 146
    sense of timing, 146
    nature of, 15, 40, 41, 144, 145-146
    and perceptual sensitivity, 146
    and sales, 145-146
    use as tool, 144
Integrity, 214-217
    and actions, 216-217
    benefits of, 216
    personal philosophy as, 215-216
    and relationships, 235
Interpersonal understanding, and
    instinct, 146-147
Intuition
    as bodily sensations, 184-185
    and concentration, 48, 178-179, 184
    and critical thinking, 194
    determinants of, 178
    and discrimination, 174-175, 176-177
    exercises
    elements of, 186-187
    journey into wisdom exercise, 187-190
    the room exercise, 190-191
    and flexibility, 179-181
    as image, 186
    and insight, 16
    knowledge base for, 177-178
    and leisure, 182-183
    nature of, 48, 176-177
    problems related to developing
        intuition, 192-193
    sense of danger, 34
    and stress, 179
    tapping intuition, 183-184
    thoughts as guide to, 185-186
    types of intuitive insights, 183
    as visionary skill, 16
Intuitive Edge, The (Goldberg), 176

J

Journey
    and developing intuition, 186-187

Journey (cont.)
    journey into wisdom exercise, 187-190
Joy, 11
    experience of, 107-108

## K

Kekule, Friedrich A. von, 126
Knowledge
    instinct, 40-41
    sensory knowledge, 40

## L

Language and mind
    changing external reality with
        words, 97-98
    chattering mind, 88-89
    clarity exercise, 98
    control of emotional reactions, 90-91
    creation of limitations by, 43
    and decision making, 198-199
    equalizer exercise, 98-99
    erasing the "should" problem, 105-106
    and personal reality, 42-43
    positive statements and reality, 99-100
    power of language, 88-89
    and self-confidence, 211-212
    word play exercise, 99
Laziness, 106-107
    elimination of, 106-107
    as resistance to change, 106
Leadership
    and confidence, 17-18
    reactions to obstacles, 18
    and self-discipline, 18
    and service, 247
    types of leaders, 17
    and will, 17
Leisure
    importance of, 182-183
    and intuition, 182-183
Life force, 35
    as energy, 35
Linear thinking, 173-174
    limitations of, 173-174
    and sensory mind, 174

Listening, paying attention, 147-148
Lombardo, Michael, 11
Love, 242-245
    and business environment, 245-246
    and fear, 245
    meaning of, 242, 245
    and non-attachment, 248-250
    power of, 19-20
    selfless giving as, 19-20
    as service, 246
    and strength, 247-248
Loyalty, 231
Luck, belief about, 202

## M

McCall, Morgan, 11
Mantras, 138
Martial arts training, 103, 240
Meditation
    centering exercise, 138-139
    and concentration, 119
    focus point exercise, 137-138
    and inner strength, 233
    mantras, 138
    meaning of, 119
    meditation exercise, 139
    and self-confidence, 213-214
Meetings, and breath awareness, 96
Mind
    balanced mind, 50-51
    being misled by, 93-95
    chattering mind, 88-89, 147
    stopping chatter, 92
    types of chatter, 89
    conscious mind, 5
    creation of fear, 88
    discriminating mind, 46-49
    and emotional energy, 166-167
    and linear thinking, 173-174
    nature of, 37-38
    and real time, 88
    sensitivity to energy fields, 40
    sensory mind, 38-46
    unconscious mind, 4-6
    versus brain, 38

Mind/body connection, 35-38, 51
Mind traps, statements/attitudes of, 164-165
Mirvus, Phil, 231
Mistakes, letting go exercise, 108-109
Muscle relaxation, 75-78
 audio cassette in learning of, 76
 benefits of, 75
 exercise for, 76-78
 relaxation posture, 75
 time for practicing, 75-76

**N**

Negative feelings, neutralizing with
 imagery, 168-169
Nervous system
 autonomic nervous system, 61
 parasympathetic nervous system, 61
 sympathetic nervous system, 61
Neurosis, 238-239
No, benefits of saying no, 241
Non-attachment
 benefits of, 248-250
 and love, 248-250
 and mastery, 251

**O**

Obstacles, empowered leader's
 reaction to, 18
Oehl, Ron, 248-249
Open mind
 benefits of, 161
 maintaining open mind, 181-182
Optimism, 11
 and success, 108-109
Organizational integrity, nature of, 144
Overreaction, language of, 89
Oxygen, and diaphragmatic breathing, 69

**P**

Pain
 imagery release exercise, 243
 and personal reality, 42
 psychological pain, 244
 shrinking headache exercise, 242-243

Parasympathetic nervous system
 and depression, 73
 functions of, 61
Peak experience, and concentration, 111,
 125
People watching, for diversification, 161
Perception
 and creativity, 42
 distortion, effects of, 41-42
 and events of sensory mind, 42
 as reality generator, 41
Perceptual sensitivity, 33
 accessing unconscious mind
 through, 33-34
 breath awareness exercise, 147-148
 creativity, 15
 developing inner sensitivity
 standing in another's shoes
 exercise, 149-151
 walking exercise, 148-149
 imagination, 15-16
 and instinct, 146
 instincts, 15
 nature of, 144
 sensitivity exercise, 33
Performance, and imagery, 167, 168-169
Persistence, and success, 218-219
Personality
 compared to computer, 27-28
 control center of, 51
 integration of, 53-55
 levels of
 balanced mind, 50-51
 discriminating mind, 46-49
 mind/body connection, 35-38
 physical body, 28-35
 sensory mind, 38-46
 traveling exercise, 26
 recreation of, 10-11
Peters, Tom, 159
Playfulness, 182
Pleasure, and personal reality, 42
Positive reinforcement, and relationships, 235
Positive thinking
 basics of, 222

Positive thinking (cont.)
 changing language of mind, 97-100
 example of, 222-223
Possum response, 88
 activation stage, 63
 alarm stage, 63
 atrophication stage, 64
 goodbye stage, 64
Posture, 37
 body/energy/mind exercise, 37
 for practicing concentration, 135
Power functions
 emotional power, 43-44
 habits, 44-46
 language, 42-43
 perception, 41-42
Power of Myth, The (Campbell), 252
Priorities
 exercise to discover priorities, 217-218
 steps in development of, 221
Problem solving
 and creativity, 145
 critical thinking, 193-196
 and sleep, 195-196
Projection, language of, 89
Prophyasic thinking, 135
Psuedo-concentration, 122
Psychological pain, 244
 letting go of, 244-245
Psychoneuro-immunology, 14
Pulse, and autonomic nervous system, 67

**Q**

Quiet Mind, The (Harvey), 89

**R**

Reading, for diversification, 160
Reasoning
 barriers to, 16
 as visionary skill, 16-17
Rechelbacher, Horst, 173, 201, 215
Reflection, 250-251
 benefits of, 250-251
Relaxation
 autonomic relaxation, 78-79

Relaxation (cont.)
 benefits of, 74-74
 and concentration, 82-83
 conflict management, 207-208
 deep relaxation, 74-75
 deep-state breath relaxation, 79-82
 meaning of, 74
 muscle relaxation, 75-78
 progression to deep relaxation, 82
 relaxation posture, 72
 scanning technique, 207-208
 sleep exercise, 82
 structural relaxation, 75-78
Response ability, development of, 12-13
Restraint, conflict management, 209
Room exercise, 190-191
Ruch, Richard, 158
Russell, Bill, 125

**S**

Sales, and instinct, 145-146
Scanning technique, 207-208
Self-confidence, 210-214
 confidence exercise, 214
 destroyers of, 211
 increasing self-confidence, 212-213
 and language, 211-212
 and meditation, 213-214
 and success, 210-211
 10-80-10 Rule, 210-211
Self-discipline
 development of, 18, 218-219
 and leadership, 18
 training for, 219-221
Self-doubt
 and decision making, 198
 development of, 211
Self-preservation
 feeling of, 101
 and instinct, 146
 versus fear, 101, 102
Self-rejection, 104-105
 forms of, 105
 and guilt, 105

Sensory knowledge, 40
    quality of, 40
Sensory mind, 38-46
    development of power functions
    emotional power, 43-44
    habits, 44-46
    language, 42-43
    perception, 41-42
    effects on language on, 88-91
    and instinct, 40-41
    and linear thinking, 174
    mistakes of
    fear, 101-104
    laziness, 106-107
    self-rejection, 104-106
    and organizational integrity, 144
    and perceptual sensitivity, 144
    and sensory knowledge, 40
    tasks of, 144
Servan-Schreiber, Jean-Louis, 251
Service
    and leadership, 247
    and love, 246
    selfless, types of, 249-250
Sexual activity, and exercise, 83
"Should," erasing the "should"
    problem, 105-106
Simonton, Carl, 168
    61 points exercise, 116-118, 261-263
Sleep
    exercise to induce sleep, 82
    and problem solving, 195-196
Sleep apnea, 71
Space, and personal reality, 42
Specialization, profile of specialists, 159
Spiritual skills
    humility, 19
    importance of, 18-19
    love, 19-20
    sense of community, 19
Standing in another's shoes exercise, 149-151
Strength, and personal philosophy, 216
Stress
    balance and control of, 66

Stress (cont.)
    cause of, 58
    controlling reactions to, 11-12
    costs related to, 28
    and diet, 84
    and employee effectiveness, 232
    environmental stress, 83
    fight or flight response, 61-63
    and intuition, 179
    and lack of exercise, 83-84
    myths related to, 59-60
    and performance, 30
    physical reactions to, 60-61
    possum response, 63-64
    stress-related disease, 28, 30, 58
Stress management
    benefits of, 31
    biofeedback, 30
    early program, 30
Stretching exercises, benefits of, 185
Structural relaxation, 75-78
Success
    and focus of mind's energy, 165
    and persistence, 218-219
    and self-confidence, 210-211
Superego, and guilt, 105
Sympathetic nervous system
    fight and flight response, 61-63
    functions of, 61

**T**

Tao Teh Ching, 246
Task absorption, 125, 131
    creating with breath awareness, 92
    and efficiency, 91
Teamwork, 229
    10-80-10 Rule, self-confidence, 210-211
Tension, and excess energy, 128
Tension headaches, 31-32
Thoughts
    discrimination, 46-48
    as guide to intuition, 185-186
Time
    and personal reality, 42

Time (cont.)
    stepping outside constraints of, 251
Timing, sense of, 146
Torbert, William, 234
Traffic, handling stress of, 96-97
Transition, from levels of consciousness, 135
Travel, for diversification, 161

### U

Ulcers, 61
Unconscious mind, 4-6
    accessing unconscious through perceptual
    sensitivity, 33-34
    and destructive habits, 8-9
    examples of experiences of, 5
    power of, 5-6
    subconscious, 4-5
Unitary consciousness, 120

### V

Vaughn, Francis, 175-176
Visionary mind
    and discrimination, 174-175
    nature of, 173
Visionary skills
    decisiveness, 17

Visionary skills (cont.)
    intuition, 16
    reasoning, 16-17
Visualization
    and imagery, 167-168
See also Imagery

### W

Walesa, Lech, 18, 202
Walking exercise, 148-149
Wholistic medicine, methods of, 14
Will, 202-210
    and confidence, 17-18
    destructive aspects of, 215
    development of
    building foundation, 203-210
    execution, 218-219
    readiness, 210
    enhancement of, 17
    and leadership, 17
    nature of, 17
    versus will power, 204-206
Withdrawal, possum response, 63-64
Worry. See Fear

### Y

Yoga, benefits of, 185

# MIND RESOURCE
# TECHNOLOGIES, INC.

In the final analysis, it is not the technology, the computer, the space satellite or the sophisticated competitive information systems that really make a difference. It is the human mind behind the system that makes the decision.

We believe that the vast potential of the human mind can be fulfilled through education and training, but that this training must involve all levels of our personality—physical, mental, social and spiritual. We are committed to the discovery and fulfillment of individual potential and response ability, and to bringing this potential into our personal, social, political and corporate environments.

Dr. Nuernberger and Mind Resource Technologies are dedicated to the highest quality of training and education to produce the highest quality of leadership, vision and performance...the achievement of personal and professional empowerment. To address these critical personal performance and leadership issues, MRT provides personal and professional seminars in the five key areas of human potential:

- Health/Wellness Skills
- Leadership Skills
- Visionary Skills
- Perceptual Skills
- Spiritual (Live Value) Skills

Many of the exercises and information discussed in this book are available on audio cassette. For information concerning training materials, professional and corporate seminars, or for information regarding a keynote address, contact:

Mind Resource Technologies, Inc.
RR 2 Box 1035
Honesdale, PA  18431
(717) 253-4754

Keys:
- diaphragmatic breathing
- Breath awareness
  - Go to breath
  - Go to silence

- concentration

start with
  alternate nostril breathing

POWER:

Concentration
Mental Clarity
Self-confidence
Creativity